A Powerless Humanity

About the Author

 S J Hussain is a highly educated individual with a Master's degree in History and an LLM from Kingston University in the United Kingdom. He has dedicated the last 20 years of his life to education and currently works at a higher education institution in the UK.

He is not only an academic but also a well-respected historian, intellectual, journalist, political and social critic, and legal expert. His writings focus on highlighting the bitter realities and mindsets prevalent in global socio-political societies. Through his work, he aims to heal the moral, cultural, and ethical wounds of these systems and societies.

His writing delves deep into various issues within social and political systems, often exposing the flaws and cancers that exist within them. His thoughts are rooted in profound philosophical wisdom and knowledge, reflecting his open-mindedness, liberalism, and sentimentality.

Rather than promoting false promises or sugarcoating unpleasant truths, Sheikh Jawad prefers to provide a clinical analysis of polluted politics and social dogmas. His words are seen as thought-provoking yet painful to swallow and digest due to their realistic nature.

Currently, S J Hussain writes columns for "Daily Pakistan" and "The Nation" on a regular basis. He continues to passionately write books, critical analyses, poetry, and other forms of writing that challenge conventional thinking and shed light on societal issues.

A Powerless Humanity

S J Hussain

Copyright © 2022 by TedPen

The accuracy, credibility, and completeness of information entered in this book is the sole responsibility of the Author, assuming no responsibility for errors, inaccuracies, omissions, or inconsistencies included herein. Any slights of people, places, or organizations are completely unintentional.

The publisher is providing this book and its contents on an "as is" basis and makes no representations or endorsements of any kind with respect to this book or its contents.

All inquiries should be addressed to:
tedpenuk@gmail.com

First Printing: 2022
ISBN: 9798367246667

TedPen Publications, United Kingdom
272 Bath Street, Glasgow, Scotland, G2 4JR, United Kingdom
publications.tedpen.uk

Ordering Information:
Special discounts are available on quantity purchases by corporations, associations, educators, and others. For details, contact the publisher at the above listed address.

Acknowledgement

To my dearest mother Dr. Ansar Begum (Late), you were not only a mother but also a mentor, a guide, and a friend. Your love, support, and endless sacrifices shaped me into the person I am today. You instilled in me the values of compassion, empathy, and perseverance. Your wisdom and knowledge continue to inspire me every day. Though you are no longer with us physically, your spirit lives on within me. May Allah bless her soul and grant her the highest ranks in Jannah (Paradise).

To my great father Sheikh Khadim Hussain, you were the epitome of strength and resilience. Your unwavering determination and hard work taught me the importance of never giving up. You provided for our family selflessly and ensured that we had everything we needed. May Allah give you long and healthy life.

To my loving wife Nadia Jawad, you are my rock and source of constant support. Your understanding, patience, and unconditional love have been instrumental in shaping our beautiful family. Together, we have created a sanctuary of love and warmth that I cherish every day.

To my lovely sons Ahmad Jawad and Muhammad Ali Jawad, you are the light of my life and my greatest blessings. Watching you grow into kind-hearted individuals fills me with immense pride. My hope for both of you is to always strive for excellence while staying true to your values.

I dedicate this tribute to all of you who have played an integral role in shaping me as an individual. May Allah bless each one of you with happiness, good health, success, and eternal peace.

Foreword

In the midst of a rapidly changing world, where social and political issues continue to shape our societies, it is crucial for us to engage in thoughtful discussions that challenge our perspectives and inspire collective action. It is within this context that I am honored to present this book – a comprehensive exploration of various social and political issues that have come to define our times.

Throughout history, we have witnessed transformative movements emerge from the depths of society, driven by impassioned individuals who refused to accept the status quo. These movements have fought against inequality, discrimination, corruption, and countless other injustices plaguing our communities. This book aims to shed light on such issues, offering an insightful analysis backed by extensive research and compelling narratives.

The pages ahead will take you on a journey through these critical topics - each chapter delving into a particular issue that has had a profound impact on our societies. From examining the roots of systemic racism and its enduring effects on marginalized communities, to exploring the complexities of gender inequality and the pressing need for inclusivity in all spheres of life – every theme covered here seeks to provoke thought and ignite conversations that demand change.

Moreover, this book seeks not only to identify problems but also propose innovative solutions. By highlighting successful initiatives from around the world – grassroots movements, policy reforms, community-driven projects – we hope to empower readers with knowledge and inspiration. It is my belief that armed with information and guided by compassion, we can contribute towards building a more just and equitable world.

However, it is important to note that no single book can provide an exhaustive examination of every issue faced by humanity today. The breadth and depth of social and political challenges are vast; they require ongoing dialogue, collaboration, and tireless efforts from individuals across all walks of life. This book serves as one part of that conversation – an invitation for readers to reflect upon their own role in creating meaningful change.

I extend my deepest gratitude to the authors whose expertise and dedication have made this book possible. Their commitment to shedding light on these critical issues through rigorous research, personal experiences, and persuasive arguments has been truly exceptional.

I hope that this book will inspire readers to critically engage with the social and political issues discussed within its pages. May it serve as a catalyst for dialogue, compassion, and collective action towards building a more just and inclusive world – one where no voice goes unheard, and every individual is afforded equal rights and opportunities.

Let us embark on this journey together, armed with knowledge, empathy, and an unwavering belief in our ability to create positive change.

Stephen Ozam

Writer and Publisher

Preface

In the labyrinth of life's complexities, certain phenomena defy all attempts at understanding issues around the typical socio-economic and political lifestyles of a nation and the world around it. Their rationale remains elusive, demanding a retrospective journey into history to untangle the intricate mess and glean insights from past experiences. It is within this convoluted landscape that we confront the core dilemmas explored in this tome — the delicate dance between politics and ethics, personality and nationality, sincerity and fractionality, and the seemingly omnipotent power dynamics that render humanity powerless.

Irrefutably, the democratic system serves as the backbone of any nation. Derived from the Greek political philosophy, democracy embodies a government representing its citizens, working for their greatest benefits across political, moral, economic, and social dimensions. The success stories of Japan, Germany, and England, rising from the ashes of war through determination, hard work, and persistence, resonate as global testaments to the potential of democratic ideals.

The crux of the matter becomes starkly apparent when examining the Pakistani political landscape. Incumbent parties routinely employ tactics that go against the very principles of democracy — framing opposition members, leveling baseless allegations, and reneging on promises, all justified under the guise of 'all is fair in love and war.' Such actions, however, collide with the limits set by Allah for human endeavors, as elucidated in the Holy Quran.

From historical episodes of Bhutto's hanging to the more recent trials of Musharraf and Nawaz Sharif, S J Hussain has brought the narrative of treason and political victimization weaves itself into the fabric of Pakistani politics into bear. This scholar dwelled extensively on the inexplicable logic behind putting political leaders on a pedestal only to later label them as traitors reflects a deep-seated inconsistency in our political standards.

Dictatorship, despite its fleeting allure, has proven fruitless when contrasted with the enduring success of democracies that flourish in letter and spirit. Unfortunately, Pakistan's trajectory has been marred by a tradition of turning heroes into traitors.

The book argues for an end to this tradition, advocating the burial of political victimization and the integration of moral values into our political system. Bridging the chasm between government and opposition, it contends, is the only viable path towards enhancing accountability, economy, society, and politics.

Drawing parallels with international agreements and historical initiatives, the narrative underscores missed opportunities and the imperative of seizing the present moment. The potential encapsulated in Gwadar and China's ascension beckons, demanding strategic planning and legislative reforms to avoid historical pitfalls.

In addressing the diaspora, the writer advocates for comprehensive measures beyond the superficiality of banking services. Doubting the loyalty of Pakistanis abroad is deemed regrettable, as their patriotism is no less fervent. The emphasis, however, remains on enabling expatriates to serve Pakistan optimally while recognizing the distinct roles of citizens within the country.

As we embark on exploration of this Powerless Humanity, full of topical issues, concerns and wisdoms, without sensationalism, we delve into the heart of a nation's struggle to reconcile its political trajectory with the moral compass that should guide it. In unravelling these complexities, we seek not just understanding but a call to action — a collective endeavours to steer our beloved country towards a future where ethics reign supreme in the realm of politics.

This book is no doubt a navigator for the nation's building champions, politicians, a prolific resource for the academics and researchers, and citadel for the historian and enthusiasts to derive great benefits of investment of purchase and reading time.

Barrister AS Orisankoko

BA (Hons) Islamic Studies (Ilorin), LLB (Hons) Common & Islamic Law (Ilorin), LLM - Economic & Industrial Law (Ibadan), LLM - Commerce & Information Technology Law (Reading, UK), MA - Islamic Law (London, UK) MSc – Cyber Security (Wales, UK) and, PhD Law (Sheffield, UK).

Table of Contents

First Chapter: Unwinding the Mess

Politics vs. Ethics

Certain things in life make no sense at all. No matter how hard you try, you can make neither head nor tail of them. Not only that but you can't even understand the rationale behind them. At such a time we must look towards history to untangle such a tangled mess so that we can solve the problem based on past experiences. It is an irrefutable fact that the democratic system of any country is its backbone (Sidney, 2006: 499).

The word democracy is derived from two Greek words: 'demos' meaning citizens living within a particular city-state and 'kratos' meaning power or rule. It refers to a government that represents people and works for their benefit. In other words, democracy is a political, moral, economic, and social structure that takes a country to new heights of success[1].All over the world, democratic governments have led their nations out of difficult situations through sheer determination and hard work (Forbrig, 2005: 134).

Japan, Germany, and England are some of the countries that were devastated by wars and were able to emerge as successful developed nations on the world map through their determination, hard work, and persistence (Jeffrey,1989: 89). But the democracy in which we are living isn't aware of even the basics of the 'demos' or democracy. There is neither democracy nor democratic values. I met Professor Michael

---

[1] https: www.britannica.com/democracy

Sandel of Harvard University through my benefactor friend, Ali Azam. Michael has propounded that in the modern era, many political problems can be solved through the propagation 7of moral values.

The importance of the fact can't be denied that this is the actual problem facing Pakistan. It is a matter of routine for the incumbent party to frame the members of other parties in fictitious cases, to level baseless allegations, and above all to renegade on the promises that they have made with the people. All this is justified by claiming, 'all is fair in love and war', which is essentially in the wrong.

Whether it is love or war, politics or business, power or government, Allah has specified certain limits for every human action and endeavor. Just have a look at the Holy Quran, all those who have transgressed were obliterated whether they were the Sabbath Breakers or people of Sodom, all of them were eventually brought to book. Sooner or later the Will of Allah prevails because the long arm of the Almighty makes no sound when it strikes. We should get our affairs in order, guide our beloved country towards the right path, and shouldn't go astray. Our politics has weird standards. Over the years we have remained in a quandary as to who should be labeled a traitor and who should be called a patriot.

From Bhutto's hanging to the disqualification of Yusuf Raza Gillani and Raja Pervaiz Ashraf, Musharraf's trial for treason and Nawaz Sharif's conviction in Panama case and Aqama case, echoes of the treason and Aqama trials against Khwaja Asif and Ahsan Iqbal have been a regular feature of Pakistani politics (R.Geraid, Ryan, 202: 925-936).

The expatriate Pakistanis are judged for their patriotism and then Moeen Qureshi is called from America and made prime minister of Pakistan. At one time government machinery is run by manufacturing Q League, the experiment of MMA and at other times the alliance of MQM and JUIF with every incumbent government keeps creating commotion in the national polity.

The logic behind all this is, at least, beyond my comprehension. We put political leaders on a pedestal and shower them with accolades and then we give the same leaders titles of traitors and incompetents and start exploiting them. Even today the Indian Army is terrified of Pervaiz Musharaff, and tales of his bravery are on everyone's tongue.

Nawaz Sharif's order for a nuclear test and his stand against American dictation is as clear as a bright sunny day. Bhutto's passionate speech in the UN and then his efforts towards making Pakistan an atomic power is still alive in the memories, similarly, the successful war of General Zia and General Hameed Gull against Russian Colonialism is an undying proof of their services for Pakistan (Institute Of Strategic Studies, 1998:131-141). Above and beyond these facts the reality is that dictatorship has never proved fruitful for any country if democracy is allowed to flourish in letter and spirit. Regrettably, Pakistan has remained highly unlucky in this regard because our tradition is to make heroes of today into traitors of tomorrow.

It is easier to comprehend the allegations of malfeasance, exceeding the limits of authority, or even rigging the elections but the melodrama of treason is extremely regretful. We will have to put an end to this tradition, bury this type of political victimization and make moral values a part of our political system.

This is the only way out of this quagmire. Government and opposition have never been on the same page for improving the systems of accountability, economy, society, and politics (Jawad, 2020:2). Things are run on adhocism. The welfare and wellbeing of the people have never been a top priority of our successive governments.

It's pertinent to mention a few examples here. Japan, Korea, Saudi Arabia, and UAE, have entered into mutual agreements with Europe and America which allow their citizens to travel to these countries without a visa for six months (Kuznets, 1988: 11-30). Similarly, the European Union and America have also entered into agreements that have made mutual trade and travel easier. Up until 1962, Germany was one of the biggest recipients of American aid. 14 countries of the world were providing Germany aid and Pakistan was one of those countries (Jawad, 2020: 2). In the era of Ayub Khan Pakistan gave Germany a loan of Rs. 120 million for 20 years. German Chancellor wrote a formal letter of thanks to the government of Pakistan for this at of beneficence. This letter is still a part of the archives at the Foreign Ministry.

Turkey and many other countries entered into lucrative agreements with Germany in place of the assistance provided but surprisingly Pakistan made no such effort that could have benefitted the general public (Luigi, 2021: 1-10). There is time yet, Allah has provided Pakistan with another opportunity in the form of Gwadar. China is going to be a world superpower within the next decade. Pakistan should work on devising ways and means that aim at easing travel and trade for Pakistani people. If this opportunity is squandered away, then there is no chance of availing facilities that weren't available to the Pakistani nationals in the past 70 years as well.

Apart from this, the laws about the transfer of land should be amended such that any foreign national who doesn't enjoy Pakistani nationality, couldn't buy land so that a repetition of the history of the East India Company and the Israeli settlement of Palestine, could be avoided[2].Most importantly it is the government's responsibility to provide the Pakistani's living abroad with the best facilities and opportunities to serve the interests of Pakistan. Just providing banking services like opening an account isn't enough; more thought has to be put into measures that could enable these expats to serve Pakistan properly and to the best of their abilities.

Doubting their loyalties is highly regrettable and disgraceful. Pakistanis living abroad aren't any less patriotic than the Pakistanis living within the country. But at the same time, there is nothing wrong in giving pREFERENCESto the people living within Pakistan for important and high-profile jobs. There are no two opinions about the fact that expats believe in serving and not in designations.

---

[2] https://www.britannica.com/topic/property-law/Acquisition-and-transfer-of-property-interest

REFERENCES:

Forbig J. [2005], "Revisiting Youth Political Participation". Europe: Council of Europe.

Institute of Strategic Studies [1998], "Text of Prime Minister

Nawaz Sharif's Speech At the UN: September 23,1998"

Jawad S. H [2020], "Politics and Moral Values".

[https://academia.edu/477755671/politics-and-moral values/]

Jeffrey E. Garten [1989], "Japan and Germany: American

Concerns". Jstor: Foreign Affairs, vol. 68. No.5(Winter,1989), pp. 84-101.Council of Foreign Relations.

Kuznets P. W.   [1988], "An East Asian Model of Economic

Development: Japan, Taiwan and South-Korea". Jstor: Economic Development and Cultural Change, vol. 36, No.3 [April,1988] pp. s11-s43.

Liugi S.   [2021], "From Partners to Rivals? The Future of

EU-Turkey Relations" Policy Brief [pdf].

R. Geraid H. Ryan S. [2021], "The Bhutto Family and Pakistan:

Power, Politics and the Deep State". Independent Scholar: Department of International Politics.

Two Nation Theory and Today's India

Almost a century ago the streets of the sub-continent reverberated with the slogan of Two Nation Theory. The actual creator of these words was Sir Sayed Ahmed Khan who gave the concept of two nations for the first time in India but these words were brought to life by and written by Allama Iqbal who wrote them in golden letters by dreaming of Pakistan and untiring efforts of Quaid e Azam not only gave beautiful colors to this dream but also turned it into reality (Prakash, 2003: 1049-60). Muslims migrated towards this Promised Land and traversed rivers of blood to reach their destination.

Thus, the foundations of an Islamic welfare state were laid. My family was among the lucky millions who migrated from India to Pakistan. I can proudly proclaim that the blood of my forefathers has nourished the foundations of Pakistan as they sacrificed their lives and livelihood for the motherland. I am proud to be a descendant of martyrs. I am proud that I am no longer a Mohajir but a Pakistani national.

I am proud that like those countless millions my forefathers gave up their lands, businesses, and homes in India for the sake of motherland and migrated to Pakistan. That is the reason why I not only understand the importance of this sacred and exalted land, but I can also feel the agony of the hardships that our forefathers bore. I can comprehend how the Muslims went through hell, what anguish and torment they bore and how they enriched this sacred motherland with their blood, and how they wrote undying stories of sacrifices to obtain this sacred piece of land.

At the time of migration from India, Muslims sacrificed everything to attain the benevolence of Allah so much so they left their clothes, bedding, wares, even wealth and cattle. The lofty idea for which they crossed rivers of blood and fire and sacrificed millions of lives was only the formation of Pakistan (Sarkar,2018:1-15).

The Muslims of India responded to the call of the Quaid to realize the beautiful dream of Allama Iqbal with this faith and belief that whatever Quaid e Azam is saying is the truth (Al-Mujahid, 2001: 87-101). Today history has proved yet again the varsity of the Quaid's vision. Time has proved once again that his thought and direction were absolutely accurate. His practical version of the two-nation theory stands vindicated in the annals of time (Akbar, 2019:1-5).

There was a time when Quaid e Azam joined Congress only with the thought that he would be able to deliver Muslims from the subjugation of Hindus and the British and make a new day of freedom dawn with his struggle and relentless efforts (Kutty, 1996: 9-15). But his political wisdom and acumen soon made him realize that Congress isn't working to promote the interests of the Muslims but instead it is striving for the wellbeing and freedom of the Hindus. Its objective behind the freedom struggle against the British was to establish a new country for the Hindus.

Muslims weren't even in the picture. As soon as Quaid e Azam realized this cunning of the Congress he left it and went back to England. Meanwhile, Allama Iqbal took a stock of the situation and requested Quaid to return to India. He offered him the leadership of the All-India Muslim League and stressed upon the need for improvement in the condition of the Indian Muslims and the importance of the struggle for the rights of Muslims. In 1906 Quaid e Azam gave up the comfortable life of London and lucrative practice and returned to India to assist the Muslims against the wicked designs of Congress by leading and guiding the Muslim League (Louise Beker, 2013).

Till his last breath, he valiantly fought for safeguarding the rights of Muslims and didn't sit still until the Muslims were free from the yolk of British rule and the evil intentions of the Hindus (Ahmad, 2021:1-3). Quaid had effectively realized that Hindus are a prejudiced nation, the Muslims will always keep proving their loyalty in India, but no one will believe them. Many Muslims of India, at that time, refused to believe this and vehemently opposed him as well.

REFERENCES:

Ahmad A.S [2019], "Understanding the Quaid's Vision of Pakistan". School of International Service, American University, Washington D.C.

Al-Mujahid S. [2001], "Ideology of Pakistan". Islamic Research Institute, International Islamic University.

Kutty B.M [1996], "Quaid-e-Azam's Presidential Address to Pakistan's First Constituent Assembly". Jstor: Pakistan Horizon, vol. 49, No 4, pp. 9-15. Pakistan Institute of International Affairs.

Louise M.B [2013], "The All-India Muslim League ,1906-1947: A Study of Leadership in The Evolution of a Nation". Karachi: Oxford University Press.

Prakash O.M [2003], "Roots of Islamic Separatism in Indian Subcontinent". Jstor: Proceedings of The Indian History Congress, vol. 64, pp.1049 - 1065. Indian History Congress.

And the Game Changed

India, which was trampling the whole region like an untamed and irrepressible animal and was under the delusion that its foreign policy, is reaching new heights so much so that it started considering itself the so-called regional superpower (Roy, 2020).

Maybe one factor behind this was undue favor shown to it by the world powers mainly because India is a major global consumer and trading market, which serves the interests of many countries. America as well as European countries sell their products here and earn hefty foreign exchange. Due to this trade volume, even China sorted out the recent conflict over Ladakh with enormous intellection and astuteness but at the same time, it reprimanded India on a limited scale (Singh, 2022).

This demonstrates that a solution to Pak- India conflicts isn't in the interest of the world powers and that is the reason that they enter into contracts and maintain relations with both India and Pakistan and keeping in view their own interests. Their real target is to expand their trade and to earn maximum foreign exchange. That is why numerous countries consider raising Kashmir or other contentious issues a suicide for the sake of their interests (Cohen, 1995).

In this backdrop, the patronage of the world powers led the Indian government to believe that the time was ripe to make the countries of the region accede to Indian hegemony. Due to this fanciful notion, India decided to browbeat China to prove that it had the complete backing of its allies but the whipping from China and flat refusal from Iran has burst India's bubble. It seems that India is now losing grip over the game. The snub from China in Ladakh was going on and simultaneously Iran backed out of the Railway line project which exposed Indian failure completely and trumped India effectively. Have a look at history and you will find out that whichever country tried to create hurdles for its neighbors eventually fell prone to its own trap even its own geographical integrity was put at stake.

The latest example in this regard is that of Russia which broke apart because of using similar tactics. Later on, Iraq and Germany faced a similar fate. Now India is on the path of repeating this history. Sneakiness and cunning are part of India's disposition (Chari, 2014:4298). It has never given up a chance of tormenting its neighboring countries and because of this attitude, Pakistan and China including Bangladesh, Nepal, and Bhutan are exasperated with New Delhi.

China is the bona fide reason for political change in the region. After announcing CPEC it started construction of Diamer Bhasha Dam in collaboration with Pakistan and has recently started a joint venture with Iran which will span almost 25 years (Laura et al, 2022:1-15). This will not only benefit China but will also bring much sought-after relief to Iran which has been suffering under economic sanctions for a long time. Iran will lay down railway tracks from Chabahar port to Zahedan located near the Afghan border, without Indian assistance.

This project is estimated at 0.4 billion dollars and will be completed in 2022. Iran made this decision keeping in view the lack of India's interest and because of new strategic planning with China. The tilt of Indian policy towards America also played a huge role in this switch over as to win American favor India was dragging its feet on this project for the past four years and didn't move ahead despite repeated reminders from Iran (Kumar, 2012: 5-8).

Quite surprisingly, America didn't sanction India because this project may be the reason behind this complacency as part of a plan to sabotage CPEC. Iran was under strict US sanctions hence turning a blind eye and giving half-hearted approval for this project could only be due to some kind of self-interest but India lost the game while trying to curry favor with its masters.

In any case, it is a big setback for the Modi government. At present; on one hand, India, America, Israel, and Europe are busy in projects of mutual cooperation while on the other hand China, Russia, Turkey, Iran, and Pakistan are working on their own mutual projects (Ningthoujam, 2021: 1-5). The need of the hour is that Iran, Turkey, Afghanistan, and Pakistan should work together so that in addition to economic improvement, the region could also experience peace and stability (Mazhari,2021:1-5). Later on, Uzbekistan, Turkmenistan and Azerbaijan can also become a part of this alongside China and Russia.

This can result in the rapid economic growth of this region. To some extent New Delhi is also thinking along the right lines that time has come but the time has come to break Indian slumber and to give it a wakeup call, to reveal the facts, to illuminate the darkness of lies with the light of truth, to get justice for the blood of Kashmiris, to raise voice for the rights of minorities in India, to expose the true face of Indian spy and terrorist Kalbhushan Jadhav to the whole world, to throw light over Indian role in terrorism in Baluchistan, Khyber Pakhtunkhwa and Baluchistan[3].to remind the world of the reasons for breaking up East and West Pakistan and to declare that Iran and Pakistan are brotherly countries, Gwadar and Chabahar are not in competition with each other rather they are the heritage of one single ummah. They cooperate and collaborate.

God willing their brotherhood will continue till the end of time. Pakistan and Iran can't even contemplate putting each other in harm's way. At the same time, the Afghan peace process will bring a new dawn of peace and harmony in these parts which will add to the significance of Pakistan in the region. In this regard, the whole world bears witness to the professional capability, acumen, abilities, and preparedness of the Pakistan army.

If we talk about ISI which is just one of its departments, we find out that it is the topmost agency in the world. The reason that BBC in one of its reports gave for this phenomenon is that Pakistan's intelligence agency has kept Pakistan safe for seventy years in one of the toughest and most difficult geostrategic regions. No doubt that after the assistance and benevolence of Allah Almighty, it is all because of the untiring and unremitting efforts of the Pak army. India should now come to its senses, accept these realities and move towards establishing peace in the region. The interests of both countries as well as world peace rest on this.

---

[3] https://indianexpress.com/article/pakistan/

REFERENCES:

Chari P.R [2014], "Can India Be Cunning?". Institute of Peace and Conflict Studies [IPCS].

Cohen S.P [1995], "Kashmir: The Roads Ahead" Seminar Organized by MCISS, Asia 1992.

Kumar S. [1999], "India-US Relations: From Estranged Democracies to Strategic Partnership". Southern Asia Studies Programme, School of Social Sciences and International Studies, Pondicherry Central University.

Laura S. et al [2022], "How Global Public Opinion of China Has. Shifted in The Xi Era". Pew Research Centre.

Mazhari M. [2021], "Iran, Turkey, Pakistan Have Great Task to Solve Afghanistan Problem: Turkish Politician". International Multimedia Tourism.

Ningthoujam A. [2021], "India-Israel Ties: New Opportunities in the Middle-East". Symbiosis School of International Studies, Pune, India.

Roy T.T [2020], "The Indian Empire of Burma, 1909". The Churchill Project, Hillsdale College, Cambridge Review of International Affairs, 2018.

Singh S. [2012], "India's China Policy Is Confused". Centre for Policy Research in India.

Student Unions: Importance and Efficacy

use them for their own personal and factional interests. These political pundits used the youth like tissue paper and later threw them away in the dustbin. Now whether we name them, elite or mafia, to some extent they have been successful in their plans because the dreams that Iqbal had for the youth never saw the light of the day.

The eagle envisioned by Iqbal is now a mere vulture who is away from religion, away from his parents, away from contributing to national development, away from morality, away from hard work and passion, away from dignity and intellect and is also far away from self-reliance and loyalty to the extent that instead of making mountain tops his home he lives on the internet and PUBG [Erum et al, 2018:1-15].

Have a look around, you will see that all political parties have established their respective student wings in the form of student organizations and use them for their political ends but never were these organizations allowed to grow into student unions after a specific time so that they don't get empowered and continue to be used as pressure groups [Alan, 1962:152-159].

These political parties issue some funds to their student wings so that they continue dancing to their tune. This is a horrifying fact that many refuse to accept but this is pure truth. I want to address these youngsters and ask them which patron political party of these student organizations hasn't ruled Pakistan. Almost all parties have enjoyed the perks of power to some extent but not even one political party resurrected student unions, even though most of today's political leaders were groomed in these unions back in the day [Siphesihle et al, 2019:91-104].

Javed Hashmi, Khwaja Saad Rafique, Ahsan Iqbal, Jaffar Iqbal, Arif Alvi, Siraj Ul Haq, Liaqat Baluch, Shehla Raza, Aijaz Ahmed Chaudhry, Faisal Sabzwari, Qamar Zaman Kaira, Sheikh Rasheed, and many others are a product of these student unions but except a few political parties, no one has ever risen their voices for the revival of student unions and those who even did that never got enough power to bring about a meaningful change.

History shows that except for the reign of Zulfiqar Ali Bhutto, all other rules have had banned these student unions in one way or the other. I remember that 36 years ago in 1984 during the rule of the Ex-Army Chief and President General Zia Ul Haq, the student unions were completely banned.

Ghulam Jillani, who was the then Governor Punjab and Martial Law Administrator, issued Martial Law Order No. 1371 and banned the student unions, simultaneously their offices were shut down and their bank accounts were frozen [Khalid ,1959: 72-79]. Punishment of five years in jail and a fine was also announced if the order was not followed. You must be thinking that I have moved away from the topic but that isn't the case.

The fact of the matter is that the whole issue starts and ends with not reviving the student unions. Had there been student unions today then they wouldn't have had to face so many difficulties in getting their voices heard in the corridors of power neither would they have had to come on the roads to get their protest registered. Ever since the breakout of Corona education and education system has come to a standstill. As soon as Corona hit Pakistan, schools, colleges, and universities were shut down in the very first stage.

It was a good step but the problem is the same; neither the educational institutions did any homework nor the government showered any blossoms of its wisdom. Online classes were arranged after many months for the students to some extent, but before starting these classes provision of internet facilities to the students living in far-flung backward areas weren't ensured but they were charged full fees, which is downright unfair.

In complete contrast, America, England, and Europe started online classes before lockdown and set an example of excellent homework and a love for knowledge. The Vice-Chancellor of Punjab University Dr. Niaz Ahmed Akhter became the first drop of rain and gave a relief package to the students.

A formal policy of fee reduction was introduced and the fees for medical, transport, and library were abolished. Moreover, the university administration has announced that students won't be charged sports fees, hostel fees, and laboratory fees and the students will only pay tuition fees during online classes which is a good step but the availability of internet facilities is the problem that remains.

The Punjab government has also provided the facility of online lectures for college students but the backward areas will remain backward still. Aside from this, Governor Punjab Chaudhry Ghulam Sarwar has given a big relief to the students by ordering that Government and Private Universities will take fees in installments.

All the Vice Chancellors of Government and Private Universities were issued a letter instructing them to provide relief to the students. All this is the result of the untiring efforts and hard work of the student organizations. They achieved this through protests and meetings otherwise the government remained oblivious to this problem for months.

Now all these measures may temporarily halt the storm of the problems of students, but effective measures for revival of student unions, provision of internet facility in backward areas, career planning, job opportunities after education, overcoming self and self-confidence issues; are yet to be taken.

All the political parties of Pakistan need to repent completely as per the anecdotes of Rumi and give students their due rights. Students should be provided a platform for resolving their problems by reviving the student unions [Marianna, 2021: 1-10].

In fact, I believe that if the students have to be emancipated from the influence of the political parties then the only solution is the restitution of student unions so that they are funded by the educational institutions, they don't have to become tools of political parties and beg them for resolution of their problems. The student unions should be barred from supporting any political party so that a wise, noble, and excellent future political leadership could be prepared. The bright future of Pakistan is also veiled in this.

REFERENCES:

Adeline I.A et al, [2015], "Roles of The Youths in Nation building". Journal of Policy and Development Studies, vol 9, No 5, November 2015.

Alan P. [1962], "Education, Muslim Elite and the Creation of Pakistan". Jstor: Comparative Education Review, Vol. 6, No 2, pp.152-159. University of Chicago Press.

Erum H. [2018], "Growing Population of Pakistani Youth: A Ticking Time Bomb or a Demographic Dividend". Journal of Educational Devlopment, Institute of Business Management, Pakistan.

Khalid B.S. [1959], "Martial Law Administration in Pakistan". Jstor: Far Eastern Studies, vol. 28, No 5, May 1959, pp. 72-79. Institute of Pacific Relations.

Marianna P. [2021], "Philosophy of Education in Times of Crises and Pandemics". Philosophy of Education Today: Diagnostics, Prognostics, Therapeutics and Pandemics.

Siphesihle E.M et al. [2019], "Political Parties and Students Union Government Elections in South Africa's Tertiary Institutions: The Case of University of Zululand". Journal of African Renaissance, vol. 16, No 3, pp.91-104.

Think Tank [2020], "Next Generation or Lost Generation? Children, Young People and the Pandemic" European Parliament.

Outdated Education System and Pakistan's Future

The progress of a country and its success depends on its education system [Samuel ,1980:203-206]. The teachers and educational institutions play a vital role in the success of the education system of any country but at the same time, it is the responsibility of the government to make a solid plan for the progress of the educational system, curriculum, its direction, and ultimate destination [Sharon et al, 2019: 1].

Over the past seven decades, while growth in every sector remained stagnant, advancement in the education sector, its development, and effective planning have also stayed sluggish. The previous governments never aimed for the advancement of education and serious planning to achieve this end. It wouldn't be far from true to say that education has always remained at the bottom of the previous governments' priority list. That is the core reason why the future of the new generation has always remained in the hands of a few predaceous private education institutions instead of builders of the nation [Taiwo ,2005: 63-69].

These institutions for the sake of material gains have been introducing multiple systems of education instead of trying to mold the young generation according to the principles of religion and nationalism. You all know that in this beloved land of ours there are multiple education systems instead of one.

One education institution is following the American syllabus and the other is teaching according to the British syllabus while still another is pursuing the Turkish system not to mention the so-called Islamic education institutions that teach syllabus crafted on the sectarian lines.

Surprisingly every educational institution has its school of thought. Every institution is taking the youth, who are the future of the nation, in a separate direction determined by its curriculum [Shamim ,2019: 1-20].

Do they give little thought to the questions like what kind of manpower Pakistan needs?

What is the future of Pakistan?

Where should Pakistan stand ten years down the road?

As a nation, we cannot get positive results without effective planning in any sector. We have reached the extent where still haven't implemented the same syllabus in the country even after seventy years of independence.

Obviously when the education system, which is the backbone of nation-building, isn't going in the right direction then why shouldn't the nation raise slogans of Sindhi, Baluchi, Pakhtoon, and Punjabi?

Why shouldn't Dhaka fall?

How would Kashmir gain independence?

Why shouldn't the country be in the clutches of the economic system of usury?

Why wouldn't be the Islamic Republic of Pakistan be far away from Islam?

Why wouldn't the innocence of children be trampled and thrown in the trash?

Why shouldn't there be extrajudicial killings?

Why wouldn't the doctors and lawyers be at each other's throats?

Why wouldn't the nation remain deprived of the blessings like dams?

Why shouldn't be graft, nepotism, adulteration, commendation, and greed be our fate?

Why shouldn't there be a dearth of good teachers?

Why shouldn't some poor man go to eternal sleep while begging for justice?

When we haven't determined a direction in our syllabus for our children, how can a nation come into being?

How can we get the best possible people to serve our institutions?

How can we stop the ever-growing yellow journalism, corrupt politicians, tax-evading businessmen, and sectarianism?

How will we leave the country in capable hands?

How will we give the nation, teachers like Faiz and Iqbal?

During the Second World War when the matter of the death of some important people came to Hitler's attention, he guided his nation with these historical words, 'Go, and if you can, hide your teachers somewhere. If your teachers survived they will educate more such important and intelligent people who will become a part of your rank and file'[Lucy ,2020 :250-310].

Just spare a thought for the fact that war-ravaged Germany asked Pakistan for assistance, after going through that tough time, that great nation paid full attention to revamping their education system and infrastructure. Now Germany doesn't earn anything from its education system and universities but spends on the development of the education system.

Students from all over the world who come to Germany for studies get free education. This German education system has produced experts who manufactured exceptional vehicles like Audi, Mercedes, BMW, and Volkswagen that made Germany a force to reckon with in the international market. They modernized production processes. We were blessed with great thinker philosopher Allama Iqbal [Ishrat ,2013: 1-13].

This very same education system gave us outstanding pathologists like Dr. Mansoor ul Hassan Alvi who is a beacon of light for us. He played a leading role in the establishment of the Institute Of Health Sciences under the auspices of Sheikh Zayad Hospital, Lahore. I was serving as a teacher of Pakistan Studies and got to learn a lot from him.

During the era of General Zia ul Haq, some efforts were made for the betterment of the education sector. At the start of these efforts, a fund was set up which was named Iqra Surcharge [Andreas, 2016:1-7]. To date, numerous successive governments have collected millions through this surcharge but not much of this was spent on education. Under General Pervaiz Musharaff many colleges were upgraded to universities, Dr. Atta-ur-Rehman's efforts in this regard a highly appreciable [Rathman, 2004: 259-282]. The issue, however, isn't the number of educational institutions.

The real question here is whether the direction of the syllabus was right?

Was a unified syllabus introduced?

Will, the coming generations be groomed in a way that will enable them to run and manage the affairs of the country properly?

At present aren't we preparing a workforce that wants to settle and work in America, Britain, and Europe?

Aren't we producing a crowd of people that have gone astray and have no real idea of the destination?

The heroes of this crowd are Michael Jackson and Jackie Chan instead of Salah ud Din Ayubi and Tipu Sultan. They are so impressed with the western civilization that given half a chance they will high tail it out of Pakistan. I don't want to imply that traveling outside of Pakistan is condemnable.

Our Holy Prophet Hazrat Mohammed Peace Be Upon Him, has categorically stated, 'seek knowledge, even if you have to travel to China'. Traveling for the sake of education or migrating for business purposes isn't wrong, but not having any feelings of being one nation for the sake of your own country is very distressing.

In the early days of Islam when any literate person came as a prisoner of war, he was treated very well by the Prophet Hazrat Mohammed Peace Be Upon Him. He also told such prisoners of war, 'if you will educate a Muslim, your sentence will be commuted'.

This was the importance of education in the eyes of the Holy Prophet Hazrat Mohammed Peace Be Upon Him. The first revelation of the Holy Quran was also Iqra (read); that is the importance of education in Islam. Islam gives a complete code of life and it gives guidance in every sphere of life. We find directions regarding the law, social system, economy, and education all that is required is following these directions properly.

Have we established any university where research is carried out on every verse of the Holy Quran and then this research is used as a guiding principle for the formulation of policies and system?

Has anyone ever thought of establishing 6666 departments in this Quran Research University, every department conducts researches on one verse for the benefit of the whole of mankind?

If we could achieve this we might find salvation. In the past seventy years; how many researchers, scientists, philosophers, lawmakers, and history teachers have we produced who are valued like Bu Ali Sina and Jabir Bin Hayan?

This archaic and rusted education system is neither benefitting anyone nor will it take the nation to any destination. I beseech Allah that we may be granted knowledge that is beneficial and then give us guidance to do good deeds. In the end, I will only say this that may Allah have mercy on us, give us the insight to learn from our elders, and make us rise as one nation on the world map with the help of a unified syllabus that has some direction and destination..

REFERENCES:

Andreas R.   [2016], "The Zia ul-Haqq Era, 1977-1988". Sociology and Anthropology of Religion. Oxford Scholarship Online.

Ishrat A. A. [2013], "Pakistan's Participation in the War on Terror and US Concerns: An Analysis". Department of International Relations, University of Sindh.

Lucy N. [2020], "Dying For the Nation: Death, grief and Bereavement in Second World War Britain". Cultural History of Modern War: Manchester University Press.

Rathman I. [2004], "Musharraf's Regime in Pakistan: The Praetorianism Faces an Uncertain Future". The Indian Journal of Political Science, vol. 65, No 2, pp.259-282. Indian Political Science Association.

Samuel E.N.O[1980], "Education as a Source of Economic Growth and Development". Jstor: The Journal of Negro Education, vol. 49, No, pp. 203-206.

Shamim I [2019], "The British vs American Education Systems". REFERENCESto IGCSE vs SAT Exams.

Sharon K. et al [2019], "Improving 21st Century Teaching Skills: The Key to Effective 21st Century Learners". Research in Comparative and International Education, vol. 14, Issue 1.

Taiwo M. [2005], "Problems of Policy Implementation in Developing Nations: The Nigerian Experience". Journal of Social Sciences, Vol. 11, No 1, pp. 63-69.

British Education System and Lessons for Pakistan

The education system and education have always been my favorite topics of discourse. Its reason maybe lies in my long journey as an educator which is still keeping me attached to an eminent university as a teacher.

Whenever there is a discussion about regression or progression of education, there is a strange restiveness in my heart and my pen comes into motion that makes my handwriting of its own volition. The restless heart yearns to share something from its bag of experiences with the readers.

A few days ago, a long list of issues regarding private education institutions that quite compassionately drew the government's attention towards these issues and difficulties. The list discussed numerous issues but a few of these points are very significant as Pakistan's future is connected with them. In my opinion, it is a crucial requirement of the modern era that the government should listen to these problems rationally and then resolve them effectively.

The topmost point that needs to be mentioned is that the government doesn't include private education institutions i.e. private schools, private colleges, and especially private universities in the key phase of education policy formulation. They aren't included in any consultation [Milton ,1955: 123-144].

To me, this is highly ludicrous and imprudent. There are numerous reasons for this that I will mention later on. Before that just know that apart from Pakistan the private education institutions are made a part of the important affairs like consultations and process of formation of the education policy [Maleesah, 2022: 1-6].

The aim of this exercise is to make use of the experiences and valuable services of the teachers and experts of the private sector in order to form a comprehensive education strategy for the nation. This policy is then used to set and achieve targets for the best future prospects of the country. In other words, this means that you will put into effect an education system and set targets according to your vision of the nation that you want to see five years down the road.

I have been associated as a teacher with a British university for the past fifteen years. In this capacity, on the British government invitation, I have represented my institution in numerous conferences and debates organized by their policy-making institutions like Department of Education, OFS, Leadership Foundation, Higher Education Academy, Education of the Home Office Department, UCAS and QAA. In all these meetings and conferences, the British government, aside from public institutions also invites private institutions as a major stakeholder [Maria et al., 2010: 1-16].

They are all gathered together under one roof a year or two, prior to the formulation of the policy and after deliberations and detailed discussions of almost two years, different proposals are prepared of the policy that is to be approved. They are approved after taking into account the input of these public and private institutions in accordance with the law. The process doesn't end here.

A detailed booklet providing guidance about the upcoming educational year is published and then the staff of all these public and private institutions is trained so that not only a unified education system could be established in the country but all the institutions could be made part of the national stream through annual reporting and audit.

OFC also called the Office of Students that monitors these institutions for safeguarding the rights of the students studying in the educational institutions working under the umbrella of the Department of Education, its job is to maintain the education standards and review them on regular basis [Catherine, 2018:1-10]. Quality Assurance Agency (QAA) conducts an audit of education institutions for its parent institution OFS and publishes the merits as well as demerits of the concerned institution on its website.

The job of all these government institutions is to guide and assist the educational institutions and the students so that they could get awareness about the standards of the educational institutions and judge their rank before applying for admission there.

Moreover, all the admissions in colleges and universities are done under the auspices of UCASE. All these departments report to the department of education and in this way the whole education system is working in tandem. Aside from this, every educational institution is not only answerable to the government but also considers itself an important element of the system [Adeniyi et al, 2015: 205-217].

The British students are granted student loans for their Bachelors, Masters, and PhDs for an unlimited time. The students don't have to return these loans as long as their pay doesn't exceed 21000 pounds and only 9% of the income above 21000 pounds is taken per month without any interest [Chris, 2014: 1-10].

On the other hand, the teachers are trained rigorously so that they could comprehend the individual educational requirements of every student and guide them towards an accurate future course of action and make every student a shining star of the country. Due to this cohesive education system, every year millions of students go to England for acquiring education and this high education standard is the backbone of the British economy.

The only reason for explaining this whole process is to make you understand how the nations gain success and the amount of hard work that goes into it. All this becomes possible when they are able to implement an organized and consistent education system because the ladder of success starts and ends with education [Alasdair et al, 2017:1-15]. Now let us come to the actual subject matter.

The second significant appeal of the private educational institutions was that the HEC creates unnecessary delays in approving new courses and they have to wait a long time. This could easily be understood by the following example; if I am desperately in need of a glass of water and you give me that glass of water after two years, will I still be in need of that?

That is the situation here as well. The experts who are required by the job market today after completing specific courses and the companies are looking to give them jobs if these courses are approved after two years and the experts are prepared five years after that then what will be their future?

Now if the private educational institutions want to serve the nation by making a sizeable investment, then the government will have to co-operate with them for a better future. In fact, I am in favor of government patronage of the private institutions, students, and education and in given circumstances consider private institutions indispensable for Pakistan to some extent. In this regard, I have mentioned some important reasons at the start of this column.

The most important thing is that private education institutions provide the best employment opportunities; cooperation in economic progress, increase in investment, increase in the number of experts, providing learned youth to industry and businesses is due to these private institutions after the public institutions.

I have always stressed that the public education institutions will have to raise their standards through government support and guidance and improvement in their lot should be the first priority of the government and taking all stakeholders on board is also a need of the hour. In a country where students, education institutions, and teachers are a part of the whole education system, the industrialists and business sector should also be a vital element of the system.

Like England they should be a part of the advisory panel of the educational institutions and their recommendations should be considered before forming new courses so that when the students leave these education institutions, the industrialists and the businessmen get manpower according to their requirements, all this happens in England, America and Europe [UNESCO, 2021:1-10].

The representatives of the multinational companies are members of the advisory board of every university. They give grants to the universities and give recommendations to get courses formulated to suit their requirements because they are in the best position to have knowledge about the realities of the market. This grant is also utilized to give scholarships to those students who take these specific courses.

They can easily get employment as soon as they complete their courses. I hope that the rulers will take leave of their usual heedlessness and procrastination and will take a close look at the problems of private education institutions and will resolve them expediently and will allow everyone to participate in the development of the country.

REFERENCES:

Adeniyi et al [2015], "Corollary of Government Policies On University Admission: A Review of Nigerian Universities". International Journal of Management and Social Sciences, vol. 3, No. 8, pp. 205-217.

Alasdair et al [2017], "Secrets of Successful Change

Implementation." Mckinsey's Sydney Office, Mckinsey & Company.

Catherine B. [2018]," A Beginner's Guide to the Office for Students". Whonke Policy Watch, pp.1-10.

Chris H. [2014], "Understanding Student Loans: How Exactly Do They Work?". Students' Award Agency for Scotland.

Maleelah et al[2022], "The Role of the Private Sector in, Pakistan, pp.1-6. Pakistan's School Education". Education Sector Development, Pakistan, pp.1-6.

Maria et al. [2010], "Teacher-Student Relationship: The Meaning of Teacher's Experience Working with Underachieving Students". Journal of Pedagogy, pp.1-16.

Milton F. [1955], "Role of Government in Education: Capitalism and Freedom". University of Chicago Press, pp.123-144.

UNESCO [2021], "Global Education Monitoring: What is Neck?". Global Education Monitoring Report, UNESCO Office.

Revamping the Police Department

In Pakistan, every department is setting new standards of appalling performance and corruption but the fact also remains that it is very tough to meet the expectations of the Pakistani people [Maryam, 2016; 49-72]. I believe that silence is better and is perhaps the best form of supplication than aimless discussions and undue critique. Criticism, however, gains immense merit and significance when it is carried out for bringing about an improvement [Vest, 1945: 162-168].

A cursory glance at the prevailing scenario shows that the department which takes the most heat is the Police Department. People censure and disparage this department openly and without giving it any thought perhaps this is the case because criticism is effortless and reform is strenuous.

At the same time, it can be said without a shadow of a doubt that authority has to be held to strict accountability but accountability and critique has to be carried out under the ambit of specified rules and regulations in the society.

Keeping in view this whole state of affairs I think that in Pakistan the Police Department is getting the short end of the stick because at times this department is vilified by every quarter. It has to bear Political, social, and economic pressures, work overload, and then to top it all there are bureaucratic demands that have to be met [Hassan ,2016: 1-8].

Few people acknowledge the sacrifices made by this department and its tireless efforts that are a source of pride for this nation. A recent example in this regard is the performance of Inspector Shahid and three security guards of the Karachi Stock Exchange Mohammad Iftekhar, Khuda Yar, and Hasan Ali, who laid down their lives while countering a terrorist attack on KSE and embraced martyrdom [Yifeng, 2021: 1-6].

They are our real heroes. The family members of these martyrs should be looked after properly by the government. The valor, bravery, and courage with which these sons of soil fought the terrorists are laudable. This is just one case in point. The history of the Pakistan Police is packed full of countless such examples of sacrifices and tributes [Adnan, 2014: 177-202].

Whether it's a case of petty street crimes or a menace of terrorism, these police officers remain vigilant and ever ready for serving their country with very limited resources. At this point it will be highly unfair if we don't give due recognition to the services of the Policemen who have laid down their lives while fighting in the war against COVID 19, they need to be as much extolled as the martyrs from any other section of society.

The government should provide the police force with protective gear and consider setting up virtual police stations so that the policemen could perform their duties safely and their sacrifices don't go in vain.

I salute those Lions of Allah and sons of the soil who have laid down their lives. I also salute those dedicated officers who serve the nation quietly on the frontlines without having any regard for their own lives. I don't deny the fact that just like other departments; the police department is riddled with its shortcomings and numerous failings. There are black sheep here who bring disrepute to their department. This necessitates improvement in the accountability mechanism within the police department. Many reputable, upright, and diligent people are an integral part of this system.

When we point out the corrupt and inefficient employees, we should also appreciate the hard-working, honest, and morally sound police officers as well. In fact, we need to think outside of our traditional approach and take practical measures. Today we have to make up our minds that we will keep the positives in view while pointing out the negatives and that we will show the public both sides of the story.

One of the sayings of Ashfaq Ahmed Sahib often resonates in my mind [Samir, 2013]. He used to say that sometimes we have to think, setting our egos and traditional approach aside. Acting on his thoughts, he once went to his nearest police station on the occasion of Eid. He gave them gifts and felicitated the employees on duty there. The SHO had tears in his eyes after such a display of genuine affection and sincerity. He complained about the lack of resources and said that it was the first time in his twenty-five years of service that someone came to visit him in the office.

The sentiments brought a tear to his eyes but the lack of resources was a problem then and even today this issue is the biggest hurdle in the discharge of duties. In fact, this action on part of Ashfaq Ahmed shows the way forward and provides stimulus to the thought that while we denigrate different government departments, we should also commend their meritorious services because they are doing their job diligently despite all the difficulties and limited resources. If truth be told this is incredibly laudable. They neither complain of hardships nor seek out comforts they just continue providing their services with gusto.

I want to pay tribute to IG Punjab Shoaib Dastgeer after Nasir Durrani who despite having inadequate resources at their disposal, took many important steps like trust-building measures and staff training for the progress of the police department. These measures can help the police department in regaining its lost dignity in the eyes of the general public. Things are improving rapidly after the transfer and appointment of 83 police DSPs all over Punjab. On the other hand, there is an acute dearth of essential amenities and modern technology. The lower staff personnel have no fixed duty timings as they remain on call all the time during emergencies. This should be the responsibility of a response force but here again, insufficient funds are a stumbling block.

Rest assured that every sector has its share of good and bad people. The good ones win laurels for their departments while the bad ones bring disrepute to their organizations. A relevant example in this regard that I have personally witnessed is the police station of Harbans Pura in Lahore where the traditional approach of doing things has been done away with. Within a short period, numerous positive changes have taken place.

Research showed that the driving force behind this revolution is the SHO Mohammad Naveed. He gave up conventional methods and played a vital role in this journey of change despite having insufficient funds. The professionalism of the police force of this station, their constant meetings with the people of the locality, trust-building, consultations, and revival of mutual trust was the turning point that made the citizens partners and helpers of the police. This markedly brought down the crime rate. As Iqbal [Faruqi,1979:97-107] has so eloquently said:

> *Iqbal hasn't given up on the unfruitful fields*
> *A little moisture will make this soil fertile*

I, personally, think that change becomes apparent when society as a whole start trusting the police force. Continuity of this thought and line of action can breathe new life in the police department. Unfortunately, for the past seventy years, there has been an acute lack of public relations in the police department. To some extent, this deficiency is being met now but a lot has to be done in this re gard. As long as the public trust isn't entirely restored things can't be improved completely. This might be the first drop of rain and maybe it will eventually bring an end to the environment of fear and suspicion that currently exists between the people and the police force.

According to my understanding, a few years ago, this model was followed in England in which the local councilors, council, the general public, and local NGOs, all joined hands and played their part in tackling the crimes [Hans, 1940:69-94]. Believe me these produced far-reaching results and greatly increased public trust in the police force. Later on, a network of cameras was established under the Safe City project across the whole of Europe and Britain. This gradually decreased the crime rate. The notable fact here is that the police force in Britain is provided with top-of-the-line protective gear.

You won't see any member of the British police force working without a bulletproof jacket. The British government has allocated a budget of 14 billion pounds for the police force in the current fiscal year. This is 980 billion pounds more than the last year. In Pakistan the Punjab government has allocated 115 million rupees, Sindh has allocated 98 million rupees, Khyber Pakhtunkhwa allocated 44 million rupees while Baluchistan has allocated 28 million rupees which is merely 10% higher than the last year. Our governments need to take up this matter seriously.

In 2016 a report 'Good Management Standards' was published which clearly stated that Pakistan's police force isn't provided with even the basic facilities. Here we encounter another problem which is that we allocate funds the Pakistani way and expect our police force to perform at the standard of British police. This expectation is nothing more than a mad man's dream.

The thing to celebrate now is the fact that the 'safe city' project has been introduced in Lahore as well as many big cities of Punjab. This can help in countering the rising crime rate, but it is imperative, that Model Police Stations and Safe City System should be established all over the country so that the crime rate can be brought down further, police could get assistance from this system and Pakistan could become a cradle of peace.

REFERENCES:

Adnan N. [2014], "Police Capacity and Insurgency in Pakistan". Policing Insurgencies, Oxford Academic Journal Online, pp. 177-202. Comparative Politics, International Relations.

Faruqi K.A [1979], "Iqbal- The Humanist". Indian Literature, 22, No 3; Aspects of Modern Poetry, vol pp.97-107.

Hans K. [1940], "The Genesis and Character of English Nationalism". Journal of History of Ideas, Vol. 1, No. 1, pp. 69-94. University of Pennsylvania Press.

Hassan A. [2016], "Role of Pakistan Police in Counterinsurgency". Belfer Centre, Harvard University. Counterinsurgency and Pakistan Paper Series, No. 5, pp. 1-8.

Maryam T.et al [2016], "Reforming a Broken System: A New Performance Evaluation System for Pakistan Civil Servants". The Pakistan Development Review, vol. 55, No. 1, pp. 49-72.

Samir T. [2013], "Remembering Ashfaq Ahmad: Through His Stories, He Will Live Forever in Our Hearts". The Express Tribune, 2013.

Vest C.M. [1945], "A Critique of Criticism or The Critic Criticised". Peabody Journal of Education, vol. 23, No. 3, pp. 162-168. Taylor and Francis Ltd.

Yifeng et al. [2021] "Self Sacrifice at Work: A Synthesized Definition and An Identity Based Framework". Academy of Management Annual Meeting Proceedings, pp.1-6.

World Press Freedom - The Way Forward

It was the year 1734 when New York City Paper took the British government to court for the cause of press freedom [Ruma, 2009: 271-285]. At that time there were only two newspapers. One was The New York Journal which was the mouthpiece of the government. It was published by an American journalist John Peter Zenger who was a bosom buddy of the then governor William Cosby. The other one was New York City that was a severe critic of the government. At that time many harsh restrictions were imposed on the press by the British government [Anthony, 1983: 281-297].

The newspapers weren't allowed to publish any news without the approval of the government. This prompted New York City to take this monumental step and it went to court in search of justice. It was a historical case that became an important landmark in the history of journalism. The court decided in favor of New York City and then this judgment morphed into a movement.

This reminds me of an incident of the Second World War when some people visited Churchill and said that the war has destroyed everything and now it seems that defeat is our fate. At this Churchill uttered these historical words, "If the courts are working, nothing can go wrong." Even today the British justice system is exemplary [Simon, 2019: 1-8].

This judgment compelled the government to recognize the freedom of the press and in 1754 this decision stirred up a storm in America. Due to this movement, America gained independence in 1776. It was this judgment that allowed Congress to raise the issue of freedom of the press in the American parliament for the first time. It was also the first time that freedom of the press was practically acknowledged. As a result of this decision, the banner of truth was raised in the history of journalism, and for the first time, any institution asked for the rightful place of journalism in a subjugated state of America.

After gaining independence the American government had to amend the first ten articles of the constitution to include freedom of expression as well as freedom of the press and it was made part of the national mainstream [Melissa, 2020: 1-4].

Following these amendments, the journey of press and journalist's freedom entered the 20th century after going through many thorny intricacies. Many movements started along these perilous paths and several precious lives were lost along the way. These aficionados sacrificed their positions, their possessions, their homes, their futures, and even their lives for this lofty and sacred purpose. There are many luminaries in this list of journalists who have given their blood to achieve the grand aims of journalism but for me, Rachel Corrie easily tops the list [Timothy J. R, 2003: 1-15].

She was a Christian American journalist. During discharging her duties as a journalist, she found out that the Israeli government is demolishing the homes of the Palestinians. She stood in front of the armored bulldozers. She couldn't stop them and was crushed to death but her death created a new standard of humanitarianism and journalism. She became the battle cry for righteousness and left an indelible mark of professional ethics on the barren landscape of hearts. The gruesome murder of Daniel Pearl in 2002 is also proof of the sacrifices made by the journalists; a proof that speaks for itself [Carlo, 2022: 1-6].

Over the past two years, alone over 272 journalists were jailed and so they ended up paying the price of fighting for what is right. They were tried under laws of terrorism and for corruption because they dared to unmask their governments' oppression and cruelties. I firmly believe that their sacrifices won't go in vain. These journalists include many cameramen, reporters, and media persons who work in the field. In Pakistan too at least 61 journalists have been brutally murdered just because they were doing their duty honestly [Geo, 2015: 1-5].

It is very excruciating and shocking that even after offering so many sacrifices the press in Pakistan didn't get the freedom that it requires and deserves. Undue censors and restrictions over the past 70 years have posed monumental challenges for the journalists in Pakistan but at the same time, the blood of the martyrs has written new tales of valor and courage. Recently world press Freedom Day was celebrated I salute all those journalists who laid down their lives while working in the field during this emergency imposed by the advent of COVID 19. Undoubtedly, they are a source of pride for the whole journalist tribe.

Now with an aching heart, I want to say to my fellow journalists that today there is an immense need for introspection. We need to ask ourselves, have we done our duty towards our fight with the pen?

Are we guiding society in the right direction? Are we making good use of whatever press freedom we are left with?

Have we raised our voices for the oppressed?

Have we challenged the oppressors?

Will we leave a free and clear environment for our coming generations?

If our consciousness is satisfied with the answers to these questions then it means that things are going fine, if not then it's crystal clear that we haven't done our job yet. We have to get rid of the black sheep who are working among us.

We have to give a new direction to this sacred profession. We have to adopt a new course of action so that anyone who picks up a microphone doesn't get to call himself a journalist. Moreover, professional workshops should be conducted so that this noble forum of journalism could be used to breathe a new life into this morally dead world [Richard et al., 2018: 45-55].

The need of the hour is the rejuvenation of this sector. Its standards have to be restructured. Its importance must be highlighted around the world under new guidelines. This sector should not fall prey to the interests of ruthless capitalism. It should be mandatory for the entrants in this profession to possess a certain level of education and experience. There should be grading based on experience and research.

The press club should be given a position from which it could ensure the establishment of high journalistic standards [Yamamoto, 1989: 371-388]. We need to acquire better products from the existing anchor industry. Numerous other steps need to be taken so that value of this sacred could be enhanced and every professional who is working as a journalist could feel safe.

To those who consider this profession as a factory, I would like to say that this sector isn't meant to do what they think it should do. Those who use this sector for the satisfaction of their ego will have to change their standards now.

REFERENCES:

Anthony A. [1983], "The British Government and the Media,1937-1938". Journal of Contemporary History, vol. 18, No. 2, pp.281-297. Sage Publications Ltd.

Carlo M. [2022], "The Tragic Murder of Daniel Pearl Explained". The Grunge Archives.

Geo E. [2015], "71 Journalists Killed in Pakistan Since 2001". PPF Media Violence Index Report.

Melissa D.W[2020], "When Thomas Jefferson Penned----". Stanford News Service.

Richard P.et al [2018], "The Seminar-Workshop Experience in Journalism Class: A Best Practice?". Rizal Technological University, Mandaluyong, Philippines. International Journal Humanities and Social Sciences, vol. 10, No. 3, pp. 45-55.

Ruma C. [2009], "Printer Hugh Gaine Crosses and Re-

Crosses the Hudson". Jstor: New York History, vol. 90, No. 4, pp.271-285. Cornell University Press.

Simon W. [2019], "The Inside Story of How Three Unlikely Allies Won World War 11". National Geographic Project.

Timothy J.S. [2003], "The Truth About the War Memorial to Fallen Journalists". Boston Globe.

Yamamoto T. [1989], "The Press Clubs of Japan". The Journal of Japanese Studies, vol. 15, No. 2, pp. 371-388.

Pakistan's Fight Against Polio

The history of Polio is as old as that of human society. In 1916, New York witnessed a severe outbreak of Polio after which this disease became a pandemic [Donald et al,1957: 254-265]. Two years later another pandemic occurred which was named Spanish Flu. Due to this new development, Polio wasn't paid proper attention. Right from the start of the Polio epidemic, 9000 cases were reported in America resulting in 2343 deaths [Madeline, 2022: 1-5]. On the global level, 27000 cases surfaced causing the deaths of almost 6000 children. This was the longest epidemic of the century. According to the records of 1952, 57628 cases were reported in only America.

Historically speaking the disease of Polio has existed for centuries. The antiquity of this disease can be judged from the fact that research revealed some petroglyphs belonging to the period of 1430 - 1365 BC that depicted Polio patients [Sintayehu 2022: 1-6]. This proves that this disease has always been with us. This disease like Corona starts with difficulty in breathing due to which British scientists Philip and Louie introduced Iron Lung in 1928 that helped in breathing, this, later on, evolved into the modern ventilator.

The first vaccine of this disease was developed in 1952 by Dr. Jonas Salk which helped greatly in controlling the disease. This was followed by the oral vaccine of Albert Sabin which is effective still. England adopted this in 1962 [Siang et al, 2019: 1-10]. After 1982, not a single case of Polio was reported in

England. Not only this but after 1982 Polio was eradicated from England, America, Australia, Europe, and 125 other countries [Sarah, 2002:1-3]. The World Health Organization (WHO) declared the American region in 1994, the Chinese region in 1997, and England along with the rest of Europe Polio free in 2002 [WHO,1994: 1-414].

By 2013 the four countries that still suffered from Polio included India, Afghanistan, Nigeria, and Pakistan but after 2015 both India and Nigeria exited the list [Edna et al, 2014: 468-472]. At present only Pakistan and Afghanistan are the two countries where Polio still exists and this is very alarming because as long as there is a single Polio patient in Pakistan, the coming generations can never have a bright future [WHO, 2019: 1-8].

There are many reasons as to why this deadly disease couldn't be eradicated from Pakistan, among them lack of knowledge and awareness in the general public is of paramount significance.

The bungling performance of different government institutions is also one of the factors. Even the staff responsible for dispensing vaccines isn't trained enough to know how to protect and administer the required dosage of the vaccine properly. According to The World Health Organization not only the children are overdosed but the vaccine isn't even stored appropriately.

Effective measures aren't taken for transporting the vaccine safely due to this in 2019 hundreds of children were hospitalized with symptoms of stomach ache, vomiting, and even unconsciousness after being vaccinated. The main reason was the carelessness of the staff that administered the vaccine.

To make a bad situation worse a few miscreants started spreading rumors about the Polio vaccine which created further problems for the staff administering the vaccine.

The Khyber PakhtoonKhwa Government countered the situation after protests by the parents by bringing the rumor mongers to book, but regrettably, no concrete steps were taken to eliminate this ignorance and neither was any effective planning undertaken [Gurmeet, 2013: 1-8]. Last year 53 new Polio cases were reported. Since then 147 more cases have surfaced. This rising number of Polio cases is a warning bell for the days to come. If this situation persists then God Forbid, Pakistan may have to face an emergency in the next decade. The Polio drive suffered badly due to months' long lockdown during the Corona pandemic.

The Government of Pakistan has recently resumed this campaign which is a step in the right direction but their government needs to uproot the deficiencies and weaknesses of this drive to wipe out this disease. To this end along with better planning, capable staff should be inducted. Health workers, who are of great significance in this whole system and work as front-line force, should be given training at least twice a year and this should be done on regular basis. At the same time, special attention should be paid to the monitoring of the health workers so that these problems could be eliminated.

Moreover, the government of Pakistan should run awareness campaigns about public health so that the doubts and misunderstandings in the minds of people regarding the side effects of the Polio vaccine could be laid to rest. The most significant in this regard is the issuance of the individual medical record book. Its lack is being greatly felt in Pakistan.

This book should be mandatory for everyone but more so for children up to five years old so that if these children visit any doctor in the country he/she could check whether the child has been inoculated and could get a clear picture of the medical history and enter the same in that book to provide effective care to the children.

If this record is maintained from the very beginning in the medical record book, it will greatly facilitate the compilation of the medical and vaccination record of the children. Later on in the future, making use of modern technology, a medical record app can be introduced which should hold the medical records of every child. This can easily be accomplished with the help of NADRA [Evans ,2016: 48-61]. The pediatricians should be given complete access to this app so that whenever a child comes to his/her clinic or hospital, the doctor should be obligated to check the vaccination record of the child and then provide accurate information to the parents as well as the health department.

It is pertinent to mention here that aside from the government it is our responsibility as well; the intelligentsia should propagate the importance of fighting polio and create awareness among the general public especially among those who reside in rural areas so that this lethal disease could be eradicated from Pakistan once and for all.

REFERENCES:

Donald et al. [1957], "Estimates of the Infection Rates for Poliomyelitis Virus in the Years Preceding the Poliomyelitis Epidemics of 1916 in New York and 1945 on Mauritius". The Journal of Hygiene, vol. 55, No. 2, pp. 254-265. Cambridge University Press.

Ednak et al. [2014], "Progress Toward Polio Eradication". National Library of Medicine: National Centre for Biotechnology Information, Microbiology and Mortality Weekly Report, Vol. 63, No. 21, pp. 468-472.

Evans R.S. [2016], "Electronic Health Records: Then, Now and in the Future". National Library of Science: National Centre for Biotechnology Information, pp. 48-61.

Gurmeet K. [2013], "Pakistan's Internal Security Challenges: Will the Military Cope?". Jstor: https://www.jstor.org/stable/resrep 09151//., pp. 1-8.

Madeline B. [2022], "Polio Vaccines: New Developments on the Road to Eradication". American Society For Microbiology, pp. 1-5.

Sarah B. [2002], "Polio is Eradicated From Europe". Health Editorial, The Guardian International Edition, pp.1-3.

Siang et al. [2019], "Jonas Salk [1914-1995]: A Vaccine Against Polio". Singapore Medical Journal, Vol. 60, No. 1, pp.1-10.

Sintayehu T.T [2022], "The Disease That Re-emerged-----". Infectious Disease Epidemiology, Infection Biology, Phytochemical Analysis, Ethiopia, pp. 1-6.

WHO-a- [1994], "Summary of 1994 Activities of the WHO Collaborating Centres in the Western Pacific Region". Language: English, pp.414.

WHO-b- [2019], "Pakistan and Afghanistan: The Final Wild Poliovirus Bastion". Language: English.

A Rare Gem

Certain core principles lay down the foundations of society. These principles include mutual relationships, justice, brotherhood, and values. Acting upon these principles, an Islamic welfare state can be established [Kwame ,2010: 1-15].

We generally see that when a state comes into existence; on one hand, many state institutions work for the welfare and wellbeing of the society, and on the other, many God-fearing men help out people to gain Allah's favor [Chris ,2005: 27-82]. These people play the role in society that perhaps even the government and many so-called charities don't play. Neither are looking for fame nor for fortune or power.

It has always been my intention and goal to bring forth accounts of such people and hold them as an example for others. The character of these fine people leaves a very positive impact on society. Somehow, they become the synonym for service and upholding human values.

Their role not only gives stability to the society but also restructures it. These are the beacons of light that brighten the darkness and lead astray to the right path. These people play the role of a father and while doing so, one day they leave this world quietly and no one even gets to know. Only those people are affected who are benefitting from their generosity.

Mr. Mehboob Ilahi is one such rare gem [Jamee ,2015: 1-10]. He dedicated his whole life to the service of his own people as well as he set extraordinary examples of love for mankind. His actions may appear ordinary and insignificant but the far-reaching impact of these small measures will force you to acknowledge that such people are the center of gravity for the people around them because this is the section of society that is neglected by the government and they look towards these great people for the solution of their problems and are never disappointed.

Respected Mehboob Ilahi was the caregiver of the oppressed and downtrodden. He treated every illness selflessly and without any hunger for reward or monetary gain. He gauged the pulse of society and cured it. He was the balm for the pain and anguish of the people and worked day and night to alleviate their suffering. His own life started as an orphan, he was a child when his father passed away and he spent his life tackling immense hardships. He was the youngest of the family, yet he married off his elder siblings, arranged jobs for them, and even stood by them when their children were getting married.

He started his business as an ordinary worker from a small shop. Due to his untiring efforts and hard work, his business expanded to London. He was always a loving and affectionate patron for those around him. Whether it was London or Rawalpindi he always served humanity. The locality of Dhoak Assu was facing an extreme shortage of clean running water. He made arrangements for water supply for the whole area from his own well.

The family members complained that the water level in the well had dropped and the people of the area shouldn't be given water otherwise they would suffer as well. To this, the friend of Allah gave a beautiful reply. He said that even if the well is about to go dry, it's not right to deny the public the use of this water. When the water will end for them it will end for us too.

Allah is their Guardian and ours too. Every person who attended his funeral was singing his praises. Countless people recounted his good deeds. Helping the poor and needy, paying for the construction of the mosque quietly, even jumping in the well to save the life of his elder brother, and being unable to walk around due to multiple fractures as a result of his efforts.

Although he couldn't save his brother, he brought up the children of his brother and gave them the best possible education. He worked as a laborer in the construction of his home and spent the money thus saved for the construction of a mosque and the rest he set aside for helping the poor.

Mr. Mehboob Ilahi spent his whole life toiling hard [Samad, 2019: 1-14]. He never overspent in dressing, eating, or living but whether it was the construction of mosques in London or helping out Pakistani youth stuck in difficult circumstances, he was always way ahead of everyone else.

My only purpose in highlighting some aspects of the life of this legend life was to make sure that his life could serve as a beacon of light for us and could brighten our lives that are enveloped in darkness. We could also be motivated to follow the edicts of Allah and the teachings of the Holy Prophet (Peace be upon him) and become helpers of the poor, orphans, impoverished, and the needy. Whether we have more or less we could lend a hand to others. In this month of Ramazan due to its benedictions, may Allah give us the fortitude to spend our lives according to the Sunnah of the Holy Prophet (Peace be upon him) and give us the wisdom to spend our wealth in the way of Allah instead of extravagant and wasteful spending. May Allah fill the whole world with the fragrance of the life of

Mr. Mehboob Ilahi and accept his good deeds and give his family and friends the fortitude to bear his loss. Amen.

REFERENCES:

Chris N. [2005], "Recognizing States and Governments". Canadian Journal of Philosophy, vol. 35, No. 1, pp. 27-82. Cambridge University Press.

Jamee H. [2015], "Mehbub-e-ilahi's Spiritual Legacy Continues to Foster the Sufi Way of Life in India: Syed Mohammed Ashraf Kichauchwi". All India Ulma & Mashaikh Board.

Kwame G. [2010], "African Ethics". Stanford Encyclopedia of Philosophy, The Metaphysics Research Lab, Centre for the Study of Language and Information.

Samad A. [2019], "Academic and Religious Services of Mohammed Maqsood llahi [Mahboobllahi] and Its Effects on the Society". The International Research Journal; Department of Usooluddin ,vol. 3, No. 2, pp. 1-14.

Banks of Euphrates and A Battle for Life

Martyrdom of Hussain is actually the death of Yazeed.....Islam is revived after every Karbala

The month of Moharam marks the start of the Hijri calendar. In this sacred month, the banks of Euphrates witnessed that epic battle between truth and falsehood that will forever echo in the east and the west until the Day of Judgment. No discerning person can overlook the significance of this encounter [Sheikh, 2020: 1-3].

This month edifies the values of troth, altruism, sacrifice, faith, unity of ummah, mutual lenience, and peaceful coexistence. Allah Almighty declared this month as the sacred month. Verse 36 of Sura Toubah proclaims four months as sanctified (Minha Arba'ata Haram); Moharam is one of those months.

The question that arises here is what is the philosophy of Karbala?

What lesson is concealed in this sacred month for Muslims?

We will have to stand in the court of our own conscious and ask ourselves, had we led our lives in the footsteps of the grandson of the Last Prophet Hazrat Muhammad (Peace Be Upon Him)?

Have we understood the spirit of the struggle and timeless sacrifices of the martyrs of Karbala?

Have we passed this message on to the coming generations successfully?

If not then we will have to ponder over it, only then will we be able to comprehend its true message and denotation. We will understand the purpose of our lives, and the rationale in being declared the paramount creation.

The philosophy of Karbala is actually a philosophy of pain and anguish ("Karb-o-Bala")[Saroosh, 2022: 1-3]. It is a heartbreaking account in which history has proven effectively that the cause of Islam was harmed more by the hypocrites than by the outsiders. These hypocrites crossed every limit of brutality in order to make Islam hostage to their own desires. They avulsed delicate buds from the limbs and spilled the blood of dearly loved ones in the streets. Their viciousness made the heavens cry. This battle was a faceoff between truth and falsehood.

Bizarre is the jest with the providence of Islam

Hussain (AS) was martyred while chanting the name of Allah

The grandson of the Last Prophet Hazrat Muhammad (Peace Be upon Him) sacrificed 72 people who embodied innocence in the path of Allah but didn't bow down to falsehood and usurper [Sadaf, 2022: 1-6]. He preferred death over pledging allegiance with Yazeed. He laid down his life and gave eternal life to Islam.

This altruism and sacrifice and teach us that the actual purpose of life is gaining the approval of Allah. Submission to the will of Allah should be a focal point of life. We should aim to achieve Allah's blessings that will validate our existence. This should be the legacy for our eternal life.

If we can achieve this objective then nothing else matters. There is no desire nor yearning for anything else. The tale of Holy Shrine (Haram) if told, is simple, strange, and of different hues. It ended with Hussain (A.S) and started with Ismail (A.S)

This modern era has its own predicaments [Michael, 1994: 1032-1054]. We love our religion dearly but practically we don't want to follow the edicts of the same religion. We are like a hollow building, a human-like marionette made of flesh and skin whose insensitivity and incapacity should be pondered upon. We have grown farther apart from wisdom, insight, perception, and sensitivity. We don't even stop for a moment to think about the real purpose of our existence.

The fact of the matter is that in the race of life we have forgotten our benefactors whose enduring sacrifices gave us the knowledge of the true faith. Someone was worrying and shedding tears for us a thousand years before our births. Someone was anxious about our future. Someone was pleading for us in front of Allah and that someone gave his blood for the blooming of this garden.

Alas! Which direction are we heading in? who are we? What are we doing? Why are we impassive and inert? Where are we going? What will be the impact of our inconsiderateness, insensitivity, selfishness, conscienceless behavior on the young generation? What are we contributing to their grooming? Are we a source of joy for those around us? Do we make their lives easy? If not then we should make a solemn oath that we will change our way of life in this sacred month. We will enforce the rule of Allah on this land of Allah.

We will have to move forward in the right direction. We will have to destroy the deity of factionalism in this holy month.

We will have to spread the spirit of brotherhood, humanitarianism, and humanity in order to make Pakistan the cradle of peace and love [Beat, 2007: 163-165]. We have to ensure that the purpose for which the martyrs of Karbala laid down their lives carries on till the end of times.

We will have to make our struggle unadulterated and incessant. We have to pull out the poisonous plant of religious abhorrence from its very roots. We will have to stand with the truth and stand firm in the fight against falsehood.

We need to spread the culture of tolerance and benevolence in order to safeguard the sanctity of this month. We have to lend a hand to the law enforcement agencies for maintaining law and order in the country. Concrete measures need to be taken now to meet any unforeseen situation. Just like previous years, we have to stand together to defeat any possible threat of terrorism in this holy month of Moharam.

Keep another thing in mind! Coronavirus is on the decline but we haven't eliminated it yet so take care of each other in this blessed month and follow the SOPs issued by the government so that the dangers of the second wave of Covid 19 could be avoided [Seth, 2021:1-5].

REFERENCES:

Beat S. [2007], "The Spirit of Geneva; Humanitarian Diplomacy and Advocacy". Refugee Survey Quarterly: vol. 26, No. 4, "The Spirit of Geneva in a Globalized World: The Twelfth Annual Conference of Webster University, Geneva (2007), pp.163-165. Oxford University Press.

Michael S. [1994], "A Guide to Truth Predicates in the Modern Era". The Journal of Symbolic Logic, vol. 59, No. 3, pp.1032-1054. Association of Symbolic Logic.

Sadaf F. [2022], "Al Hassan: The Beloved Grandson of The Prophet Mohammed". Online Islamic Library, Karachi, Pakistan, pp. 1-6.

Saroosh A. [2022], "A Philosophical Significance of Karbala". Research Gate: Aligarh Muslim University, pp. 1-3.

Sheikh J.H [2020], "A Battle For Justice ". The Nation Editorial, pp. 1-3.

Seth B. [2021], "How to Prevent the Next Pandemic". Public Health Opinion: Scientific American Journal, pp. 1-5.

Hope and Misery

Cancer is a highly insidious and deadly disease. According to the World Health Organization's (WHO) 2020 figures, 10 million people worldwide have died of cancer so far [Hyuna et al, 2021: 209-249]. While a recent study by Cancer Research UK and the American Cancer Society estimates that 19.3 million new cases will be registered by the end of 2020 [Rebecca et al, 2020: 7-30]. There has been a gradual increase in the number of cancer patients over the past few years. The whole world is taking special measures to prevent this disease as well as spreading awareness. Governments, welfare organizations, and the people are constantly working together to eradicate cancer from its roots.

But, the governments in Pakistan never paid special attention to the research, diagnosis, and treatment of this disease. Especially now because of COVID-19, all other types of patients are being completely ignored. According to a report by WHO, the total number of cancer patients in Pakistan is 329547, out of which 11714 deaths and 17888 new cases have been reported this year, which is much more than in previous years [Muhammed, 2017: 1-13].

But so far only five cancer hospitals are functioning; Shaukat Khanum Hospital Lahore, Baitul Sukoon Hospital Karachi, Kiran Cancer Hospital Karachi, Nuclear Medicine Oncology and Radiotherapy Institute Islamabad, and Anmol Institute of

Nuclear Medicine and Oncology Lahore Hospital. They are playing their part in the treatment and eradication of cancer in Pakistan day and night.

Anmol Hospital Lahore was established for the first time in Pakistan in 1984 for the treatment of this contagious disease and is still engaged in the service of the people of Pakistan without any discrimination.

Although its capacity and facilities are much less than the number of patients coming in, due to the excellent performance of Dr. Maqbool Shahid (former director of the institute) and Dr. Abu Bakar Shahid (the current director) the poor cancer patients are getting better and free treatment facilities instead of stumbling door to door.

This organization is working under Pakistan Atomic Energy Commission (PAEC). According to the Chairman Atomic Energy Commission, 80% of cancer patients in Pakistan are treated in 18 medical centers of the PAEC, and in recent years, four new machines have been installed here including State of the Art Radiation Machine, MRI, Spect-Scan, and Dexa-Scan which was the need of the hour [Ali,2022:1-18].

On the other hand, the Prime Minister of Pakistan Imran Khan also dedicated the 1992 World Cup victory to Shaukat Khanum Hospital and then laid the foundation of a great dream to cure the suffering of the people by working day and night. Prime Minister Nawaz Sharif also allotted land for the hospital by the government so that this great dream could be realized.

The Shaukat Khanum Hospital was finally established in 1994 and the project was completed in a very short time. The project grew significantly until the Shaukat Khanum Memorial

Hospital and Laboratory Center became the largest institution in Pakistan and was introduced to the public as a free cancer treatment institution [Nausherwan, 2019: 1-10].

Who knew that this great institution was targeted by some evil elements and an attempt was made to damage its structure which in my view is condemnable.

Recently, my hopes turned to sadness when I learned from my personal observation and research that only the treatment of patients up to the age of 40 is free in this institution, even if the patient meets the standard requirements and conditions of this institution.

Otherwise, he is handed over to Shaukat Khanum's business manager, who despite listening to all the poor conditions and difficulties of the patient tries his best to advise him on private treatment. Even if he is a Stage-One cancer patient, Rs. 2.5 to 3 million is demanded his treatment. And if he does not have the money, he is refused treatment straight away; even he is not offered charity (Zakat) money which is very painful.

I know that the resources of the hospital are limited and it is not possible to provide free treatment to every patient. But I would urge the Prime Minister to provide equal opportunities to the people by eliminating the age limit. Because people under the age of forty have the same right to live as people over the age of forty, and also life and death are in the hands of Allah.

Who knows how long the patients are going to live? Such a policy is also against human rights because the treatment should be equally available to all. If the resources are scarce, then instead of starting Peshawar and Karachi projects, the work should be completed on one project first. This way the money can be spent right on the welfare of poor patients.

However, it is still not understood that the Prime Minister started this project to help cancer patients, but after becoming the Prime Minister of the country, the government is still not working on building more hospitals and getting the modern machinery in such a way that was expected from his government.

At this time, there is a need for immediate action to be taken against this disease, as well as against the divided policy for treatment from Shaukat Khanum Hospital. Treatment should be done on a first-come, first-served basis.

REFERENCE

Ali A. [2022], "The Burden of Cancer, Government Strategic Policies and Challenges in Pakistan: A Comprehensive Review". Frontiers in Nutrition, Vol. 9, No. 7, pp. 1-18.

Hyuna S. et al [2021], "Global Cancer Statistics 2020: GLOBOCAN Estimates of Incidence and Mortality Worldwide For 36 Countries". American Cancer Society: A Cancer Journal for, Clinicians, Vol. 71, No. 3, pp. 209-249.

Muhammed R. S. [2017], "Cancer Prevalence, Incidence and Mortality Rates in Pakistan in 2012". Cogent Medicine, Vol. 4, No. 1, pp. 1-13.

Nausherwan K. B. [2019], "Establishing A Tertiary Care Cancer Hospital in a Developing Country: The Story of The Shaukat Khanum Memorial Cancer Hospital and Research Centre", Cancer Control, Shaukat Khanum Memorial Cancer Hospital and Research Centre, Pakistan, pp. 1-10.

Rebecca L. et al., [2020], "Cancer Statistics 2020". American Cancer Society: A Cancer Journal For Clinicians, Vol. 7, No. 1, pp. 7-30.

Civilized Nations and Racial Riots

If we take a closer look at the racial riots in America, history teaches us that racial riots aren't a new problem for America [Zara,2021: 1-48]. The American government, American police, and African Americans have faced this situation many times in the past as well [Colleen,2021: 1-10]. This is a basic social principle that if viciousness isn't stopped the first time around then after one or two incidents this brutality becomes a tradition in the society which encourages the oppressor and makes it a matter of routine for the oppressed [Samuel, 1945:6-12].

A few days back I went through a book of Philip Kotler in which he said that humans have a very weak memory [Vikas, 2021:1-6], maybe this is the reason that African Americans put up with this injustice time and again and then repeatedly forget about it. If this viciousness was countered with full might the first time around then maybe the African Americans didn't have to live this day again and they wouldn't have been brutalized in this way, now it may take many more centuries to uproot this brutal system.

Anyway, I don't see an immediate end to this in American society rather I feel that this may never end and there are many reasons for it but the major reason is the inherent racism in human nature since if it is in his power every person wants to prioritize his own race and nation in every matter.

There is only one way out of this predicament that Islam has taught the world i.e. no black has any superiority over white and no white has any superiority over any black except by piety and fear of Allah. The Holy Prophet (Peace Be Upon Him) gave the world a practical illustration of these teachings by being affectionate towards Hazrat Bilal (May Allah be pleased with him) and by treating him exceptionally well. In any case, racism started centuries ago in America when we see the struggle of African leader Kunta Kinte against racism and the practical form of his sacrifices but its second stage started a little bit earlier than the modern era in 1824 and later in 1831 when the homes of the blacks were brutally razed in the areas of Hardscrabble and snow town, the ensuing movement resulted in the destruction of many buildings and countless people were injured and incarcerated [Melissa, 2022:1-15].

Following that, these incidents kept happening regularly after every year or two and this is still going on. Until now almost 159 black movements against racism have been documented on the national level [Keisha, 2020:1-8]. During these protests, thousands were jailed and thousands of others died. In these 159 black movements, many leaders raised the issues of human rights and the end of racism but some black leaders deserve to be named and we will talk about them later on, lamentably these leaders were either murdered or made to commit suicide over the past century, which has kept the black community deprived of real leadership.

Whenever the blacks raised the voice for equal rights it took the form of a mob or riots because there is no comprehensive purpose to guide them and no proper course is determined, there is just anger and grief that results in making looting, arson, and plunder, the destiny of America.

Another episode in this connection was witnessed a few days back in Minneapolis when racial riots broke out across America following the murder of George Floyd by the police after brutal torture [Farrah, 2020: 1-9]. As a result, things haven't come back to normal as of yet. Special Forces have been called up to assist the police in 24 states.

Arson and violence are going on everywhere, more than 200 buildings have been set on fire, more than 300 police vehicles have been torched and this is still going on. To top it all President Trump is adding fuel to the fire. It would have been better had he handled things sensibly but he recently gave another proof of his irresponsible behavior by saying that where there be riots there will be bullets by the government [Khaled, 2018:1-2]. After this, the American government, which claims the Americans to be a civilized nation, stands fully exposed.

After this pat on the back by the government, the American police started treating its own people like the enemy. The sky even witnessed such scenes where the policemen were dragging the African American women on the roads. This was the frightful face of the American police. Anyways, the discussion was about the prominent personalities who raised their voices against racism, one of these was Malcolm X who later on embraced Islam [Allison, 2007: 261-272]. He said that Islam was the only religion of the world that teaches equality among humans.

He even said that only Islam gives the solution to racism and racial riots. He further wrote that he has never seen love, brotherhood, and equal human rights anywhere but among Muslims. Another outstanding figure was that of Martin Luther

King who raised his voice against American prejudice and talked about equal rights, converting black African Americans from a race into a nation [Clayborne, 2023: 1-25].

Despite being black, he won the love and admiration of the American public more than anyone else and even reached the American National Assembly. In 1955 with Montgomery Bus Boycott, he started the civil rights movement and in 1962 this morphed into a movement to end racism. In a few years, Martin Luther King made this into a national movement so much so that he started working on naming the national department of Washington DC after the movement of the poor people. In 1964, he won the Nobel Peace Prize, he was also given Presidential Award but a conspiracy led to his death in 1964. He didn't even live to see his 40th birthday but he contributed so much towards ending racial prejudice from the world that he will always be remembered in American history.

The need of the hour is that all the communities in America should work together and take practical steps for ending this racial prejudice. In this regard, the most appreciable efforts were made by the Pakistani Muslims in America. Sajid Tarrar the advisor to the American President and Mubashar Warraich the president of the DFW Muslim Community both have not only taken particle steps but have also given superb suggestions for solving the issues between the police and the black community [William,2019:95-98].

They have stressed upon giving all Americans equal rights free of racial discrimination, perhaps the American President will understand their stance. DFW has started its work from a few cities and has shown positive results by increasing police-public interaction on the public level.

At the moment, American city AEVLES is among one of those cities where not even a single incident of confrontation between the police and the public has been reported yet, not even stone-throwing or arson or any other kind of racial unrest has surfaced which is due to the efforts of the Pakistani community which is really admirable.

Now it's time for America to correct its course which is desperately needed so that the American economy doesn't get devoured by the Corona as well as the racial riots. The words of Hazrat Ali (RA) keep reverberating in the mind that enunciate that a system based on refuting the presence of Allah can survive but a system based on oppression cannot. If America can't see the writing on the wall even after the defeat in Afghanistan, the crisis of Corona, and now these racial riots then I think that this system of oppression is not going to last long as well.

REFERENCES:

Allison J. [2007], "Giving Voice to Children's Voices: Practices and Problems, Pitfalls and Potentials". American Anthropologist, Vol.109, No. 2, pp. 261-272.

Clayborne C. [2023], "American Civil Rights Movements". The Editors of Encyclopedia Britannica.

Collen W. [2021], "Solving Racial Disparities in Policing". The Harvard Gazette, pp. 1-10.

Farrah T. [2020], "After the Fires: Re-building Minneapolis in the Wake of Black Lives Matter". The Sidney Morning Herald, pp.1-9.

Keisha N. [2020], "The Fight Against Racism Has Always Been Global". Civil Rights International: Department of History, University of Pittsburgh, pp. 1-8.

Khaled D. [2018], "Trump Adding Fuel to Fire". Al-Ahram Weekly Journal, 2018 Edition, pp. 1-2.

Melissa D. [2022], "Examining Systemic Racism: Advancing Racial Justice in America". Stanford University Communications, pp. 1-15.

Samuel H. [1945], "Principles of Social Interaction". American Sociological Review, vol. 10, No. 1, pp. 6-12.

Vikas D. [2021], "Review of Select Contributions of Philip Kotler to Marketing Theory and Practice". Neville Wadia Institute of Management Studies and Research, pp. 1-6.

William E.   [2019], "The President and Intelligence Communities". Vol. 36, No. 2, pp. 95-98. National Military Intelligence Foundation.

Zara A. [2021], "The Fight Against Racism Must Continue". American Psychological Association, vol. 52, No. 1, pp. 1-48. Continue". American Psychological Association, vol. 52, No. 1, pp. 1-48.

The Danger of Racial Riots in England

After the brutal murder of George Floyd an African American, a few days ago, at the hands of the police, the situation is very tense, so much so that army had to be deployed across America [Melissa, 2021: 1-3]. The anger of the African Americans isn't abating. Now the current situation is that these violent protests have reached London. For the past few days protests have been going on in London and dozens of policemen have been injured in these protests, which is very disturbing [Antoine, 2020: 1-5].

If these protests gained strength in London too, then England will have to fight on two fronts. On the one hand, there is the Corona pandemic and the lockdown and on the other epidemic of racial riots and anarchy. The most disturbing aspect of this whole scenario is that during these black public protests all the preventive rules and regulations to avoid Corona were completely disregarded.

This could bring a new wave of Corona for Britain. If this happens then God forbid, the deaths could increase from thousands to millions. Corona has played such havoc in Britain that lockdown and its effects are starkly visible on the British economy [Becca, 2021 :1-4]. Now there is this new predicament. The fact is that it's the first time that economic, social, and political problems have knocked on the doors of America and Britain together which is a big challenge for these governments [Cross, 1950: 359-365].

Now at this point, the question arises that why the British government gave permission for this kind of protest right in the middle of a deadly pandemic, and even if this permission was granted then why were Corona preventive measures ignored, knowing full well that it could have extremely adverse fallout for England [Malcolm, 1979: 305-323]. If the purpose was to channelize the grief and anger from the death of George Floyd in a positive direction, then this could have been better organized in such a way that could have minimized the danger of the spread of Corona. In any case, it can't be denied that now we will have to live with Corona until an effective treatment is discovered.

The only solution at present is just being careful and nothing else because our Allah is angry with us and we can't fight this pandemic without seeking His forgiveness. Let's have a look now at the racial riots in England [Vivekanandan,1982 :51-63]. These violent demonstrations have a long history but some incidents are worth mentioning. In 1189 when Richard first came to the throne he dismissed some Jewish courtiers for some reason, the result was that some people spread the rumor that the king has ordered the killing of the Jews, that was all it took and the people laid foundations of first racial riots in England [Ted, 2021: 1-821].

In London the people started destroying the homes of the Jews; the devastation was such that Jews even had to convert. Upon getting the knowledge of this mayhem King Richard the first who was the third son of King Henry the second stopped this massacre and gave the Jews reprieve.

Later in 1768, the racial riots broke out when John Vex who was a member of the British parliament, wrote a column on slavery which was published in his own newspaper 'The North Burton'. Many demonstrations were held against this racist and poisonous piece of writing. Some members of the government ordered the army to open fire on the demonstrators and as result, countless died [Jeff, 2023: 1-20].

The Notting Hill riots of 1957 are also worth mentioning that were the first such riots between the black and white communities of England [Christopher, 2022: 47-68]. This was the first time that blacks were made a target of systematical racism. All this started when The White Defense League kidnapped black families.

At that time more than 500 people every day came out on the roads, destroyed property, and attacked white people. Within no time this spread to the whole country. In 1977, The Battle of Lewisham took place, in which more than 4000 people marched against racism [Jenny, 2007: 1-4]. In1981, the demonstration of the blacks took place in Brixton which was later dubbed as Bloody Week, in which thousands died and got injured.

All this was repeated in London in 2011 and now it has started again in 2020. In spite of all this, at present England is less racist as compared to America and the rest of Europe. The human values that are taught to us by Islam are still alive here. Justice is provided by the courts and institutions and racism is relatively low but it's impossible to eradicate it completely. Recently the British police bowed its head in front of the black protestors and reiterated the promise to give their race respect which was a beautiful display of British democratic behavior.

I saw a glimpse of a mature democracy in this. Had the British government dealt with the demonstrators in the same way that the American police did then the situation here would have been far worse but the government realized the gravity of this critical situation and keeping this in view made the best possible decisions.

My criticism, however, stands that the demonstrations to protest the murder of George Floyd could have been better organized and these matters could have been handled in some other way just like Jacinda Arden tackled racism exceptionally after the Mosque Attack in New Zealand and became an example in the history [Jason, 2021: 1-4]. Similarly, England recently passed a Police Reform Bill, so that such racial riots could be stopped.

This is an extremely laudable step of the British Parliament. America should learn a lesson from the way England and New Zealand have taken steps to eliminate racism. Trump's government shouldn't become a police state otherwise the race suffering from slavery could follow in the footsteps of the gladiators who rose against slavery in Italy whose origins can be traced back to Sparta in Greece.

There is time yet, things can be brought to normal. All that is required is to give up obstinacy and stand in other person's shoes to get a better understanding of the problems. A small step can bring the people of the world together and a wrong step can take them towards a civil war.

REFERENCES:

Antoine J.et al., [2020], "How Do Black People Channel Their Anger----". Washington Post, June 2019 Edition, pp. 1-5.

Becca B. et al., [2021], "Understanding the Impact of Covid-19 on UK Population". Directorate of the Centre For International Migration, UK, pp. 1-4.

Christopher H. [2022], "Mapping the Notting Hill Riots: Racism and the Streets of Post-War Britain". History Workshop Journal, Vol. 93, No. 1, pp. 47-68.

Cross R.S. [1950], "The Modern Predicament". The Philosophical Quarterly, Vol.6, No.25, pp.359-365, University Press.

Jason S. [2021], "The Global Impact of George Flyod-----". The CBS News International, UK, pp.1-4.

Jeff W. [2023], "Boston Massacres: United States History". The Editors of Encyclopedia Britannica, pp.1-20.

Jenny B. [2007], "Lewisham'77: Success or Failure". The Institute of Race Relations, UK, pp. 1-4.

Malcolm R. [1979], "The British Government and Mormon Question, 1910-1922". Journal of Church and State, Vol.21, No. 2, pp.305-323. Oxford University Press.

Melissa D. [2021], "Anger and Sadness Soared Following George Floyd's Death". Directorate of Stanford Report, pp.1-3.

Ted B. [2021], "The Massacres of the Jews Under Richard [A.D 1189-1190]". Department of History and Religion,

Lincoln Memorial University, Harrogate, Vol.12, No.10, pp.1-821.

Vivekanandam B. [1982], "Riots in Britain: An Analysis". India Quarterly, Vol.38, No.1, pp.51-63.

Message for the New Year

Dear readers, many good wishes for the upcoming year. May God bless you all with happiness and joy and prolong everyone's age, health, and prosperity, and may He grant us the wisdom of self-critique and the courage to tread the right path.

Yesterday I read very meaningful advice of Hazrat Ali (May God exalt his face) in which he addressed the faithful and said, 'always pray for a long life because even a moment before death is worth more than a thousand months after death'. This guidance is incredibly profound and full of wisdom; it is not only a treasure trove of guidance but also holds the secret for the longevity of the Muslim Ummah and the rest of of the humanity. Just ponder over this, what does a Muslim and all others need, apart from the guidance and pleasure of God and God's forgiveness for his sins?

The significance of the moment mentioned by Hazrat Ali (May God exalt his face) is also amplified by the fact that if in that last moment one asks forgiveness for one's sins then that instant could be the moment of deliverance but after death, there won't be any such moment for even a thousand years. Allama Iqbal has beautifully reiterated the same advice when he said,

That one prostration that is tough for you
Delivers you from a thousand prostrations

[Aatif, 2008:1-3]

There is a mention of that one tear which if shed with remorse before the Exalted One, saves one from wandering pillar to post without any avail. The Sunnah of the Holy Prophet (peace be upon him) also teaches us that this life is the crop of eternal life. We will reap as we shall sow and it is imperative that we critically examine our actions.

One of Ashfaq Ahmed's sayings often keeps coming to the mind, he says facilitate people, which means that be generous and good to others and make things easy for them. Treat others kindly and take care of their lives, property, and honor. If you do this, then I can say with complete certainty that every good deed of yours will be honored by God and you will be rewarded both here and in the hereafter.

I know that self-criticism is very complex and tough because the biggest weakness of a human being is that he always sees wrong in the other person. His worst habit is to think of himself as pure and he always makes excuses for himself.

In fact, just as one doesn't overlook the faults of others, similarly one should also not lose sight of one's shortcomings to overcome them. A successful person always succeeds after prevailing over his failings. We will have to examine our flaws honestly and decide how to triumph over these weaknesses and make them our strengths. We will have to see if knowingly or unknowingly we are committing the sins that are hampering our prayers from being accepted by God. I don't want to talk here about the theology of religion, but wisdom of life.

Shouldn't we replace mistrust with fear of God, the foul language with the remembrance of God, anger with compassion, laziness with the struggle for gaining knowledge, narcissism with the common good, hopelessness with faith in

God, lies with truth, deception with honesty, backbiting and false accusations with mutual reform?

Don't we insult others on the pretext of improving them?

We need to give serious thought to these points. With these small alterations, we can transform ourselves into a complete person and a genuine Muslim, a Muslim who facilitates others in the society and whose every moment in life is precious.

Now if we take a look at the past year as a nation, we could easily find out what we have gained and what we have lost. We need to reform individually as well as collectively. We have to let go of racial prejudices like Punjabi, Sindhi, Baluchi, and Pathan and become a unified nation [Charles, 1984:688-703]. In the same sense I believe that the humanity is first and foremost element for good life.

We desperately need to promote the values of tolerance, care, mutual respect, and showing favor to others and at the same time, we have to strive to uproot social evils [Tariq,1997:833-839]. We will have to nurture our democratic system and take practical steps to create a balance among the national institutions in the accordance with the true spirit of the constitution [Peter, 2018:1-2]. We have to include ethics as a subject in the curricula of the universities that produce journalists and other professionals so that responsible experts become a part of society [Manzoor et al, 2016:385-396].

We have to rein in the growing unemployment and widespread economic adversity. We need to check the rise in scarcity of resources such as gas, power, and water by adopting effective practical measures. We will have to protect the lives and honor of our children [Sarah, 2023:1-10]. We will have to perk up our education system. We will have to duly acknowledge the sacrifices made by our armed forces on every front because our army is one of the greatest armies in the world. We will have to learn from our past mistakes and make Pakistan a strong and stable country and live with neighbours with harmony. We have to plan for the coming year and the challenges that it will bring.

All this is possible only through the above-mentioned ways and means. First of all, we should pray for long life, then help out our friends, critically analyze our actions and then our actions as a nation, and then meet those challenges head-on that is staring us in the face. May God protect and help us to give great care to other humans beside the religion. Amen

REFERENCES:

Aatif A. M. [2008], "Iqbal's Vision of a Muslim State". International Iqbal Society, Vol. 944, No. 1656, pp. 1-3.

Charles H. K. [1984], "Policies of Ethnic PREFERENCESin Pakistan ". Asian Survey: University of California Press, Vol. 24, No. 6, pp. 688-703.

Manzoor H. et al [2016], "Ethics and Education in Pakistan: Principles, Policies and Practice". Children and Sustainable Development Journal: Chapter 10, pp. 385-396.

Peter C. [2018], "How to Nurture A Democracy". Institute for The Study of Complex Systems, Vol. 459, No. 2, pp. 1-2.

Sarah E. [2023], "The Rights of Children Over Parents". Aljumuah Magazine, pp. 1-10.

Tariq R. [1997], "Language and Ethnicity in Pakistan". Asian Survey: University of California Press, Vol. 37, No. 9, pp. 833-839.

Home of the Heartless

It was a beautiful evening a few days back. The weather was quite chilly, cold wind was blowing, accompanied by a drizzle. I was walking to the market with a cup of coffee in my hand. I was going on the footpath enjoying the weather suddenly I felt a jab on my ankle. Someone had hit me with a stick. Hurt and in pain I turned around furiously but my anger dissipated and turned into compassion when I saw that the man who had hit me was blind. He was feeling his way with a stick.

I held his hand and helped him to his destination. That day I realized that when one's point of view changes their feelings change as well. As soon as this realization dawned on me, I got lost in deep thought for a while. A notion kept bothering me that someday an ordinary citizen's view about these special people will change in Pakistan as well.

When will these deprived and destitute people be considered an important element of Pakistani society? [James,1911:39-50]

When will their equal rights come out of books and become a practical part of society?

May Allah protect us all from such a tribulation. Just ask those parents who have a special child, how they become an object of disdain, how their beloved is ridiculed, how they are considered a burden on society, how they are scoffed at in the streets, markets and offices. To some extent, our upbringing as a nation and our environment is to blame for this behavior. This uncivilized attitude starts from our homes and enters the schools.

In the schools, these children are not only called names but are also mocked in front of other students.

Living in Pakistan, have we ever taught our children or given them any awareness about these special children? [Zaeem, 2017:1-2].

Have we ever taught them the significance of these special, underprivileged, and disadvantaged people and how they should be treated? [Emma et al., 2019: 1-12].

How can we make our society more sensitive to their needs?

How can we uproot the insensitivity and lack of conscience and make them a part of the national mainstream?

How can we benefit from their immense potential?

How can we take them out of the sense of being neglected and make them pillars of society?

In this modern era, we really need to understand the fact that no creation of Allah is meaningless. His justice is supreme and eternal. If he deprives someone of one thing then he blesses them with countless others. If he takes from one hand, then he gives countless blessings from the other.

Islam holds the deprived and disadvantaged in high regard. The biggest example in this regard is that of an elderly man who came to visit the Holy Prophet (Peace be upon him) when he was busy convincing the prominent leaders of the Quraish and said that he wanted to talk to the Holy Prophet (Peace be upon him).

The Holy Prophet (Peace be upon him) asked him to wait a while as he was busy. That man again beseeched, O Prophet of Allah I am blind and I have come to you to ask about Islam, please inform me about the word of Allah. The Holy Prophet (Peace be upon him) told him,'Wait a while. Let me talk to the leaders of the Quraish first.' Allah SWT revealed in Surah e Abas,

> *'He frowned and turned away. Because there came to him a blind man.'*

(Chapter 80: verses 1,2)

This blind man was so honored that his narrative was immortalized in the Holy Quran. Similarly, Hazrat Bilal (May Allah be pleased with him) who was held in high esteem by the Holy Prophet (Peace be upon him) spoke with a lisp. He couldn't pronounce *'Ash'Had'* properly and instead said 'As'Had' when calling for prayer, and when some Muslims objected to this Hazrat Bilal (May Allah be pleased with him) didn't say the Azan, and that day the morning didn't dawn. All these examples teach us the lesson that there is a crucial need to award the special people due regard and along with that they have to be given their rightful place in the society.

Have we ever thought of making ramps for wheelchairs while constructing shopping malls?

Have we designated a separate space for wheelchairs on our roads?

Have we provided a network of schools for the special people?

Have we provided them with equal employment opportunities? [Abel, 2017: 1-12].

Have we ever thought of helping them on a permanent basis instead of providing them temporary relief?

How many of us give them equal regard instead of merely taking pity on them?

Trust me they don't need our pity, what they need is equal opportunity and standing in society. Have we considered giving them equal opportunities instead of reserved quotas on the government level?

Have we ever provided them with any out-of-the-ordinary facilities in our homes, streets, markets, railway stations, cafés, schools, offices, and places of entertainment?

The bitter truth is that we have never given this a thought and tried to do something different for these people. They also have feelings and sensitivities; they also have an insightful heart beating within the chest, they are living breathing people just like us, they also get hurt from our conduct, they also experience grief and pain, they are neither made of stones nor are they dwellers of stone burgs.

A very dear friend of mine Prof. Rauf Ahmed used to teach mathematics in the Government College of Science, Wahdat Road. He was visually impaired. After moving abroad, I lost touch with him but he had a very unique quality. Once you had met him you won't have to introduce yourself again; he would recognize you by the touch of your hand, or through your tread, or maybe by your scent. This loving friend of mine is exceptionally intelligent, believe me, people like him are an asset to the nation.

My affectionate teacher, the first visually impaired Muslim judge in England, Mr. Ameer Ali Maajid who aside from being a teacher of Human Rights at Metropolitan University; also served as an Immigration Judge. He is a shining example of courage and graciousness who glorified the name of Pakistan internationally [Mncube et al., 2021: 1179-1187]. I met a Pakistani student Irfan this year; he couldn't speak or hear but never lagged in the studies despite his disabilities.

I was pleasantly surprised when he told me the reason. I knew about it to a great extent but I liked hearing it from him but the next instant I felt sad that this kind of facility isn't available to special people in Pakistan. Irfan told me that being the president or office holder of the British Deaf Association he helped numerous Muslim students who are deaf. He further informed me that when Azan is called or the Holy Quran is recited then they understood it in sign language. He said that he longed to hear that beautiful recitation.

I can't tell you what I felt when he said this. This got me thinking that there are many Muslims among us who don't even open the Holy Book for days on end. The value of this should be asked from those who aren't able to hear or speak. Irfan taught me to love Holy Quran. He further told me that he can hire a sign language interpreter whose fee is paid by the government.

I understood all this conversation through the interpreter. He further told me that all of his expenses such as tuition fees, rent, medical, books, and traveling are paid by the government and he is given many other special facilities. The visually impaired are provided guide dogs by the state. These dogs safely take them to their educational institution and then back home, safely.

What is more, the great British scientist Stephen was funded generously for years until his death by the government for research with the help of modern equipment and state-of-the-art wheelchair [Sarah, 2018: 1-5]. That is the way of the nations who are alive; this is how they honor their gifted people. Now think about the way we treat our deprived and destitute.

Don't we ridicule them by calling them names like one-eyed, deaf, cripple, lame, fat, dwarf, etc?

How cruel are we, how brutally we break the hearts of those who live with us as if we are heartless?

Are we really that stone-hearted?

Don't we possess a heart?

I fail to understand how we can be so vicious?

I think that we really live in the city of stones where everyone is devoid of emotions and feelings, where everyone is trying to sniff out the light of the fireflies so that they can't show others the way. In fact, these deprived and destitute are the ones who are like fireflies in darkness who guide others and show them the straight path [Hilary, 2019:1-7].

The straight path that teaches us the fear of Allah, the straight path that teaches us compassion, the straight path that our religion shows us regarding the rights of others, and humanitarianism. If only our nation's point of view could change, if only we could sense the light that is definitely somewhere closer to us.

REFERENCES:

Abel I. [2017], "Education of People with Special Needs". Department of Economics, National Open University, Jabi-Abuja, Nigeria. The 3rd International Conference on Social Science, pp.1-12.

Emma C. et al., [2019], "The Challenges of Inclusion for Children with Disabilities: Experiences of Implementation in Eastern and Southern Africa". UNICEF Think Piece Series, pp. 1-12.

Hilary S. [2019], "Social Exclusion". Brown University Publications, pp1-7.

James S. [1911], "The Problem of Destitution: A Plea For the Minority Report". International Journal of Ethics, vol. 22, No.1, pp.39-50.

Mncube D. et al., [2021], "Novice Teachers' Experiences of Teaching Visually Impaired Learners in the Foundation Phase", Universal Journal of Educational Research, Vol.9, No. 6, pp.1179-1189.

Sarah C. [2018], "Stephen Hawking's Final Theory About The Big Bang", SciTech Daily: University of Cambridge, pp.1-5.

Zaeem M. [2017], "Legal Rights of Children Under Laws of Pakistan". Pakistan's 1st Legal News and Analysis Portal: Courting the Law, pp.1-2.

The Shade for the Trees

Loving trees is equivalent to cherishing humanity because the trees are our life source. They provide us with oxygen, shield us from the hazardous effects of global warming and protect us from rains, typhoons, storms in addition to sheltering us from the devastating effects of floods and earthquakes [Alan, 2019: 1-10].

At present, global warming is the biggest challenge facing the world which means that due to deforestation the temperature of the earth is gradually rising every year [Jackie, 2019: 1-4]. This will cause the water from the earth to evaporate thus depleting water resources. Lack of clean drinking water will not only adversely affect the whole of mankind but the scarcity of available water for farming may result in widespread famines.

The slowly melting ice caps provide us with water all over the year to quench our thirsts and to meet other needs. If these ice caps melt at a rapid pace, the resulting water will reach the oceans at a greater speed which in turn will raise the sea level. It is being predicted that megacities on the shores of oceans will come under water due to this expected rise in the sea level. It is imperative that awareness should be raised among the people world over, regarding the importance and necessity of more trees [Foluke, 2004: 41-52].

At the moment the level of pollution and weather changes in Pakistan requires that the plantation drives should continue all year long so that the environmental problems could be tackled as soon as possible. The government of Pakistan has again initiated a plantation drive this month which is very heartening [Muhammed, 2020: 1-16].

The main driving force behind this initiative is not only recognition and awareness of this problem at the government level but also the Bonn Challenge. It is a global agreement among dozens of countries that requires the participating countries to restore forests on 150 million hectares by the year 2020 and 350 million hectares by 2030 [Bravo,1987: 1-5].

 Fortuitously Pakistan is also one of the signatories of the Bonn Challenge Agreement and is playing an important role in the efforts to meet the challenges posed by global climate change. Over the past years, the temperature has been gradually rising in Pakistan and there is a threat of shorter winters if there is a further rise in temperature.

This is why an increase in the number of trees takes precedence over an increase in the number of people. In this modern era, the world needs to curtail and limit the number of not only factories, cars, buses, and rickshaws but it is also essential to regulate and improve the use of vehicles/ machinery in the agriculture sector. In order to reduce environmental pollution, it is imperative that the government should consider legislation that should make it mandatory to get government permission prior to cutting trees [Haibo et al, 2022: 1-10].

In this regard, the PTI government laid the foundation of the Billion Tree Tsunami Project in 2014 from Khyber Pakhtunkhwa [Salman, 2017: 1-7]. During this campaign, efforts were made at the government level to make Pakistan green and lush. Unfortunately, many irregularities surfaced in this whole process but steps were taken to bring the culprits to task.

According to a report of BBC, in England alone 15 million trees were planted during the current year [Patrick, 2021: 1-3]. The British government aims to take this number to 100 million in the coming decades. Similarly, America is planning on planting around 60 billion trees over the next two decades. In the same vein, Europe has started a campaign for planting 30 billion trees over the next decade [Bruce, 2020:1-4].

In order to reduce pollution from fuel emissions, Europe and America have started working on achieving a 100% increase in the use of electric cars by the year 2025 [Hannah, 2020:1-4]. The government should make use of the services of British NGOs like AFHAE, continue the plantation campaign all year round to ensure the permanent safety of the plants.

Unfortunately, this sector remained badly neglected in the past. In spite of annual floods, storms, heavy rains, sweltering heat, environmental pollution, and ever-lowering underground water table, tree plantation wasn't paid due attention. Instead, those who claimed of converting Lahore into Paris chopped down the trees on the sides of the roads, constructed bridges and Orange Line.

All this was done while knowing that the presence of trees reduces air pollution by releasing oxygen and absorbing carbon dioxide and is basically hope for the bright future of our coming generations. Had even a little thought was spared for this problem, the environmental disaster wouldn't have reached the present scale in Pakistan. Lahore is just one example; Sindh and Baluchistan are not in any different situation. If only a billion olive trees are planted in Baluchistan, which is extremely suited for growing olives, it can compete with the billion-dollar olive oil industry of Spain [Rafiullah, 2022: 1-5].

The previous governments have merely paid lip service and never worked diligently on this issue. A few days ago a video got viral on social media that showed a mob pulling out trees ruthlessly as if they had stones instead of hearts. If these trees had to be pulled out for any reason whatsoever, they could have been carefully transplanted elsewhere but sadly that wasn't the case. I would call this environmental terrorism because such actions are an act of terror against us and against our coming generations. I fail to understand how anyone could be so ignorant and heartless? No one can deny the fact that even the person who cuts trees, sits in the shade of a tree to refresh himself. Planting trees is not only Sunnah, the way of the Holy Prophet (Peace be upon him) but is also an act of perpetual charity.

We should plant trees for our descendants so that we can pay the debt that we owe to our ancestors who have left us the priceless treasure of trees. We continually benefit from the fruits, shade, and wood of these trees. Planting trees is neither difficult nor time-consuming; it is very easy and simple. The difficult task is ensuring the safety and looking after these trees, which in Pakistan is almost negligible.

It is essential that almost 25% area of a country should be covered with forests but according to a report after Afghanistan, Pakistan is the country with the least area under forests in this region as forests constitute only 4% of the area [Martin et al, 2021: 1499-1509]. On the other hand, among the neighboring countries, Iran has forests on 7%, India has 23%, China has 22% and Russia has 44% of its total area covered with forests.

It is high time now to take part in the plantation campaign at an individual level. Not only should we plant trees but also pledge to look after them. If we can't increase the area under forests, then at least we could plant trees and make our streets and localities green. Let us all join hands, work together, do our part, meet our obligation and make our country and the safe. We will have to include lessons that highlight the importance and efficacy of trees so that they could become shade for every shady tree and we could have a brilliant future. Amen.

REFERENCES:

Alan B. [2019], "Examining the Viability of Planting Trees to Help Mitigate Climate Change". Global Climate Change: NASA's Jet Propulsion Laboratory, pp. 1-10.

Bravo A. [1987], "The Driving Forces of Environmental Change". United Nations University Website: http;//unu.edu/, pp.1-5.

Bruce L. [2020], "The Pros and Cons of Planting Trees to Address Global Warming". Yale Climate Connections: Bruce Liberman Freelance Archives, pp. 1-4.

Foluke O.   [2004], "Environmental Sustainability in Nigeria The Awareness Initiative". African Issues, vol. 31/32, No. ½, pp. 41-52. Cambridge University Press.

Haibo R. et al., [2022], "Government Trust, Environmental Pollution Perception and Environmental Governance Satisfaction". National Library of Medicine: National Centre for Biotechnology Information, Vol. 19, No. 16, pp. 1-10, PM/D: 36011557.

Hannah R. [2020], "Climate Change and Flying: What Share of Global CO2 Emissions Come From Aviation". The Editorials: Our World in Data, pp. 1-4.

Jackie S. [2019], "How Artificial Intelligence Can Tackle Climate Change", National Geographic, pp. 1-4.

Martin J. et al., [2021], "Areas of Global Importance For Conserving Terrestial Biodiversity, Carbon and Water", Nature, Ecology and Evolution, vol. 5, pp. 1499-1509.

Muhammed H. [2020], "Climate Change and Health in Pakistan: Impacts and Adaptation Policy". PMAS and Agriculture University, pp. 1-16.

Patrick B.   [2021], "Row Over UK Tree Planting Drive". The Editorial: The Guardian, pp. 1-3.

Rafiullah M. [2022], "Olive Farming is Key to Saving The Forests in Balochistan". Olive Oil Times, Pakistan, pp. 1-5.

Salman G. [2017], "An Environmental Analysis of the Billion Tree Tsunami Project in Khyber-Pakhtunkhwa Pakistan". South-Asia Forestry and Environmental Sustainability, Himalayas, pp. 1-7.

Have You No Shame Left

Out of countless heartbreaking tales from this beloved land of ours, one is that of Arsalan Haider who belongs to Jarranwala [Rokus, 2011:61-93]. When he was terminated by the factory where he was working, he reached home empty-handed, troubled, destitute, and with shattered dreams; he saw his brother who on his death bed was asking for the last ray of hope from his family especially his penniless brother.

Arsalan almost lost his senses at seeing his brother in such a pitiful state. Instead of his treatment, Arsalan was consumed by another thought entirely. Teary-eyed he begged his brother not to die and said, 'My brother! Don't die yet. I don't have money to pay for the funeral'.......

Isn't this state of affairs enough to move one to cry tears of blood?

Isn't this the story of every middle-class family that is living below the poverty line in this beloved land of ours? [Veronica, 1971:14-18].

Isn't this the story of every person who is running from pillar to post just to make ends meet?

Isn't this the pain of every family where the daughters grow old waiting to be wed, but no one comes to their rescue?

These words of Arsalan Haider are tearing my heart out and will be a thorn in every intelligent person's heart. Every person would be extremely hurt by this accident who has considered this not a mere accident but a national tragedy. In this Islamic Welfare State, every day some Arsalan Haider has to go through these circumstances. Every day in some nook or cranny there are dead bodies waiting to be buried and placed in some morgue lament our nationality and humanity or tease us by being a picture of our helplessness and insensitivity.

What kind of human beings are we?

What kind of Muslims are we that we take bodies to the graveyard on our shoulders but never stop to think about the expenses involved in the burial rituals?

Do we never think who had paid for the funeral?

How was it arranged and by whom?

Does the family have enough to pay for this in these trying times without any worry or even this is the responsibility of the family that has suffered this loss?

Just think for a moment whether we'll arrange our own funerals?

Do we have any knowledge of the place, time, and circumstances of our deaths?

If not, then believe that we are all interdependent. After Allah we turn to each other in the times of pain, we trust that we will put balm on each other's wounds, we will share each other's hurt and pain, we will be there for each other in difficult times, but we are so caught up in gathering more and more wealth that we have forgotten death itself.

Mosques and philanthropic organizations are doing this job to some extent but the question isn't who will bury the dead, the real question is why isn't there someone to cater to the needs of such people and families in this Riyasat e Madina?

Why is the poor dying to get two meals a day and medical treatment?

Why are they running hither thither for getting medical treatment?

Someone should ask these rulers; why, why the people are still deprived of the solutions to everyday problems like treatment for dengue? [John, 2021: 1-3]

Every year many people pass away without getting treatment facilities and thousands remain under treatment in the hospitals, why aren't different areas sprayed timely? [Gabriel et al, 2019: 1-4].

Why isn't the vaccine for rabies available in the hospitals?

How long will this farce continue?

Where is the health department?

Where is the Auqaf Department?

Why aren't they facilitating the people?

Whenever the people need their help, the process is so complicated and long drawn out that either the patient dies without treatment or his body ends up in a morgue paying its last respects to this governance system and is awaiting a messiah who would send them off to their final journey.

Recently after the breaking out of Corona, the Pakistani students stuck in China are awaiting the government's help. Every day government representatives were seen consoling them on the television screens and uttering the line that they have probably learned from Trump that he uses in the case of

Pakistan-India issue, 'we are closely watching the whole situation'.

The advisor for health is also continuously repeating this line, on the other hand, these students are facing so many hardships yet no one in the Pakistani Consulate is even answering their phones. You should have at least that much moral courage as to console them after listening to their problems. If you can't help them then the least, you could do is to get their issues resolved by the Chinese authorities. They shouldn't be left helpless like this.

Is this the new Pakistan?

Is this the value of overseas Pakistanis? Is this the way of lively nations that they should abandon their citizens vulnerable in dire straits? [Sayed, 2019: 1-7].

I agree that we don't have as many facilities as China but are we lacking in honor as well?

Isn't even listening to their phone calls and getting them help from Chinese authorities is possible?

For God's sake please wake your national honor up and help these Pakistanis as much as you can, otherwise how will you face Allah?

I humbly seek an apology from fro those Pakistanis who consider themselves alone and helpless in China. I beseech them to trust Allah because He will not leave them alone like the government of Pakistan. He is the one who takes care of everything, He will definitely help you. I want to salute the PIA, which despite all its handicaps and shortcomings has taken up the task of transporting the dead bodies of Pakistanis back home free of cost, for a very long period and doing this job rather well.

Why can't other relevant institutions do their jobs well, like PIA?

Despite tall claims made by the government, the effective performance of the government institutions is yet to be seen. Things are as haphazard as they were before. These institutions should learn something from PIA. They should help out the poor and helpless so that they could easily get treatment and if the situation demands things should be made easier for funerals etc.

The health department should take strict notice of this situation and ensure that the poor and needy get health facilities. Health Card is a good step but taking it to 100% of the citizens and improving the condition of the hospitals should be the government's top priority.

The Auqaf Department should introduce 24-hour services for the poor and the needy. The hospitals should be given special funds by the Auqaf Department that can be given to the family who can't afford the expenditure, along with the dead body. Here things go exactly the opposite way. The family isn't even handed over the dead body, let alone the money to cover the expenses.

The government should shoulder the responsibility of meeting these expenses and it should provide permanent packages to the vulnerable and the deprived families so that the poor laborers, orphans and the destitute don't have to face such hardships [Malcolm, 2019: 1-12]. No other Arsalan Haider has to be anxious about the funeral expenses instead of grieving for the loss of his loved ones.

It is our moral obligation as well to be cognizant of the needs of the disadvantaged and underprivileged those are living around us and help them out as much as possible so that a healthy society could be established [Schurman,1894: 1-15]. No one should have to come to you with their problems, they should be taken care of before asking and in a way that no one else gets to know so that their self-respect remains intact and we could earn Allah's favor as well.

REFERENCES:

Gabriel G.et al [2019], "Every Year Nearly 6 Million People Die". Global Health: World Economic Forum, pp.1-4.

John H. [2021], "Good Leadership is About Asking Good Questions". Harvard Business Review: Global Peter Drucker Forum, pp. 1-3.

Malclom S. [2019], "The Fiscal Responsibilities of Government". A Modern Guide to State Intervention: University of Leeds, pp. 85-96.

Rokus D. [2011], "Rumi and The Abyss of Longing". Mawlana Rumi Review, Vol. 2, pp. 61-93.

Sayed B. [2019], "The Future of Pakistan and Its Overseas Diaspora", Journal of International Affairs, Pakistan, pp. 1-7.

Schurman J. G. [1894], "The Consciousness of Moral Obligation". The Philosophical Review, Vol. 3, No. 6, pp. 641-654. Duke University Press, pp. [1-15].

Veronica S. [1971], "The Myth of The Middle-class Family in American Family Sociology". The American Sociologist: Vol. 6, No. 1, pp. 14-18.

The Problems of Government Servants

There is a Persian proverb 'TANG AAMAD BAJUNG AAMAD' (even a cornered rat will fight). Over the years, the plight of government servants hasn't registered any positive change, in spite of repeated reassurances by the government [Alex, 2002: 498-517]. Pakistan's history bears witness to the fact that whenever the working class has raised their voice, imprisonment, torture, and oppression become their fate [Raja et al, 2020: 215-229].

This time when driven by adversity, these government servants protested, the government showed its hospitality by teargas shelling. Afterward, when the government saw that things are starting to get out of hand, it had to back down and the pays were raised by 20% to 30%, but the government has failed to increase more than 10% in the budget.

I want to ask the government what recourse is there for the public that is facing the brunt of rising inflation for the past two years. The unfortunate government servants neither have the right to protest nor can they voice their grievances. No matter who is in power, the government servants and the pensioners were never given proper relief packages even in the current budget 2021-22.

The truth of the matter is that no single government has given serious thought to their problems.

In reality; the developed nations always maintain a balance between the ratio of income and prices of goods and services otherwise the tsunami of inflation, graft, and dishonesty can't be countered [Rakesh, 2015: 1-10]. If the government couldn't bear the pressure of the protests, why weren't these demands met earlier? Why did they have to take to the roads in the first place? The rulers who claim to be great humanitarians have become so insensitive that they can't see anything except their own problems? [Hugo, 2020:1-3] I would urge the officials, kindly spare some time and have a look at the dire situation of the government servants who are condemned to a state of perpetual poverty and are barely making the ends meet while trying to maintain a semblance of respect and dignity.

Their problems are eating away in their lives. In England, protests against inflation were held in every era including those of Margret Thatcher, Tony Blair, and David Cameron. Millions took to the roads but never once did the government resort to force [David, 2023:1-44].

Similarly, during last year's recession in Spain and Greece, the public protest was not stopped with force and brutality neither the employees were laid off because of the peaceful protests.

In sharp contrast, here Riyasat-E-Madina is held as an example but the actions are worst than that of a banana republic. There should be some rules to regulate a protest, however, whether the protest is being held outside the Parliament or in some remote, little-known area; it should be given due importance. The rulers should listen and respond to the grievances voiced thus because that is the true spirit of democracy.

According to a report of CEIC, the GDP growth rate registered a minuscule increase but prices were increased manifold so that the poor may never become financially independent. There is no doubt that the people of Pakistan have always been stolen from in the name of the Islamic Welfare State [Raja,1972: 17-22]. The past governments gave this lollipop and the present government is also following in their footsteps and is duping the nation with the same empty slogans. If the present government is serious in transforming Pakistan into an Islamic Welfare State in letter and in spirit then it must start working to get rid of the current Riba (interest) based economic system. The importance of this effort was realized by Luxemburg. In spite of being a Christian country in the middle of Europe, they have completely gotten rid of interest-based systems and have established their economy on Islamic economic principles. This is a strong slap in the face of all those who claim to establish an Islamic Welfare State.

An Islamic Welfare State ordains that the laborer must be paid for the labors even before the drying of the sweat and also that the rights of none be usurped under any conditions. Ashfaq Ahmed used to recall that once he had to go to court while his stay in Italy where he was serving as a teacher. The judge and the court employees stood up in his honor saying that a teacher was in the court [Tahir, 2019: 1-4]. But we are outlandish people. If teachers, lawyers, doctors, laborers, farmers, and even the visually challenged people raise voices to get their rights; we give them bullets, tear gas, baton charge, and jail cells. Islam has given rights even to stray dogs and no one is allowed to treat them brutally. How can followers of Islam treat humans worse than animals? It is shameful, to say the least.

The decency of our ministers is such that instead of putting salve on the wounds of the underprivileged and the downtrodden, they feel pride in inflicting wounds. We have seen the protestors in this very same Islamabad attacking Supreme Court and the PTV headquarters; we have seen them burning electricity bills and heard them talking about civil disobedience while standing in the red zone.

Why this wrath over the protest of the poor and the needy now? This culture needs to end now. The incumbent government came to power raising the slogan of justice and with the mandate to end injustice. If they are also going down this route then the direction of 'change' isn't quite right. There are many ways to end such protests in the world and the dominant amongst them is improved performance and fulfilling of promises. This is followed by talks and if that doesn't do the job then accepting defeat is the brave thing to do.

REFERENCES:

Alex S. [2002], "Civil Service Reform in Post-Independence Nigeria: Issues and Challenges". Public Administration Quarterly, Vol. 25, No. 4, pp. 498-517.

David B. [2023], "Consumer Price Inflation, UK: July 2023". Office for National Statistics, pp. 1-44.

Hugo S. [2020], "You Don't Have to Be Neutral to Be a Good Humanitarian". The New Humanitarianism, pp. 1-3.

Raja Q. et al., [2020], "The Rise of Peripheral Nationalism in Pakistan and The Pashtun Tahafuz Movement". Asian Ethnicity, Vol. 23, No. 2, pp. 215-229.

Raja T. R. [1972], "Some Foreign Policy Problems of Pakistan". Pakistan Horizon, Vol. 25, No. 3, pp. 17-22. Pakistan Institute of International Affairs.

Rakesh K. [2015], "A Global Middle Class is More Promise Than Reality". Economy and Work: Pew Research Center, pp. 1-10.

Tahir K. [2019], "Ashfaq Ahmad's Warning and The Apathy of The Educated". The Editorial: The News On Sunday, pp. 1-4.

Second Chapter: Modus Operandi of Politics

The Troika That Matters

Pakistan is passing through the most critical period of its seventy years' history. On the one hand, the Iran-America conflict has created a problem of peace and stability while on the other hand ever-increasing Indian aggression is creating a profound impact on Pakistan as well as South Asia [Sawaf ,2020: 1-7]. In addition to these problems, Pakistan is facing a plethora of other problems as well. To face all these challenges and predicaments Pakistan needs wisdom and acumen as well as mutual cooperation and unity of thought.

The most important issue among these delicate problems was legislation on the Army Act [Shahzeb,2023: 1-8]. To pass the bill, the government needed a simple majority in the national assembly. Since the government didn't have the requisite majority for legislation, it needed to take the opposition into confidence to tackle the legal crisis and to solve future problems with its help.

With the Grace of Allah, Army Act 2020 and Air Force Act 2020 were passed in the National Assembly without any hitch but this whole process was completed in undue haste. The lower legislative chamber i.e. the National Assembly cleared the bill in one day and the upper legislative chamber i.e. the Senate passed the bill in less than one hour.

On the one hand, this is a good omen in that a very crucial national issue was resolved decently and expediently but on the other hand this whole affair has given birth to numerous questions. The question isn't as to why were these bills passed; the question here is why was this done with undue speed?

The consensus of opinion on this matter isn't surprising in any way, but still, this issue should have been thoroughly discussed and debated. Only after laying the issue and its relative pros and cons bare, should it have been given the status of an Act of Parliament. In contrast, if we look at the process of legislation in Britain, we find that although it's very complicated the acts are passed and amended pretty quickly.

For legislation in Britain, first of all, a government committee is constituted, then a white paper is issued which is followed by the green paper that is prepared only after detailed discussions and debate [Jess et al., 2023: 1-7]. In this way, a bill is passed after months of deliberations and discussions. Another thing to keep in mind here is that in the British legislature discussion and critique is constructive and not just criticism for the sake of criticism. Before promulgating a law that date on which it would come into force is also declared.

Only those issues are resolved under the new law that comes to the fore after the law has been enacted. The laws aren't passed or revoked for the benefit of any individual. If it's a matter of national interest, then speeding up the process of legislation isn't undesirable just like what happened recently in Pakistan but it would still have been better if the legislation had followed adequate deliberations and open debate.

All this was done swiftly, but there is no consensus of opinion neither any flexibility is in sight when the issues concerning public problems or benefits are being raised or discussed on the floor of the house.

In Pakistan, unfortunately, the problems of the people have remained unresolved and the raison d'être is unreasonable bickering between the government and the opposition. Their difference of opinion comes to the fore only when the matters of peoples' interest are being discussed [Muhammed,2021:1-36].

The opposition thinks that its primary job is to criticize every action of the government regardless of merit or reason [Devendra, 2014: 165-170]. In the same way, the government keeps one step ahead by constantly painting a negative image of the policies of 'the previous governments' i.e. the opposition. In Pakistan, every incumbent government considers rubbishing the projects started by the previous regime its foremost duty [Shahid et al., 2006: 913-923].

Either the funding for these projects is stopped or the very same projects are continued with new names after minor adjustments and then they are touted as the projects of the sitting government. This has been the modus operandi of politics in Pakistan for the past seventy years.

Lamentably this whole process and callous attitude not only leads to wastage of national resources and time but as a result of this squabbling, the real problems of the people remain unsolved. The underlying cause of this phenomenon is not only the fact that our democracy is young but the absence of political ethics, political acumen, and its immaturity as well.

Maybe insensitivity and lack of conscience are also its defining features. One can't help but ask, what is the fault of people in this?

What is their crime for which they are being punished? Who will bring them relief?

Who will put a balm on their wounds?

Who will fulfill the promises that were made to them?

Who will pay heed to their hopes and aspirations?

Who will put the genie of hunger, poverty, and uncertainty back in the bottle?

They have been listening to the slogans of bread, cloth, and shelter for the past seventy years. They can't see any light at the end of the tunnel. They have spent ages in the grind of injustice and brutality. No one took up their cause in the past and no one can be seen doing that in the present.

From …… Why was I ousted (Mujhay Kyun Nikala), respect the mandate (Vote ko izzat do), and chewing iron pellets (loahay kay chanay) to get me out of here (mujhay yehan say nikalo) and ……. from the 'murder of Zulfiqar Ali Bhutto to the fight against the dictatorship'…….. we have been witnesses to everything [Sajjad, 2018: 1-3].

What we haven't heard or seen a practical example of is ….. respect the people, give regard to the voter and let the people live. Everyone has his own battle and his own axe to grind. People were neither given any thought in the past nor in the present.

If only this much haste was shown for the welfare of people, ending inflation, and solving the problems of health and education; then the people wouldn't have been living in such a dire state. I pray that may Allah keep this cooperation between the government and opposition going and guide them to solve public issues with this haste as well. Amen.

REFERENCES:

Devendra [2014], "Role of Opposition in a Parliamentary Democracy". The Indian Journal of Political Science, vol. 75, No. 1, pp. 165-170: Indian Political Science Association.

Jess S. et al. [2022], "The Legislative Process in Parliament". Institute for Government, United Kingdom.

Muhammed N. [2021], "National Integration: Challenges and Options for Pakistan". Islamabad Policy Research Institute [IPRI], vol. 7, No. 1, pp. 1-36.

Sajjad H.M. [2018], "Mujhey Kyun Nikala [Why Was I Ousted?]". Office of the Directorate: Delta Technology Consulting Ltd, pp. 1-3.

Shahid A.et al [2006], "Economics of Regaining Office: The Case of Pakistan [1947-2005]". The Pakistan Development Review, vol. 45, No. 4, pp. 913-923: Pakistan Institute of Development Economics, Islamabad.

Sawaf M. [2020], "The US-Iran Conflict and the Consequences of International Law-breaking". The Conversation International Journal, pp1-7.

Shahzeb A. [2023], "Can Pakistan's Military Dispense Justice?". Asia News Network.

New Strategy for Kashmir: Need of the Hour

It has been a year since India revoked Article 370 in Kashmir [Kathryn, 2020: 1-4]. Since then, regrettably, curfew and lockdown are still enforced in the valley, which is condemnable. This step by India didn't generate appropriate backlash from the international community. Although this act of changing the special status of Kashmir was protested across the world as usual, it made no difference to India [Khurram, 2020: 1-4].

At this moment all means of transportation are closed and resettlement of Hindus is being vigorously carried out in the valley. Attempts are being made to change the ratio of the Muslim population. In shocking contrast, Pakistan's role is limited to passing resolutions that condemn this act and holding country-wide protests on 5th February and recently on 5th August [Akhilesh, 2019: 1-8].

Government has yet to adopt concrete measures that were being expected. In this scenario, the publication of a new political map by the government is a step in the right direction but it is just a small step and a lot still has to be done. Pakistan will have to come up with a new strategy for tackling this problem. The need of the hour is to think outside the box.

Pakistan has to strengthen lobbying in friendly countries of the world and the world consciousness has to be awakened on this issue. In order to solve the Kashmir issue work has to be done and untiring efforts have to be made on a permanent basis [Asif, 2019: 1-6]. The international media needs to be briefed on this issue incessantly. Pakistan's proposal of launching a joint TV channel in collaboration with Turkey and Malaysia should be given a practical shape.

Pakistan has to invite researchers from universities across the world to write papers on this issue. The universities have to be convinced to start Kashmir Chair in their respective History Departments. Indian goods have to be boycotted permanently. Terrorist activities of India in Karachi, Baluchistan, and Khyber Pakhtunkhwa have to be exposed [Mir, 2017: 112-125]. There are numerous other measures that have to be given a practical shape on an unremitting basis. Pakistan now has to rethink its seventy years old Kashmir strategy and has to do more than merely paying lip service [Mobeen, 2021: 1-15].

The moot point here is that why aren't protests and resolutions effective? Why are the world nations so cold and insensitive towards this issue? One year's lockdown of Kashmir has put the whole world under lockdown but the world has adopted a heartless attitude in this regard.

In my opinion, a complete failure of our foreign policy is the biggest reason for this. We should realize that freedom is that blessing of Allah without which even the thought of life is impossible. This immense blessing can't be bought it has to be earned with blood. We should utilize our freedom to win independence for the Muslims of Kashmir. Kashmiris are sacrificing their lives and paying tribute with their blood. Their sacrifices will definitely bear fruit one day [Sarmad, 2021: 1-4].

For how long will these suffering Kashmiris be denied their rights?

How long will their voice remain soundless in front of a dead and deaf world conscious?

When will these so-called Muslim rulers lend practical and meaningful support to the Kashmiris?

For how long will Kashmir suffer the dark night of oppression?

When will Pakistan gather enough courage like Turkey and will send its army to help these victims of oppression?

Did Kashmiris side with us to see the light of this day when they are being murdered, their women are being raped and we are just silent spectators?

It is better to die rather than continue on with this unashamed and shameless existence. What is the use of living when we can't take back what is ours from an oppressive and cunning usurper who is slaughtering innocent Kashmiris with complete impunity [Catherine, 1993: 403-417]?

Ever since the curfew has been announced in the valley no conscientious person has been able to sleep peacefully. How can these world rulers get a good night's sleep in peace?

Why don't they heed the cries of these persecuted people?

What can one say about the rulers when even the actions of some political groups show that they have no conscience at all?

Their venality and selfishness have actually tried to bury the freedom movement of Kashmir at an extremely critical juncture when the rulers were getting waking up the world conscious.

The movement for Kashmir freedom would have taken a very different turn had the 'Azadi March' not thrown a spanner in the works. 'Azadi March' was nothing but an untimely and ill-advised adventure that stabbed the movement in the back [Om, 2001: 486-494].

It is better to die rather than continue on with this unashamed and shameless existence. What is the use of living when we can't take back what is ours from an oppressive and cunning usurper who is slaughtering innocent Kashmiris with complete impunity?

All such matters should be firmly dealt with in the future so that no one can harm the national interest.

It is imperative that the struggle for the solution of this issue remains active and continuous regardless of the circumstances. The government should utilize all resources at its disposal for highlighting this issue with a fresh perspective. Quaid e Azam had declared unequivocally that we can't survive without resolving this issue. It is a matter of life and death for us. In other words, it's our lifeline.

REFERENCES:

Akhilesh P. [2019], "The Origins of Hindu-Muslim Conflict in South-Asia". The Editorial: The Diplomat Press.

Asif A. et al., [2019], "A Study of Kashmiri Problem and its Solution". Scholars' Journal of Arts, Humanities and Social Sciences, ISSN 2347-9493, pp.1-6.

Catherine V. [1993], "It is Better to Die Than to Be Ashamed: Cultural and Moral Dimensions of Women's Trading in an Islamic Nigerian Society". Anthropos Ed. 88, H. 4/6.[1993], pp.403-417.

Kathryn S. [2020], "Kashmir: One Year Later". Foreign Policy Guide, Vol. 370, pp.1-4.

Khurram P. [2020], "Kashmiris Worry About a Demographic Shift". The Editorials, Jammu Kashmir Coalition of Civil Society, Vol. 5877176, pp.1-4.

Mir S. [2017], "Indian Interference in Balochistan". Strategic Studies, Vol.37, No.3, pp.112-125. Institute of Strategic Studies, Islamabad.

Mobeen J. [2021], "Pakistan-Kashmir Strategy: An Assessment and Future Outlook". Islamabad Policy Institute, Pakistan, pp.1-15.

Om P. [2001], "Freedom Movement and Emergence of Secular Politics in Kashmir [1932-40]". Proceedings of the Indian

History Congress, vol.62, pp.486-494. Indian History Congress.

Sarmad F. [2021], "Kashmir Day: A Tribute to the Story of Struggles and Sacrifices". Daily Times Editorials, pp.1-4.

Victory of Pakistan over Terrorism

Pakistan was a no-go area for the rest of the world for the past many decades [Glenn, 1968: 195-213]. Traveling to Pakistan for the sake of business or pleasure was considered a symbol of danger, fear, and uncertainty. Europe, Britain, America, Canada, Korea, Japan, and many other countries had declared Pakistan unsafe for its citizens.

That is why no economic or tourism relations could be established with these countries for a long time. As a result of these circumstances, Pakistan became isolated from the rest of the world. All the countries of the world not only left Pakistan alone on the economic front but also made Pakistan change its policy regarding Afghanistan, pushed it into the war against terror, and later on declared Pakistan unsafe [Rabia, 2021: 1-4].

In addition to this, many countries specifically asked their citizens not to travel to Pakistan in their travel guides, this led to the closure of almost everything like tourism, foreign investment, sports, and trade.

I remember in Britain whenever someone asked me for the name of my birth country, their expressions would immediately change on hearing the name of Pakistan and my heart would ache for the law-and-order situation in Pakistan. But I was proud of being a Pakistani then, I am a proud Pakistani now and I will remain proud of this till my last breath.

With the blessings of Allah, Pakistan Army has played a key role in getting rid of this menace. General Raheel Sharif and later on General Qamar Javed Bajwa have on the front lines during this war [Sharif, 2007: 25-35]. May Allah reward them for this service.

In fact, every soldier, officer, and a jawan of the Pakistan army fought untiringly and steadfastly against the anti-state elements. They took Pakistan out of the toughest violent and terror-stricken days and transformed it into a peaceful country.

According to a recent report of BBC London, Pakistan Army's department ISI is one among the intelligence agencies of the world due to its performance and expertise [Chris, 2011: 1-3]. The reason that is cited in BBC's report for this clearly states that ISI is the number one agency because the geographical region in which Pakistan is located is surrounded by enemies on every side. In such a tough region defending its country and making its defense, impregnable is conclusive proof of extreme excellence and capability.

Today Pakistan Army has uprooted terrorism completely and had proved to the world that the Pakistan army is the finest army that has eliminated terrorism in such a way, an achievement that defied the combined armies of the whole world [Muhammad, 2023:1-6].

NATO that claims to be the unsurpassed army despite having state-of-the-art equipment, resources, and unlimited wealth failed miserably in ending the reign of terror in Afghanistan and is now requesting Pakistan Army for a safe exit [Ivana et al., 2022: 1-6].

That is why due to the proficiency and bravery Pak Army, Pakistan's name has become a shining example in the world today, the forces of evil tremble at the name of the Pakistan Army [Thathiah, 2006: 119-146].

I believe that Pak Army deserves not only to be eulogized but also respected and valued. Undoubtedly over the past some time, a few political sections along with some pygmies of social media and people belonging to certain specific sectors have been criticizing this great institution of Pak Army but I challenge them all to serve for one night at the control line in their stead and then I will ask them the meaning of serving at the cost of your life.

I revere every drop of sweat of the jawans of the Pakistan Army who are sacrificing the days and nights of their lives for the solidarity and integrity of Pakistan. These are the brave lions of Allah who always remain steadfast in their commitment towards the safety and prosperity of Pakistan.

I salute the brave mothers who gave birth to the sons who brightened every corner of Pakistan by laying down their lives. Salute to the martyrs and Ghazis who are the crowning glory of the country. Salute to the great sons of the soil who delivered us from terrorism, whose vigilance gives us a peaceful night's sleep, who have protected our honor.

Pakistan's army turned this war against terror spanning decades into peace and forced the world to change its priorities and to mention Pakistan as a safe destination for its travelers [Syed, 2007: 85-107]. At present only Britain has taken this step and has hanged travel advisory for its citizens marking Pakistan as a safe country to travel to. France, Germany, Spain, Italy, and other countries are also reviewing their policies, and God willing, Pakistan will soon become the preeminent country for tourism, trade, diplomacy, sports, and diplomacy.

Credit goes to the Pakistan army and its departments for the recent successful visit of the British prince and princess which were followed by the tours of Srilankan and Bangladesh cricket teams.

I hope that very soon Pakistan Army will defeat the hostile Indian designs by bringing a permanent end to the undue propaganda against Pakistan and will bury fifth generation warfare because Pakistan and Pakistani nationals promote peace [Myra, 2016:1-6]. The efforts of Pakistan's government and army to bring peace to the world will bear fruit one day and the world will see the positive face of Pakistan. May Allah protect Pakistan and keep it always. Amen.

REFERENCES:

Chris A. [2011], "Pakistan Military Denies BBC Report on Taliban Links". Reuters: South-Asia News, pp.1-3.

Glenn V. [1968], "Pakistan: Discontiguity and the Majority Problem". Geographical Review, Vol.58, No.2, pp.195-213.

Ivana K. et al., [2022], "What is NATO and When Does it Act?". CNN Editorials, pp.1-6.

Muhammed S. [2023], "Is Terrorism Returning to Pakistan?". The Conversation Editorials, pp.1-6.

Myra M. [2016], "On India-Pakistan: Hope for the Best, and Prepare for the Worst". Reuters Editorials and Commentaries, pp.1-6.

Rabia A. [2021], "Pakistan and the Taliban 2.0: The Good, the Bad and the Ugly". Office of the Directorate, the Atlantic Council's South-Asia Centre for Security, Strategy and Policy Research, University of Lahore, pp.1-4.

Sharif S. [2007], "Pakistan: Islam, Radicalism and the Army". International Journal on World Peace, Vol. 24, No. 2, pp. 25-35.

Syed M. [2007], "Pakistan and the War Against Terrorism". Pakistan Horizon, vol. 60, No. 2, pp.85-107. Pakistan Institute of International Affairs.

Thathiah R. [2006], "Pakistan Army and Regional Peace in South-Asia". Journal of Third World Studies, Vol.23, No.1, pp.119-146. University of Florida Press.

The Truth of Freedom

Those Muslims of the subcontinent who understood the real meaning and purpose of freedom answered the call of Quaid e Azam, whether they were fully capable or lacking in some capacity they played their part in getting a separate homeland and stood like a rock in front of the foreigners to achieve this end [Ziad, 2011: 1-4].

The history of Pakistan is comprised of bloodied corpses, blistered feet that have traversed deserts, hands that were wounded by holding the rails of the bullock carts to get to Pakistan, and dusty but joyful faces [Iftikhar, 2008: 1-262]. I think that even if we sell ourselves, we would never be able to pay for this favor of Allah Almighty and the sacrifices of our forefathers for Pakistan.

We are indebted to the mothers, sisters, and daughters who sacrificed their honor for this beloved land, we are indebted to the elderly parents who sacrificed their grown sons for this land, we are indebted to those people who migrated through the rivers of blood and fire, who sacrificed their homes, cattle, and business for our future, who left their relatives, family and friends and even the graves of their ancestors in order to come to Pakistan.

It is the fruit of the sacrifices of these magnificent Muslims that history took a turn and on the auspicious moment of 14th august 1947 the caravan of truth reached its destination, the sun of a new Islamic state shone brightly on the horizons of the world, which was paying homage to the founder of the nation and to those who have laid down their lives for founding of this state.

These sacrifices gave birth to a state that bestowed a separate identity on the Muslims of the Indo-Pak sub-continent, a land where the Muslims could spend their lives in the light of the teachings of Allah and the Holy Prophet (peace be upon him) i.e. the economy, society, culture, lifestyle, civilization everything is according to the golden principles of Islam, where all minorities could consider themselves safe and pray according to their faith in their places of worship, where there is no restriction on anyone's freedom of expression, where no one could usurp the rights of others, where there is no robbery, theft, murder or mayhem, where there is no graft, nepotism, bribery, deception, hoarding, where there is no ignorance and poverty, where there is no unemployment, inflation, and terrorism, where there is no sectarianism, ethnic wars, and fights over language[Neha, et al, 2021: 1-20]. That was the Pakistan which was the true interpretation of the dreams of Allama Iqbal and Quaid e Azam, the Pakistan which was the last hope of those who laid down their lives, the last light, and was to become the avatar of the last ray of the journey of light. We have, however, diametrically altered the interpretation of this dream. The chapter of freedom was taken out of the book of life and was thrown in the dustbin, we have left it to rot and now we are aiming to conquer the stars.

Keep in mind that the nations who ignore their history end up like a dog that runs after two bones and catches neither. There is time yet, we will have to learn from our history [Justice, 2019: 1-21]. A few days back I came across Dr. Riaz Ahmed's book 'Struggle for Pakistan', which unveiled the facts that we have always ignored. We will have to face these facts and then correct our mistakes. We will have to take the road of self-accountability and take decisions for the betterment and development of the country.

We will have to snatch our rights back from a handful of elite and lay the foundations of justice, brotherhood, and equality, we will have to strengthen our institutions, we will have to uproot corruption completely in order to lay down the foundations of a truly Islamic Welfare State [Nelson, 2017: 117-136]. Lamentably we are known by our rulers in the comity of nations, who from the very first day has remained a stronghold of the elite. Even if their corruption gets caught it's not in millions but in billions. They construct plazas and petrol pumps; they indulge in corruption through sugar mills and flour, if this isn't enough to feed their greed then the national wealth is looted and transferred in foreign accounts.

Who can take them to the task? At times they have angiography at others they suffer from piles, when it is time for accountability everyone falls ill and runs to the hospital. I ask the rulers why these elite aren't given permanent treatment, they are either sent to London, Dubai, or New Zealand. Recently a REFERENCESwas filed in the corruption case of 300 billion in the Accountability Court but bravo! What a smile was playing on Zardari Sahib's lips that were telling everyone loudly that nothing has happened and nothing will.

All this will be taken care of by political catastrophes. Neither the government can prove corruption nor will these cases be pursued. Given this, the smile is justified. Had someone even laughed their heads off the rulers wouldn't have felt any embarrassment.

For God's sake enough is enough. Have some pity on this country full of corruption and dishonesty. Only lighting candles and waving flags on the fourteenth of August won't do Pakistan any good. These leeches like the elite should be stripped and hung on the roundabouts just like China hanged its elite to get rid of corruption.

Only by doing this can we end corruption, only then will Quaid's Pakistan come into being, only then will Pakistan start its actual journey on the road to development, only then will we taste real freedom [Madiha, 2023: 1-4]. Khan Sahib! you swore that you wouldn't let anyone go but you let everyone go, freed everyone, accepted defeat in front of everyone, shook hands with everyone let everyone leave from the side alley. Don't forget that even if you let them go they will not be forgiven by Allah for all that they have done to Pakistan.

REFERENCES:

Iftikhar M. [2008], "The History of Pakistan". The Greenwood Histories of The Modern Nations, Greenwood Press, pp. 1-262.

Justic M. [2019], "Sustainable Development: Meaning, History, Principles, Pillars and Implications For Human Action: Literature Review". Cogent Social Sciences, Vol. 5, No. 1, pp. 1-21.

Madiha H. [2023], "Pakistan: Five Major Issues to Watch in 2023". The Brookings Press, pp. 1-3.

Neha S. et al., [2021], "Religion in India: Tolerance and Segregation". Pew Research Center, pp. 1-20.

Nelson M. [2017], "On the Coloniality of Human Rights". Revista Critica de Sciences Socials, vol. 114, No. 114, pp. 117-136.

Ziad H. [2011], "Islam and The Early History of Pakistan". Middle East and The Islamic World Working Group: Hoover Institution, pp. 1-4.

Reply of Grievance

It isn't something that should be made into a huge issue, especially since Dr. Yasmeen Rashid has already apologized for her comments. Still, the reason for bringing this up is to unveil certain facts to clear the misunderstanding related to the way the people of Lahore have been depicted.

We have learned the art of airing grievances and then answering them from the poet of the East who had acquired knowledge from the multiversity of Lahore and bestowed wisdom and cognizance on the whole nation. Now that the lady has made a grievance public it's natural for the Lahoris to feel aggrieved and angry but with due respect, we would like to bring to your kind notice that we acknowledge your meritorious services for the Lahoris with the bottom of our hearts and that you have used these words in good faith because you love Lahore like any other patriot, this is also a fact that the Corona has become an ominous problem and it was taken very lightly in Lahore but my take on the whole issue is a bit different.

I believe that the arrival of people from other cities also added to the gravity of the situation in Lahore [Radhakrishnan, 2022: 1-3]. Secondly, you had ended the lockdown in compliance with the directives of the Supreme Court but that was done without any homework. What followed was the logical sequence of cause and effect. The Supreme Court didn't stop you from taking precautionary measures. The whole world witnessed and lived through the consequences of the second wave of Corona after lifting the lockdown [Kohale et al., 2021:1-10].

The impact was perilous in the careless countries. The example of America is there for everyone to understand this. Iran also suffered terribly from the effects of the second wave of Corona after slacking of lockdown restrictions [Ebrahim et al., 2022:1-8]. Similarly, Spain, France, Italy, and even England are grappling with the trepidation of the second wave of Corona. This doesn't mean that all these countries are ignorant and have no appreciation of the problems. Moreover, you gave an excuse that conspiracy theories are being propagated so for your information these misleading theories are originating from abroad.

Recently England sanctioned a few Israeli channels for propounding erroneous theories about Corona. This makes it very obvious that this isn't being done from Lahore but from somewhere else hence you shouldn't believe in hearsay but should focus on researching the truth and side by side you need to make your news agencies more effective so that you could remain well informed.

At this point, a few questions arise. What measures has your government taken to educate the people and what has been done to face these circumstances? This also reminds one of your 'Tiger Force', where is it these days? There are other queries as well that will be discussed in detail later on. Now if the lady has taken her words back then believe that the people of Lahore have very big hearts. Your apology was neither needed nor did we want an apology from a healer because the people of Lahore will never forget your services. Had someone said these words they might really have been unbearable but you have healed in the capacity of a healer, it's tough and impossible to pay you for your good deeds.

You know the people of Lahore extremely well. They possess immense courage as well as benevolence because the lively dwellers of Lahore whole-heartedly welcome anyone and open their doors to anyone who comes to their city.

This is the city of Data Gunj Baksh and Bibi Pakdaman and is alive with the spirit of generosity, love, brotherhood, and good intentions for everyone. It is the trustee of the 1940 resolution for Pakistan, the reason for the foundation of Pakistan and cradle of love for Islam. It is the city where there is the University of Punjab and Jamia Ashrafiya as well as Jamia Al-Muntazir and the University of Lahore, above all this city, has compassion for humanity.

As I have mentioned earlier that this great city has timeless history, this city has never closed its doors for the immigrants but has always opened its hearts and welcomed everyone wholeheartedly. Instead of making things difficult for the newcomers it has always spread its wings so that no one is disappointed.

This is the city of lively people it has as much room for all the countrymen as there is space in the hearts. This is a city of hospitable people. This city has produced countless wise and capable people including shah Jahan, Shorish Kashmiri, and Nawaz Shareef, your leader Imran Khan, Guru Ram Das, and Amjad Islam Amjad. There are countless others whose names will always remain a part of history in golden words. This city has always remained a center of wisdom and learning.

Whether it was the time of Turks or Mughals, in respect of knowledge this city has held a unique position [Frit , 1970: 125-131]. The learned people of this city are serving in every corner of not only Pakistan but also the rest of the world. The significant feature of this city is that its dwellers have never raised the slogan of Pathan, Sindhi, Baluchi, and Panjabi; rather they sacrificed their language for the cause of the national language [Stephen, 2020: 2467-2481]. Even today every person residing in Lahore prefers speaking Urdu over Punjabi.

Respected madam doctor, your personality is highly esteemed but I have acknowledged my ignorance by electing you now you should also accept that your government is inept and your ineptness has landed the country in this present situation. Had you worked adequately for improvement in the health and education sector, Pakistan would never have been in the present mess.

Now let's consider the questions that I have raised earlier. Quite respectfully, kindly tell us how many new hospitals have you constructed?

How many hospitals have been upgraded?

How many new medical colleges have been constructed?

How many nursing schools have been commissioned?

How many new laboratories have been established?

How many young doctors and nurses were sent abroad for higher education on government expenses?

Has a health card reached every Pakistani?

Wasn't it your foremost responsibility to provide health cards to elderly pensioners?

Have you raised the pensions of the pensioners in the annual budget?

Did you introduce any adult literacy program to add to the cognitive capacity and awareness of people?

Have you fixed any stipends for the poor, the laborers, and the farmers?

Have you taken any practical measures to spread awareness in society in collaboration with educational institutions especially universities?

Have you worked out any strategy to counter the water scarcity that is going to hit in a few years?

Have you taken any steps to bring transparency to the Election Commission?

Have you devised any plan to save the industrial sector?

Have you deposited the plundered money of the nation in the State Bank?

Have you converted the Governor Houses and the Prime Minister House into universities?

Have you given the poor nation its due rights from the electricity, water, and gas resources?

Have you given the media the genuine freedom that they were promised?

Have you constructed 50, 00,000 homes for the poor?

Are Kala Bagh and Bhasha Dam a reality? [Samiullah et al., 2017: 1-6].

Have people been able to come from abroad and get employment in the steel mills?

Have you made all the corrupt politicians 'cry'?

Have you improved the governance of the national institutions by strengthening them?

Have you created a new province?

Have you given justice to the victims of Model Town?

Have you punished the culprits of the Baldiya Town tragedy? [Danyal, 2018: 1-10]

Have you reformed the police department?

If none of the above has been accomplished, then envy those who are still bearing with your government. Who has compromised with the problems and compulsions of your government, who trusted you and given you an opportunity to change the fate of the country?

REFERENCES:

Danyal A.K [2018], "Quiet Burns the Fire: The Baldia Tragedy". The Editorial: Herald Magazine, pp. 1-10.

Ebrahim B. [2022], "Adverse Effects Following Covid-19 Vaccination in Iran". BMC Infectious Diseases, pp. 1-8.

Fritz L. [1970], "Urdu Literature and Mughal Decline". Mahfil, Vol. 6, No. 2/3, 1970, pp. 125-131: Asian Studies Centre, Michigan State University.

Kohade V. [2021], "Impact of Second Wave Covid-19 in the World", College of Pharmacy: Department of Pharmaceutics, Latur College of Pharmacy, Hasegaon, Vol. 8, No. 3, pp. 1-10.

Radhakrishnan R.K [2002], "Passage to India: Arrival of Economic Refugees from Srilanka Looms Large". The Editorial: The Hindu News, pp. 1-3.

Samiullah S. et al., [2017], "Causes of Delay in The Construction of Dams in Pakistan". First International Conference on Industrial Engineering and Management Applications, Mehran University of Engineering and Technology, Jamshoro, Sindh, Pakistan, pp. 1-6.

Stephen H. et al., [2020], "Locational Analysis of Slums---". GeoJournal, Vol. 86, pp. 2467-2481.

Relief in Repentance

Whenever humanity was swallowed up by natural disasters and calamities, only one act brought salvation for humanity from these trials and tribulations and that was an act of mass contrition [Malarvizhi, 2021:1-8]. After the people as a whole repented their sins, Almighty Allah delivered them from these calamities, afflictions, and pandemics and they were blessed with comfort and ease. But this requires true and heartfelt repentance.

We have always seen our elders offer mass contrition and repentance whenever there were heavy disastrous rains. The mosques continually resounded with Azans. Many times, we have seen Muslims getting out of these tough situations with our own eyes. Allah has repeatedly mentioned those people in the Quran who were wiped off the face of the earth as a result of Divine perdition. Sometimes it took the form of excessive rains, at times it was storms and hurricanes while sometimes pandemics and diseases destroyed countries and nations. Every so often humankind creates its own hell.

The Quran tells of communities and people and regents like Pharaoh, Nimrod, the elephant people, Sabbath-breakers, people of Loot, the nation of Noah, and many others who were destroyed. Those nations who transgress and become unjust and those who stay quiet on these crimes, all have to taste the wrath of Allah. Allah has the right to forgive or to test people whenever He so wishes. He wants for nothing; he is neither bound by any limit nor does he need anyone. He is the Omnipotent and we are all dependent upon him for his favors.

History has proved that Allah doesn't need an army to put a nation through turmoil or to test his creation. Quran bears witness to the fact that when Allah decided to send a calamity, he even used small insects like mosquitoes and frail birds like Swallows. He gives plenty of rope to the transgressors and after a specific time the rope is pulled, the final verdict is announced and then they face the fury of Allah, and sometimes Allah tests His subjects, many examples for this are present in the Holy Quran.

If Allah's Will can prevail through mosquitoes and swallows, then is the present Coronavirus also doing the same? Following the Plague, SARS, and Ebola; is coronavirus also a test from Allah? In these hard times, we should collectively ask for Allah's forgiveness. The catch is that in the present scenario large gatherings can further intensify the epidemic. Recently the World Health Organization termed this epidemic a pandemic.

We should all repent our criminal silence; we remained silent on the genocide of the Muslims in Burma, we should repent our silence on the solitary confinement of the Muslims of Kashmir and the rapes of Kashmiri mothers, sisters, and daughters, on the annihilation of the Iraqi Muslims, on the devastation of the Libyan Muslims, on the oppression of the Muslims of Yemen, on the subjugation of Palestinians, on the mass murder of the Syrian women and children, on the inhuman brutality in Afghanistan, on the cruelty suffered by the Muslims in China, on the lamentations of the Chechen Muslims, on the atrocious murders of Sikhs, Dalits and

Muslims in India and we should repent our sins as individuals and beseech the Actual Lord for his forgiveness and mercy.

We are facing the consequences of our own actions. Isn't Allah the Lord of those innocent victims whose cries have reached the heavens, whose curses are following us, who had declared emphatically before being killed that they would voice their grievances about their helplessness and the silence and selfishness of the whole Ummah in front of Allah on the Day of Judgment? We should learn from the teachings of the Holy Prophet Muhammad (Peace be upon him).

Rachel Corrie, the unarmed Christian humanitarian is a thousand times better than us who stood in front of the bulldozers that were razing the Palestinian homes and was crushed to death as a result of this stand in March 2003 [Neve, 2012:1-2]. We should learn from her and give humans a lesson of humanity because it's not about Muslims, it's about humanity and it's about cruelty suffered by the humans, it's about silence on these atrocities whether the victims are Muslims, Christians, Hindus, Jews, Sikhs or any other human being......even animals.

We should always raise our voices against tyranny and injustice. I hope and pray that Allah Almighty may rouse our hearts from the deep slumber, may he forgive our mistakes and misdeeds otherwise it's not hard for Him to replace us with others. Everything is possible for that Rabb the Omnipotent.

There is still time and the door to repentance is still open. We should all repent and remind ourselves that there are two benefits of repentance; firstly, if we are forgiven then this trial will pass and we will get an opportunity to redeem ourselves by reforming our ways, secondly if our repentance is accepted and we pass this test then we may be considered worthy of the paradise. Now the decision lies in your hands.

Take care of your surroundings. Look after your neighbors, family members, poor and the destitute. If nothing else at least feel remorseful in your heart of hearts about your past and pray Allah for a better tomorrow. Give up usury, profiteering, adulteration, and hoarding. There is still time if we can comprehend otherwise, it's entirely possible that we may fail this Divine test and most decidedly we aren't worthy of any trial. Just think for a moment whether Allah is so angry at us that we can't gather together for showing contrition because of this Corona Virus?

Keep in mind the detail that we are fighting a war against a virus that we can't even see. Is Allah so angry with us that we can't even see what we are up against? the earlier people at least got to see the calamities like mosquitoes and swallows that were sent by Allah. We aren't even able to see what we are trying so hard to avoid. Only Allah can save us, there is none other who can deliver us from this.

We have even been deprived of the blessing of circumambulating the Holy Ka'aba. Now there is no one to pray for the Muslims even in the Holy Ka'aba. We aren't even able to pray together. Now we will have to bow our heads before the Will of Allah. When fear rules, solace can only be found in prostration.

The world market is in the grip of recession, in the stock markets share prices are in free fall, companies all over the world are facing bankruptcy and the dollar is losing its value [Gayle et al, 2023:1-3]. Now we have to take practical steps in order to save our nation from this deadly virus and simultaneously we have to decide a time at which we could ask for Allah's forgiveness and repent, collectively and individually, at the same time.

According to recent reports, China, Iran, Russia and Israel have claimed that this virus was manufactured in an American laboratory [Mercy, 2022:1-3]. America has refuted this claim categorically. The problem isn't whether it's man-made or not the problem is, how this virus is affecting human beings and what is its impact on the world? As Muslims, we have to think of the whole of humanity and to not only pray for deliverance but have to go an extra mile and provide help in every possible manner, just as Pakistan helped China in tough times and is still assisting. Just as China had sent a team to Italy for providing assistance, Pakistan should also benefit from the experience of China.

REFERENCES:

Gayle M. et al [2023], "Recession in 2023?". The Editorial: World Economic Forum, pp. 1-3.

Malarvizhi P. [2021], "Humanity on Calamity". V.V. Vanniaperumal College For Women, International Journal of Scientific and Engineering Research, Vol. 12, No. 11, pp.1-8.

Mercy A. [2022], "The China-Russia Triangle: Alternative World Order?". The Editorial: The Diplomat, pp. 1-3.

Neve G. [2012], "No Justice for Rachel Corrie". The Editorial: The Nation Newspaper, pp. 1-2.

Challenges knocking at the Door

In every era, nations have been grappling with challenges, hardships, and problems but history has proved that only those nations come out of the whirlpool of adverse circumstances successfully who prove to be alive, who forget the divisive issues, and have the strength to fight the problems collectively as a nation with unison and mutual accord [Endalcachew, 2017:1-8].

Those nations whose rulers have an iota of natural compassion and whose leadership has the ability and good intentions, who know and comprehend the difference between designations and responsibilities, who have the ability to test analysis on the touchstone of experiments, only those nations have a bright future who can follow these golden principles [Michael,1990:1-15].

If the aptitude and intentions of the leadership become one then no challenge is big enough, its magnitude decreases to the point where it loses its form and flies away with the wind like specks of dust or evaporates in the air like water vapors just as a small ray of sunshine is enough to dispel darkness.

A practical example of this is Germany which was completely devastated after World War 2, but the leaders of this nation possessed both capability and intent, through which they made Germany a force to reckon with in the whole world [Nick, 2018:1-7]. At the moment the sound of the challenge knocking at our door is so loud that it is deafening, it could snatch the last morsel of food out of our hands through unemployment, inflation, and poverty. I am afraid that no one will be spared if we get hit by this tsunami.

I have been hearing its echo for a long that which is going to attack us in the shape of socio-economic aftereffects of the Corona pandemic. Take a look around and you will see that everyone is oblivious to this and is going about his life, as usual, no one is even bothered let alone getting on with preparation for hard times. It is very regretful that in a society where everyone claims to be a 'Messiah' no one even knows what it entails. Giving away one bag of flour and a tin of oil and advertising it to no end, is the most despicable and cheapest example of self-projection; in fact, we are completely hollow from the inside.

 If you look deep in their hearts, you will find nothing but darkness there. Islam encourages charity in a way that no one gets to know about it but in this society, even the rivers run backward. Who cares whether someone lives or dies or if someone is willing to sell their bodies for a meal; their heart doesn't break over anything. I believe that no one is born brazen; this society grinds the citizens in poverty and hunger and rips their clothes off in front of the whole world [Deborah, 1995: 245-264].

Fear the time when things will go out of our control just as the Italian Prime Minster lamented his powerlessness; American president ordered the opening of mosques, churches, and other places of worship and bore witness to his own helplessness when he said that only prayers could save America [Laura, 2022:1-5]. In Pakistan people are dying for one time's meal, children are awaiting a drop of milk, they can't even cover their bodies properly, the poor are getting poorer and on the other hand, the rich are getting richer.

Generations have to wait to see justice get done. Everything is fake and adulterated and now everything seems strange and distorted. The day isn't far enough when you will be forced to look after your neighbor out of the fear that his hunger might drive him to attack you.

This has started long ago in the form of street crimes but now this is going to enter the homes of those who have usurped the resources [Tony, 2013: 216-230]. At this moment there is a profound responsibility on the government that how it can turn the tide. How it steers the nation, how it tackles the upcoming storm with wisdom and acumen because at this moment the basic requirement is ability and intention, this is the key that will unlock the locked doors.

To some extent we are convinced of the good intentions of the government now, it has to convince us of its abilities. If the government keeps ignoring the realities then this could have serious consequences. Many endeavors have been made to solve these problems temporarily but the destination lies far ahead and reaching it requires solid planning.

As of now, not enough has been done according to the requirements because this is a war against the elite and the mafia, this is a struggle against brutality and oppression, against the landlords and the capitalists who are in complete control of the resources of this country [Olaoluwa et al, 2014:1-7]. Until the government finds a solution to the unjust distribution of resources and brings the looted national wealth back into the coffers; it can't liberate the people from this current vicious circle of futile days and nights.

I want to ask them, who is forcing you to bow before these powerful people? Who is stopping you from getting rid of these rotting fish? Who is directing this filthy farce? We would like to know who is hounding the public in the name of expediency, who stops you from apprehending these ferocious predators? Khan Sahib! Please clean up this filth from the country otherwise the confidence of people will quickly erode.

REFERENCES:

Deborah P. [1995], "Shall We Go Home? Increasing Urban Poverty in African Cities and Migration Processes". The Geographical Journal, vol. 161, No. 3, pp. 245-264. The Royal Geographical Society.

Endalcachew B. [2017], "The Legacy of Colonialism in The Contemporary Africa: A Cause for Intra-state and Inter-state Conflicts". Bahir Dar University, pp. 1-8. International Journal of Innovative and Applied Research, vol. 3, No. 2.

Laura D. [2022], "What Is Fear of Time Chronophobia". The Editorial: Very Well Health Magazine, pp. 1-5.

Michael E. P. [1990], "The Competitive Advantage ofNations". The Editorials: Harvard Business Review, pp. 1-15.

Nick O. [2018], "How Germany Was Divided: A History of Partition Plans". The Editorial: NeverWas Magazine, pp. 1-7.

Olaoluwa et al [2014], "Living Conditions and Public Health Status in Three Urban Slums of Lagos, Nigeria". SouthEast Asia Journal of Public Health, vol. No. 4, pp.1-7.

Tony P. [2013], "Street Crime: A View from The Left". Social Justice and Global Options, Vol. 40, No. 1-2, pp. 216-230.

Better to have a Wise Enemy than a Foolish Friend

An age-old anecdote goes thus…. a king had a pet monkey. He adored the monkey and always kept him by his side. Many servants were appointed for looking after the monkey and he was given the status of royal monkey.

The king loved the monkey so much that he had given up many friends who had criticized him for keeping the monkey so close to him. The only one that the king cared for was that monkey whom he thought to be very clever and the most sincere friend. No one knew the reason for this love and trust except that the monkey even fought the fly sitting on the king for hours on end so that it couldn't annoy the king.

Perhaps the monkey also suspected that the king appreciated this fight so whenever a fly came near the king, he immediately went after it. He never let an opportunity to appease the king go to waste. One day the monkey was very miserable because the king was going on a hunt in the forest by himself.

The royal guard was waiting for the king's order but the king refused to let them accompany him. Suddenly a messenger came to him and was about to say something but the king got up from his seat and quickly asked him to tell what had happened and why was he so stressed.

The courtiers were well aware of the importance of that attendant because he was appointed to serve, as per the king, his most sincere and wise friend. Without wasting a moment the attendant informed the king that ever since he had announced his intention of going for a hunt alone, the monkey had given up eating and drinking. Upon hearing this news, the king ordered that the monkey should also be prepared to accompany him. This made the monkey very happy.

The king went to his quarters and fed him with his own hands. The king and the monkey started their journey. When they reached the forest, they were too tired. The king was very sleepy; he gave his sword to his friend the monkey and went to sleep in the tent. The monkey swung to one tree after another to defend the king, he was overjoyed at the trust and faith that the king has shown in his abilities.

After some time, the monkey started missing the king. He at once went to the tent with the thought that it was too hot and he should fan the king. As soon as he entered the tent he saw a fly, he immediately took out the sword and hit the fly with all his might. Unfortunately, the fly was sitting on the king's head.

A similar mistake was made by ex PM of Pakistan Mr Nawaz Shareef and now the current PM Mr Imran Khan is also doing the same [Secunder, 2022:1-5]. They have given the power to those who let this power get to their heads. Imran Khan is surrounded by the people who are the king's well-wishers more than the king himself. Their follies could prove dangerous for PM Imran Khan and can also adversely affect the government and Pakistan Tehreek e Insaf next elections [Shah, 2021:1-4].

I have always been fond of Mt F. Chaudhry, criticism and praise aside…..may I ask him a question with all due regard? Promise you won't beat me? Where did you learn to slap like this ?….. The beating of journalists Mr Sami Ibrahim and Mr Mubashar Luqman by Mr F. Chaudhry (Minister) and taking the law into his own hands is extremely regrettable. If he had any grievance or difference of opinion then he should have brought it forward in the media, he could have asked PEMRA or the courts for redressal.

If the allegations about personal life are condemnable then 'being judge, jury, and executioner' is also isn't the way to go……. It's not as if there is the law of the jungle prevailing in the country and you can't raise your voice on any forum…..then there is the matter of Faisal Vawda bringing a 'boot' to the TV show of Kashif Abbasi. Both actions are unethical, condemnable, and appalling.

They should apologize to the journalist community and the nation as a whole. One needs wisdom, patience, and insight for politics, which seems to be extremely lacking in the present setup. When they were in the opposition, they were always frothing at their mouths about the morality of the PMLN ministers. They used to say that the ministers don't have civilised tongues in their heads. Now they are walking the same path, the same modus operandi is absolute to their liking now.

The thing is that elephants have different teeth for chewing and different teeth for showing……but in retrospect, they were a thousand times better than these crupt ministers as these crupt ministers have to rob the coffin and appropriate the grave too. They have to build funeral homes after building shelter homes, as per the government of Pakistan's theory 'peace can be only possible to find in the grave', the corruption will not let anyone live peacefully in this country if the government will not take drastic actions against the problems of the public. Suppressing the voices seeking justice and promoting brutality isn't one of the practices of political ethics [Andreas,2021:491-511].

If nothing else then they should at least learn from their leader. Government and power aren't eternal. I applaud Javed Abbasi and Qamar Zaman Kaira for their patience and placidness as they didn't resort to any extreme measures. Otherwise?..... 'It is the truth but this truth is mortifying'.....for those who graced the program with a shoe in the hand [Battilana et al,2021:1-10].

As for Mr. Kashif Abbasi, there is a small complaint as well. Why did he put up with this blatant display of uncouth behavior? He should have raised his voice against such coarseness. He shouldn't have allowed this rudeness in his program. A host is responsible for the honorable treatment of his guests, he should have fulfilled this responsibility. Recently the esteemed minister went to Uzma Bukhari's home with a lorry full of flour as he wanted to humiliate her for complaining about the dearth of flour in the market. If the very same ministers are criticized for their actions they get hypertension.

It is beyond comprehension that they used to criticize the previous government now what laurels have they won? Have the Governor Houses and the Prime Minister Houses been converted into universities? Have 50 lakh houses been constructed? Can't they find applicants for 10 million jobs? At least I can't understand what is all the hoopla about? In the present circumstances, the government should be grateful to the opposition that it hasn't created any upheaval in the country.

The opposition hasn't created any fresh crisis for the government nor has it put the country through any internal or external disruption. The government should pay attention to the internal and external affairs of the country and make an effort to bring down inflation. It should work with the opposition for solving the problems of the people as the opposition has saved the national pride and increased the dignity of the Prime Minister's office, which should be the beauty of the democracy but everything is exactly the opposite. Imran Khan should take a good look around and appoint capable people to the seats of power. He should realize who is helpful to him and who is posing a threat to his government? [Devendra, 2014:165-170] He should grasp this fact. You will end up losing these competent members of your party.

REFERENCES:

Andreas M. [2021], "Violence, Communication and Civil Disobedience". An International Journal of Legal and Political Thought, Vol. 12, No. 4, pp. 491-511.

Battilana et al [2021], "Don't Let Power Corrupt You". The Magazine, Harvard Business Review Analytical Services, vol. 9, pp. 1-10.

Devendra K. [2014], "Role of Opposition in a Parliamentary Democracy". The Indian Journal Political Science, vol. 75, No. 1, pp. 165-170.

Secunder K. [2022], "Imran Khan: What Led to Charismatic Pakistan P.M's Downfall". The Editorial: BBC News, Islamabad , pp. 1-5.

Shah M. B. [2021], "Imran Khan Is Crushing The Poor: Anger Rises as Inflation Grips Pakistan". The Editorial: The Guardian News, Islamabad, pp. 1-4.

Politics, Protest and Pandemic

The protest campaign launched by the opposition has created a ruckus in the national politics on one hand and as an outcome of this protest, the specter of CORONA is raising its head again. This is a point to ponder for the whole nation as well as a blatant challenge to the government because the government couldn't enforce SOPs at even a single gathering. The need of the hour is that the opposition and the government should take decisions according to the country's situation. If for a moment we grant that carrying out protest is imperative for the opposition parties then fine they should do so because it's their democratic and constitutional right but how much better it would be that keeping in view the COVID situation, these parties change their modus operandi and lay foundations to new traditions of protest. At the moment the whole country is in the center of the vortex and is moving towards another lockdown in this regard. The opposition would have to find out solutions that suit the situation. It's not obligatory that in every period the protest is registered by blocking roads, holding rallies, and getting into physical altercations. In my opinion protest at this time is like testing the loyalties of the political workers [Christopher, 2021: 919-942]. Many simple villagers are now Covid positive because of these rallies and gatherings and they are not in the habit of following protective measures even if they have knowledge about them. It's not possible to maintain a two-meter distance during a large-scale political meeting so if the protests have to be held then the opposition should spare a thought for the wellbeing of the gullible public

[Caspar, 2020: 1-13]. The least the opposition could have done in these trying times would have been to join hands with the government to assist it and the people. But sadly, the situation is quite different. A few days back the government called a joint session for discussing ways and means to counter corona but the opposition boycotted the proceeding which I don't see as a good step because the opposition should express its view on all the challenges facing the nation and represent the people as per democratic and constitutional norms. This is the opposition's foremost duty as well as a civic responsibility. The country is now experiencing the third wave of Corona and danger is not over, aside from the rallies and meetings the public is generally not following SOPs collectively this, God Forbid, maybe a preamble to a future catastrophe. Unfortunately, Pakistan has always suffered from a shortage of resources and as the PM has pointed out, this lockdown has caused severe hardships for the daily wage earners, but the truth of the matter is that at the moment the whole nation is going through an extremely rough time; the business has been destroyed, jobs are non-existent, inflation is skyrocketing and the poor can't even have two meals a day; in this situation, Pakistan can't afford such challenges [Cyril, 2022: 1-4].

The virus is spreading like wildfire in the country although now the situation is getting better and the infection rate is low. The intensity is such that more than 3000 corona cases have been reported in a single day at the peak. The second challenge is inadequate facilities in the hospitals. Pakistan is to some extent self-sufficient in the ventilator industry but it is still a very limited capability [Madiha, 2020: 273-278]. The vaccine is already on the market but manufacturing vaccines for the whole world might require another year. At the moment the only recourse is prevention and being careful. For the sake of God, please have some mercy on yourself as well as the country. At the moment the whole world is in lockdown. England, Germany, Ireland, especially India, America, and many other countries are in the grip of this calamity again because of the Indian variant [Muhammed, 2021: 1-14]. Europe and America are helping out their people by giving soft loans, personal loans, and providing government assistance but the Pakistan government can't do this, in spite of the desire to do so, because of the dearth of resources [Daniel, 2020: 1-5]. The opposition will now have to modify its protest tactics. A short while back the opposition in Iran, in the face of strict government restrictions, introduced the world to a novel protest technique [Ali et al, 2019: 1-8]. In spite of limited resources and government-imposed restrictions, the sound of this protest reverberated all around the world. The opposition members wrote slogans on currency notes with lead pencils made their voices heard among the masses. This was so effective that it gave birth to a movement in the whole of Iran. My purpose here isn't to suggest that protest should be registered by writing on currency notes here as well the point is that if the opposition parties want to, they can register their protest in many different ways.

As the saying, where there is a will, there is a way.

REFERENCES:

Ali A. et al [2019], "Ideology and Iran's Revolution: How 1979 Changed the World". The Global Institute, pp. 1-8.

Caspar P. et al [2020], "Monitoring Physical Distancing for Crowd Management: Real Time Trajectory and Group Analysis". Research Gate, pp. 1-13.

Christopher B. [2021], "Political Sociology in a Time of Protest". Sage Journals, vol. 69, No. 6, pp. 919-942.

Cyril A. et al [2022], "Pakistan's New Government Struggles to Consolidate Control". United States Institute of Peace, pp.1-4.

Daniel F. R. [2020], "US Foreign Assistance in the Age of Strategic Competition". Center for Strategic and International Studies, pp. 1-5.

Madiha H. et al [2020], "A National Survey of Critical Care Services in Hospitals Accredited for Training in a Lower-middle Income Country: Pakistan". National Library of Medicine: National Center for Biotechnology Information, Vol. 60, pp. 273-278.

Muhammed K. [2021], "Impact of The Coronavirus [Covid-19] Pandemic on Retail Sales in 2020". Office for National Statistics, pp. 1-14.

Lilliput of Politics

There is a fable that narrates the story of two birds. Once two birds were sitting on a branch. They saw a man coming from afar. The female said, 'I think we should fly away, I am afraid this man will kill us'. The male replied, 'I am of a different view. Just look at this man's personality, his apparel, and the obvious dignity. I don't expect this from him besides he looks like a good man why would he kill us? But as the man approached them he took out his bow and arrow, shot and killed the male bird. The grieving female bird took her case to the king.

The king summoned the huntsman and interrogated him. He confessed to his crime. Upon hearing this confession, the king gave the bird the right to sentence the huntsman. The bird requested, 'O Mighty King! Change his glorious robes as they don't reflect his true personality and aren't mirroring his misdeeds as well as his deception. Since he is a hunter, he should dress like one.' This might be a fable but it truly depicts the people currently in the government and the opposition.

I beseech them both to kindly take off their people-friendly apparel so that no bird would lose its life because of their deception.

Let's talk about the last week's APC called by the opposition parties. It was attended by all the prominent politicians of the opposition parties and they took this opportunity to severely criticize the overall performance of the government. After APC a joint declaration was also issued which stipulated that all the opposition parties will commence collective struggle and this will continue till the ouster of the government. The opposition issued a barrage of allegations and took the opportunity to vituperate the government.

On the other hand, the government members also gave their own stance in response to this critique.

Actually, we will soon witness the drop scene of this whole farce. The policy of giving and taking will come into play as usual. Recently the opposition has become increasingly bewildered because of the promulgation of FATF [Morgan, 2021: 1-5]. The main target of the opposition at this time is to achieve its objectives by pressurizing the government. As soon as its demands are met it will once again start singing songs of peace.

Regrettably, this policy has resulted in reducing the stature of some people. To me, they all appear as political pygmies because no matter what their real intentions are; their appearance is belies their objectives. An example, in this case, is the sit-in organized by Maulana Fazal ul Rehman which despite a lot of thundering, ended without a deluge as a result of a political deal. The real reason behind the sit-in was the release of Asif Ali Zardari from jail and the departure of Mian Nawaz Sharif to England. Many political secrets became part of the Chaudhry brothers' bag of tricks. Let's see where the chips will fall this time.

No matter what they preach their apparel doesn't mirror their personalities and purposes. Trust me when I say that the public issues being used to gain personal objectives, were neither solved yesterday nor are they being resolved today. It's absolutely fair to pass judgment on 'one billion jobs' but it is also our right to criticize the slogan of 'food, clothing, and shelter'. Just a few spells of rain have laid bare the futility of the claims of those who talked about turning Lahore into Paris, calling Karachi the financial hub of the country, and serving the nations over the generations [David, 2019: 1-8].

These threats and movements don't hold the same strength that used to be a hallmark of revolutionary movements. The only party to suffer from this charade and deluge of desires is the public. No one has spared a thought for them in the past nor will they do so in the future.

I don't deny the fact that criticism of the rulers is the beauty of democracy and government revenge tactics are also a despicable act to me but I humbly dare to ask the opposition, do you people define democracy as a family rule? [Gerasimos, 2007: 70-89] If you win neither the system is rotten nor the establishment has played any role, the election commission isn't vilified nor the accountability bureau is questioned, all is well and the win is depicted as the reflection of public support.

During your own rule your heart didn't bleed for the Kashmiris nor did you see the problems like rising prices of food and fuel essentials, which perpetually plague the public.[Neha, 2009: 1-20] Before politicizing the Motorway Tragedy you were deaf to the wails of the pregnant daughter in the Model Town Tragedy, you turned a blind eye to the miseries of the people dying of thirst and hunger in the Thar, you failed to see the flood affectees and the people suffering the grind of poverty[Katy, 2016: 1-4].

You have no idea whose walls crumbled and whose roof collapsed. It's been ages since you were among the people.

Sitting in your palaces, you can never understand the miseries being suffered by the people. For the sake of Allah try to feel the pain of the deprived who are in the grip of poverty and inflation. Either do something practical or get rid of this apparel of being people-friendly. The public can't bear any more deceptions.

REFERENCES:

David F. L [2019], "What Does Fair and Impartial Judiciary Mean and Why is it Important". Bolch Judiciary Institute, An Institute of Duke Law School, Duke University, pp. 1-8.

Gerasimos S. [2007], "Plato's Criticisms of Democracy in The Republic". Social Philosophy and Policy, Vol. 24, No. 2, pp. 70-89.

Katy W. [2016], "A Brief Inglorious History of "Not Politicizing Tragedy". The Editorial: The Slate Press, pp. 1-4.

Morgan K. [2021], "Political Polarization and Its Echo Chambers: Surprising New Cross-disciplinary Perspectives from Princeton". High Meadows Environmental Institute, pp. 1-5.

Neha N. [2009], "Kashmir: The Clash of Identities". The Editorial: Beyond Intractability, pp. 1-20.

Lost Reality

An old proverb narrates the story of a king who was certain that no matter how he would treat them the people will remain sincere with him at all times. His sagacious ministers always tried to make him see the light of reason. The counseled that until the situation of the kingdom isn't improved the sincerity of the people would be hard to ascertain. So, the king decided to test the sincerity and loyalty of the people.

A large cauldron was placed in the center of the city and it was proclaimed that every citizen would pour a glass of milk in it at night in order to prove his/ her sincerity. All the lanterns in the surrounding areas of the cauldron were extinguished. After that, the whole city followed the royal edict. In the morning when the king saw the cauldron, there was a small amount of milk in it while the rest was all water. This finally made the king realize his mistake. Something similar is happening with the current government.

The whole of the government entourage is under the impression that people are with them and after the resignations of the opposition members the government will easily win the by-elections. This is nothing but self-deception.

The government has to keep its fingers on the pulse of the nation and unless it doesn't put salve on the wounds of the people, it shouldn't expect any sincerity from the people because they have voted for the present rulers to see some performance not to be sold dreams to. None of the promises made to the expatriates have been fulfilled, however, this year they have been given the facility to open online accounts in Pakistani banks. A large number of expatriates started opening these accounts; this resulted in an increased foreign exchange influx.

For the first after the rule of Mian Nawaz Sharif, the current account registered a surplus to the tune of $447 billion; sadly inflation and foreign debt have risen to astronomical heights [Mosharraf, 2017: 1-5]. The dollar is at an all-time high. Circular debts also didn't exhibit any tangible reduction; the national institutions are the same as before. Every institution from the PIA to the police is in a state of decline [Badamasi, 2019: 41-50]. Balance of inflation and deflation has gone haywire and IMF is dominating the financial matters of the country same as in the past. There is rampant corruption and political instability. According to transparency international, the last ten years have seen a steady rise in corruption in Pakistan [Hongying, 2001: 25-49].

In sharp contrast, corruption has decreased in neighboring India [Myint, 2000: 1-26]. A few days back the CCPO Lahore made eleven SHOs OSDs and informed the media that their performance wasn't up to the mark even though there were many among these SHOs whose performance was appreciated multiple times in the media.

It's high time for this culture to change, such decisions should be revisited and a system should be introduced that ensures genuine justice for the employees and after the implementation of such a system the hardworking, sincere, and honest workers aren't tossed aside just because of personal prejudices, likes and dislikes. It is also imperative that the Prime Minister should take practical steps and provide authentic relief to the people instead of merely taking stock of the performance of the ministers [Catherine, 2020: 1-4]. Work should be started for the improvement of the institutions and the eradication of corruption based on solid foundations.

People should be liberated from the price hike and circular debt. Asking people to stay strong is a good thing and people will even act upon this advice but if its impact is felt in the expected by-elections and next general elections then maybe the government might be in need of this advice rather than the public. The decision is now up to you.

REFERENCES:

Badamasi Z. et al [2019], "Restructuring and the Dilemma of State Police in Nigeria: To Be or Not to Be?". Journal of Bussiness and Social Review in Emerging Economies, Vol. 5, No. 1, pp. 41-50.

Ctherine H. [2020]," Ministerial Accountability". Institute for Government, pp. 1-4.

Hongying W. et al., [2001]," Transparency International and Corruption as an Issue of Global Governance". Global Governance, Vol. 7, No. 1, pp. 25-49.

Mosharraf Z. [2017]," The Downfall of Nawaz Sharif and the Triumph of Stupidity". The Editorial: Foreign Policy Press, South Asia, pp. 1-5.

Mint U. [2000], "Corruption: Causes, Consequences and Cures". Asia-Pacific Development Journal, Vol. 7, No. 2, pp. 1-26.

Brexit and Its Impact on Pakistan

At last, after forty-seven years, England once again emerged as an 'independent and free nation on the world map [Devine, 2006: 163-180]. In fact, England has a long history with Europe encompassing centuries. This history is made up of wars and peace pacts and typical love-hate relationships. During all these times, England has passed through many ups and downs that include the journey from Churchill's blood-drenched Britain to Boris Johnson's solitary and disengaged Britain.

In 2016, 52% of British citizens voted for leaving European Union while 48% recorded their protest by voting against this proposal [Bruce, 2016: 1-3]. I had the opportunity of witnessing all these phases from very close proximity. My observations, analysis, and even public opinion polls say that majority of the people who voted for the exit weren't fully aware of the repercussions of Brexit.

Some people supported Brexit because they were of the view that Brexit meant the exit of foreigners from England while some thought that it entailed kicking out Muslims from Britain. After many ups and downs, this process was finally completed. While some welcomed this with open arms there were quarters where this news wasn't received as joyfully.

Now the moot point is that what Brexit will mean for Pakistan as this step will affect Pakistan just like the rest of the world. Presently millions of Pakistanis are residing in Britain [James,

2019: 1-10]. The economic development and current account surplus depend on foreign remittances. Any factor influencing the economic position of these Pakistanis, whether positively or negatively, will have a directly proportionate impact on Pakistan's economy [Adela, 2013: 3-19].

At the same time, Europe is a significant market for Pakistan [Rashid 2004: 29-36]. The share of the European market in overall exports of Pakistan is around 21%. Only 7% of GDP is earned from exports which are already dangerously low. In 2013 Pakistan was awarded GSP status and as a result, Pakistan's exports rose from $ 6.21 billion to $ 6.67 billion in 2014 but in 2015 the exports again declined to $ 6.67 billion. According to a recent report of Trend Economy, these exports have touched $ 117 billion in 2019 which is a huge improvement over $ 23 billion in 2018.

Whether Pakistan will be able to register an increase in its exports or will there be a decline after the Brexit, remains to be seen. Pakistan has to take concrete steps for increased economic independence [Arif, 2022: 1-4]. This cannot be achieved without the promotion of trade and tourism. Those Pakistani students who travel to England for higher education need to keep an eye on the new policies of Britain.

Moreover, growing Islamophobia is going to greatly impact the lives of Pakistanis and the Muslims residing in Britain. The European Human Rights laws are shielding the Muslim community to some extent, hopefully, things will move in a positive direction. However, many Pakistanis are scared, because due to the low number of Europeans in England, the overall temperament of peaceful coexistence that currently prevails in British society may get adversely affected due to new laws. If this happens it might take years but it will be an immense challenge for the Muslims in Britain.

If we consider the positive aspects of this move, then Pakistan ought to take full advantage of this situation since Pakistan no longer has to take Europe into confidence for conducting trade and expanding relations with Britain. Pakistan can enter into agreements with Britain with full confidence. After America, Russia and China; Britain and Germany are indisputably quite influential in international affairs. Pakistan can get the Kashmir issue resolved with the help of Britain's influence. Britain's support and access to the British market can help Pakistan get back on its feet in the economic sphere. Pakistan needs to take a leaf out of Turkey's book in this regard [Madiha, 2023:1-5].

Recently Turkey and Britain have signed deals amounting to billions of pounds. This will be a milestone in British- Turkish relationships. At the moment Britain is looking for new agreements and trade deals. Pakistan should hit the iron while it's hot and restart negotiations with the British government regarding trade, international issues, education of Pakistani students, and improvement in other economic relations in the new setup. The agreements entered into and the relations cemented in the current situation will have far impacts.

REFERENCES:

Adela S. et al., [2013], "Remittances and Their Impact on Economic Growth". Periodica Polytechnica Social and Management Sciences, vol. 21, No. 1, pp. 3-19.

Arif R. [2022], "Pakistan's Political Crisis and The Imperatives of Economic Reform". Middle East Institute, pp. 1-4.

Bruce S. [2016], "Brexit Vote Highlighted UK's Discontent with the EU, But Other European Countries Are Grumbling Too". Pew Research Center, pp. 1-3.

Devine T. M. [2006], "The Break up of Britain? Scotland and The End of Empire: The Prothero Lecture". Transactions of The Royal Historical Saociety, vol. 16, No. 6, pp. 163-180.

James M. [2019], "What Brexit Means". Council on Foreign Relations, pp. 1-10.

Madiha H. [2023], "Pakistan: Five Major Issues to Watch in 2023". Brookings Educational Press, pp. 1-5.

Rashid S. [2004]," Pakistan-European Union Relations". Pakistan Horizon, Vol. 57, No. 4, pp. 29-36. Pakistan Institute of International Affairs.

Significance of Gilgit Baltistan Elections

The third elections for the Gilgit-Baltistan Constitutional Assembly were held on 15th November, during this process the area remained a hub of political activities. Urgent visits of the political leaders and the usual promises and proclamations added to the enthusiasm of the people. Every party was trying to form the government here which could have deep repercussions on politics and the government.

The obvious reason is that if the governing party wins then the opposition's narrative will die its own death, in contrast, a win by the opposition could leave profound consequences for the government's popularity and its writ as well as future general elections.

Prior to 1839, this area consisted of Gilgit, Baltistan, and Hunza which was later annexed by the then Maharaja of the State of Jammu and Kashmir [Hermann, 2013: 1-43]. In 1947 Pakistan came into being within a year the people of this area fought a limited war and gained independence from the State of Jammu and Kashmir, as a sovereign region [Stephanie, 2022: 1-15]. Balti and Sheena are the regional languages here. The people of these areas love Pakistan as much as the people of Kashmir, which is why after independence this region was at the forefront of the movement for joining Pakistan.

The Silk Route passes from these areas, which has added to their strategic significance. After the promulgation of Gilgit – Baltistan as a province, the China-Pakistan Economic Corridor (CPEC) will be completed swiftly because this is the only region that touches the boundaries of three countries that can guarantee the success of the CPEC [Dhrubajyoti, 2015: 1-10]. In 1948 as well, this region was at the center of Kargil- Siachin war which can herald the independence of Kashmir.

The first General Elections were held here in 2009, the credit for these elections goes to the then government of the Peoples Party. The region was also given limited autonomy at that time. Sayed Mehdi Shah of Peoples Party took oath as the first Chief Minister of Gilgit-Baltistan.

In the second election, PMLN won a landslide victory and Hafeez Ul Rehman took over as the Chief Minister. Now the biggest issue for the political parties is the transparency of these elections and acceptance of the results. A look at the election results of the past decade shows that the attitude of the people here isn't that different from that of the Khyber Pakhtunkhwa. Every party is given a chance there for a limited time period, if the promises are fulfilled then it is re-elected like the last term of the PTI otherwise it is bid a loving farewell. The people of Gilgit-Baltistan also appear to be very sagacious and wise. Their thinking mirrors the thoughts of the people of Khyber Pakhtunkhwa which is to remain focused on the ultimate purpose instead of being dived amongst themselves [Martin, 1997: 83-90].

This auger well for the future, but for me, the most important thing is the fulfillment of election promises that were made with these innocent people because if they are subjected to the traditional political attitude then this behavior will have perilous outcomes. The conduct of the newly elected government Vis a Vis the people of Gilgit-Baltistan is of utmost significance as it is vital for the future of this region and particularly for Pakistan.

If we analyze the international scenario we see that India is watching these elections very closely. The Indian media and the government are spewing venom on this development which is their routine but owing to the strategic importance of this region augmented by the CPEC; India doesn't let any opportunity for propaganda, slide [DevVrat, 2022: 299-307]. Moreover, America has expressed its reservations about CPEC.

Things are expected to get better after Joe Biden's coming to power. The American policy will become clearer after January. The visit of Iranian Foreign Minister, Javad Zarif is of vital importance.

The Pakistani government has been given the mandate of holding free and fair elections in the whole country besides Gilgit-Baltistan. Therefore, it is the need of the future to reform the system of Election Commission; one that is transparent and free of reservations.

Moreover, the need to counter the effects of Indian propaganda on the international stage through effective foreign policy, establishing relationships with the new American Government on equal footing, and not taking pressure in case of relations with China and India; is a daunting challenge for Pakistan.

REFERENCES:

Dev Vrat S. [2022], "The Indian Media @2047". Central University of Jharkhand, pp.299-307.

Dhrubajyoti B. [2015]," Gilgit Baltistan, China and Pakistan". SSRN Electronic Journal: Indian Council of World Affairs, pp. 1-10.

Hermann K. [2013], "Preservation of Gilgit-Baltistan's Cultural Heritage as a Key to Development". Freie Universitat Berlin, pp. 1-43.

Martin S. [1997], "Migration and Society in Gilgit Northern Areas of Pakistan". Anthropos, pp. 83-90.

Stephanie J. [2022], "The Partition of India: Division and Violence in 20th Century". The Editorial: The Collector, pp. 1-15.

Pakistan Army

Pakistan was a no-go area for the rest of the world for the past many decades. Traveling to Pakistan for the sake of business or pleasure was considered a symbol of danger, fear, and uncertainty. Europe, Britain, America, Canada, Korea, Japan, and many other countries had declared Pakistan unsafe for its citizens [Glenn, 1968: 195-219].

That is why no economic or tourism relations could not be established with these countries for a long period of time. As a result of these circumstances, Pakistan became isolated from the rest of the world. All the countries of the world not only left Pakistan alone on the economic front but also made Pakistan change its policy regarding Afghanistan, pushed it into the war against terror, and later on declared Pakistan unsafe [Farrukh, 2021: 1-12]. In addition to these many countries specifically asked their citizens not to travel to Pakistan in their travel guides, this led to the closure of almost everything like tourism, foreign investment, sports, and trade. I remember in Britain whenever someone asked me for the name of my birth country, their expressions would immediately change on hearing the name of Pakistan and my heart would ache for the law and order situation in Pakistan.

But I was proud of being a Pakistani then, I am a proud Pakistani now and I will remain proud of this till my last breath. With the blessings of Allah, Pakistan Army has played a key role in getting rid of this menace. General Raheel Sharif and later on General Qamar Javed Bajwa have on the front lines during this war.

May Allah reward them for this service. In fact, every soldier, officer, and jawan of the Pakistan army fought untiringly and steadfastly against the anti-state elements. They took Pakistan out of the toughest violent and terror-stricken days and transformed it into a peaceful country.

According to a recent report of BBC London, Pakistan Army's department ISI is one among the intelligence agencies of the world due to its performance and expertise [Jayshree et al, :1-3]. The reason that is cited in BBC's report for this clearly states that ISI is the number one agency because the geographical region in which Pakistan is located is surrounded by enemies on every side. In such a tough region defending its country and making its defense, impregnable is conclusive proof of extreme excellence and capability.

Today Pakistan Army has uprooted terrorism completely and had proved to the world that the Pakistan army is the finest army that has eliminated terrorism in such a way, an achievement that defied the combined armies of the whole world. NATO that claims to be the unsurpassed army in spite of having state of the art equipment, resources, and unlimited wealth failed miserably in ending the reign of terror in Afghanistan and is now requesting Pakistan Army for a safe exit [Madiha, 2021: 1-5]. That is why due to the proficiency and bravery Pak Army, Pakistan's name has become a shining example in the world today, the forces of evil tremble at the name of the Pakistan Army.

I believe that Pak Army deserves not only to be eulogized but also respected and valued. Undoubtedly over the past some time, a few political sections along with some pygmies of social media and people belonging to certain specific sectors have been criticizing this great institution of Pak Army but I challenge them all to serve for one night at the control line in their stead and then I will ask them the meaning of serving at the cost of your life.

I revere every drop of sweat of the jawans of the Pakistan Army who are sacrificing the days and nights of their lives for the solidarity and integrity of Pakistan. These are the brave lions of Allah who always remain steadfast in their commitment towards the safety and prosperity of Pakistan. I salute the brave mothers who gave birth to the sons who brightened every corner of Pakistan by laying down their lives.

Salute to the martyrs and Ghazis who are the crowning glory of the country. Salute to the great sons of the soil who delivered us from terrorism, whose vigilance gives us a peaceful night's sleep, who have protected our honor. Pakistan's army turned this war against terror spanning decades into peace and forced the world to change its priorities and to mention Pakistan as a safe destination for its travelers.

At present only Britain has taken this step and has hanged travel advisory for its citizens marking Pakistan as a safe country to travel to.

France, Germany, Spain, Italy, and other countries are also reviewing their policies, and God willing, Pakistan will soon become the preeminent country for tourism, trade, diplomacy, sports, and diplomacy. Credit goes to the Pakistan army and its departments for the recent successful visit of the British prince and princess which were followed by the tours of Srilankan and Bangladesh cricket teams [Celia, 2021: 1-6].

I hope that very soon Pakistan Army will defeat the hostile Indian designs by bringing a permanent end to the undue propaganda against Pakistan and will bury fifth generation warfare because Pakistan and Pakistani nationals promote peace [Farzana, 2015: 665-667]. The efforts of Pakistan's government and army to bring peace to the world will definitely bear fruit one day and the world will see the positive face of Pakistan. May Allah protect Pakistan and keep it always. Amen

REFERENCES:

Celcia B. [2021], "Travelling is Resuming but Not for Everyone". Foreign Policy: Centre on The United States and Europe, pp. 1-6.

Farzana S. [2015], "Fighting to The End: The Pakistan Army's Way of War". A Reviewed Work, International Affairs [Royal Institute of International Affairs 1944], Vol. 91, No. 3, pp. 665-667.

Farrukh F. [2021], "Identity and Interests: History of Pakistan's Foreign Policy and The Middle-Eastern Muslim States, 1947 to 1956". Cogent Social Sciences, Vol. 7, No. 1, pp. 1-12.

Glenn V. S. [1968], "Pakistan Discontiguity and the Majority Problem". National Geographical Review, Vol. 58, No. 2, pp. 195-219.

Jayshree B. et al [2011], "The ISI and Terrorism: Behind the Accusations". Council of Foreign Relations, Foreign Affairs, pp. 1-3.

Third Chapter: **Pakistan & Economics Crisis**

Islamic Economic System: Idealism or Realism

I have spent 40 years of my life with the hope that I would live to see the auspicious times when the world created by Allah will be run in accordance with the edicts of Allah. The purpose for which 1,24,000 Prophets were sent, the faith for which Hazrat Imam Hussain (RA) sacrificed his life and the lives of his family will be implemented by someone in Pakistan [Al Muntazar, 2020:1-10].

There will come a moment when the colors of this great way of life will illuminate the whole world, there will be a day when the fragrance of this system will envelop the whole world, someday my sightless eyes get to see this radiance, someday the deprived and suppressed millions of this country will be given their due rights, someday they will be delivered from this economic exploitation, someday we will join hands for pulling the people of Pakistan out of the abyss of poverty, injustice, and ignorance.

With this idea and longing in my heart, I had to migrate from my beloved land like a bird that can't find sustenance in its own motherland, and in order to survive, it has to fly miles without any nourishment.

At times, it so happens that a man has to be away from what has been the love of his life, I am also one such person. But it has always been my fervent desire and intention that God willing I will definitely do whatever I could to serve Pakistan and the Muslim Ummah.

Sometimes living in this foreign land I feel that those who get to have a position according to their abilities in their own country are the luckiest people on the face of the earth [Nate ,2019:1-5]. They don't have to leave their parents and siblings and they spend their lives working for the prosperity of their own country. I would further add here that unfortunately at times one can't have a decent enough life in Pakistan even if one tries to live within one's own means.

Deception, lying, nepotism, bribery, dishonesty, hoarding, profiteering, and duplicity are the order of the day in Pakistan [Seumas, 2017: 106-124]; but I can say with all certainty that we have all been a part of this in one way or another even if it is done unwittingly. It would be nothing short of a miracle if anyone says that he has always remained safe from this.

The cause of these circumstances is no one but ourselves because we have made all these vices a part of our way of living. We are either tools of this system or we are the facilitators or else we are working wholeheartedly for the propagation of this system [Cohon, 2018:1-20]. In whatever capacity, we are a part of this system and it is an undesirable action in the eyes of Allah because this system is drenched in the evil of Interest and usury.

This land was obtained in the name of Allah and it was to be run according to the decrees of Allah. Millions of lives were sacrificed for upholding the name of Islam. I still remember the tears of my mother when she used to weep while telling me, 'my son, all my brothers laid down their lives for this country but Allah's proclamations have still to be established here.'

Silent and lost in my thoughts, I trembled when I imagined the horrible scenario of losing a dear one just because he is a Muslim. Only someone who had suffered through such calamity would understand this pain. Our young generation seems least bothered with the loss that was suffered for establishing this country; they seem to think that whatever happened has happened, we opened our eyes in an independent country whether the system is based on the pillars of Interest or the faith, just have fun. But think for a moment that Allah gave us this beautiful land on the promise that it will be run according to His set of laws, if we break this promise how can we succeed?

Our rulers will now have to take one step forward and think. They will have to decide that enough is enough we should get rid of this evil and seek Allah's assistance by breaking the begging bowl of IMF, the Interest-based economy will have to be replaced with an Islamic Economic system on a self-help basis [Maxwell, 2019:1-8].

Pakistan is much better placed than a Christian country like Luxembourg whose population and constitution both aren't based on Islam but even while being a part of the West; it has eliminated Interest from its economic system. Interest was the mainstay of their system but Luxembourg has adopted the Islamic Economic system even though it's not an Islamic country [Imran, 2010:1-17].

Brunei Darussalam was boycotted by the whole world because it wanted to implement the Islamic Code of Life, Malaysia and Qatar presented the finest alternate system after thorough research which was deemed practical even by countries like

England, Germany, Japan, and France [AbdulMalik, 2021:291-309]. Not only this but England has made an investment of 2 billion pounds in the Islamic bonds and declared England a center of the Islamic Economic System [Ahmed et al, 2014:37-78].

Now consider this, why can't Islamic Code be implemented in an Islamic country like Pakistan where even the constitution is Islamic? Why aren't we willing to uproot a system based on exploitation and oppression? If Malaysia and Luxembourg can get ahead by implementing the Islamic system then why can't Pakistan emulate their example whose scholars and jurists like Dr. Iqbal Asariya, Maulana Taqi Usmani, Dr. Humayn Dar, and Prof. Khursheed Ahmed; have set up and reared the Islamic economic system in different countries of the world?

How can we gain favors of Allah in our lives by earning livelihood through forbidden means and which is generated by the involvement of Interest? It the same as someone who is looking to buy halal meat with income that is Haram. Kindly let us all get together and force our rulers to end this accursed system of Interest-based economy. No power on earth can stop Pakistan's rise to greatness if we could achieve this objective. In Sha Allah.

REFERENCES:

Abdul M.O [2021], "The Whole-of-Nation Approach: The Case of Brunei Darussalam, Wawasan 2035, and The 4th Industrial Revolution". Handbook of Global Challenges for Improving Public Services and Government Operations, pp. 291-309.

Ahmed B. et al., [2014], "Islamic Finance in The United Kingdom: Factors Behind its Development and Growth". Islamic Economic Studies, vol. 22, No. 1, pp.37-78.

Al Muntazar [2020], "Hazrat Imam Husain (a.s) and Hazrat Imam Mahdi (a.s)". Al Muntazar Online Islamic Course, Pakistan, pp. 1-10.

Cohen R. [2018], "Hume's Moral Philosophy". Stanford Encyclopedia of Philosophy, pp. 1-20.

Imran N. [2010], "Pakistan's Standing in the Global Villlage". Research Gate Publication, pp.1-17.

Maxwell C. [2019]. "Aristotle and the Good Ruler". Centre for the Study of Democratic Institutions, University of British Columbia. Oxford University Press, No. 13, pp. 1-8.

Nate R. [2019], "Alone in a Foreign Land: The Emotional Challenges of Living Abroad Alone". Ascent Publication, pp. 1-5.

Seumas M. [2017], Bribery, Nepotism, Fraud and Abuse of Authority". Cambridge University Press, pp. 106-124: A Book Chapter: Institutional Corruption: A Study Applied in Philosophy.

Inflation and the People

It has been more than a year since the government of change has come to power but there are no signs of any change in the country yet. The people are as powerless, vulnerable, and helpless as they were in the past; the only change is that inflation has doubled. The poor can't even earn enough to eat a decent meal and the middle class is worn out trying to sustain its livelihood and honor.

Sometimes I wonder what should I call these blind, deaf and dumb rulers, how can I share my feelings with these insensitive people who are completely without any conscience. Trust me, at times the heart becomes so agitated that I want to lament loudly about these problems and hardships. The government keeps harping on the same tune that things aren't easy for it; it has inherited empty coffers and loads of debt.

How easier it would have been if the previous rulers had given subsidies on medicines, lentils, rice, flour, sugar, and milk instead of subsidizing the Metro then the people wouldn't have been facing the present predicament. After more than a year, now the government has given the utility stores a subsidy of just 7 billion instead of 70 billion which is a feeble attempt at hiding its insensitivity.

The government of Pakistan should have given a subsidy of 70 billion on electricity and gas each, as well. Even now instead of playing the same old tune if the government starts moving in the right direction then a change in the present circumstances of the people is possible to some extent because in a welfare state it is the responsibility of the government to keep the prices of the items of everyday use, well within the reach of the common man, aside from this, the people should get some relief [Noah, 2023:1-4]. The simple formula is that the items that are consumed by them should be made tax-free and in its place food banks should be established for the poor and the needy.

The people who can't afford basic food items due to poverty should be given free rations from these food banks. Electricity bills up to 500 units should be subsidized, gas ought to be bought from Iran and the people who earn less than Rs.50000 per month should be given free gas; petrol should be subsidized in order to give them cheaper fuel and they should either be given free or cheaper petrol up to a certain limit per month, if the construction of homes is taking time then people should be helped out in their rent payments, widows, orphans and destitute should be helped out, they should be provided with equal and free health facilities [Isabella et al, 2023:1-3].

Do the rulers not see that the people are crying for help? But like previous rulers, these rulers who claimed that they would establish 'Riyasat e Madina', are miles away from implementing any concrete measures [Guilia, 2013:1-3]. No one can even see the actual problems; the poor citizens just need decent meals and a roof over their heads with dignity.

What more do they ask for?

All over the world the items of daily use are either exempt from tax or the rate of taxation is very low but here these items are especially taxed at a higher rate, and why shouldn't the government do so?

How many in the parliament of Pakistan belong to poor families?

Who can have knowledge of the pain of the people, who has seen poverty?

Who knows the rates of the basic essentials?

Who gives two hoots about the poor?

They are all so high on power and wealth that to them the general public is nothing more than insects. Their revelries are colorful and their lives are trouble-free. Why talk about the next meal?

They have no worries for the next 50 years in this regard. If they ever come down from their lofty seats of power, they would know what grind the people are going through. The statement of Ex PM of Pakistan Nawaz Sharif keeps echoing in my ears, 'had I known that justice is so expensive, I would have done something for it.'

This clearly means that our past and present rulers are the holy cows and they shouldn't be held accountable, no questions should be asked of them and if someone does ask them, they reply that this is the accumulated filth of the past regimes, how can it be cleaned in one year? they should keep one thing in mind that 'their ignorance is more regrettable than their inaction' pretty soon they will have to answer for their deeds, God Almighty will pardon the mistakes that are about Him but He will never forgive what has been done to these weak people.

The incapability of the Punjab Government (Pakistan) is proof that they aren't up to the task [Khalid, 1966:102-110]. They have given nothing to the people of Punjab.

Neither he improved the education system nor were the parents who were protesting the increase in the fees given any relief, they weren't even given coverage in the media so that their voices might have reached the high seats of power, police corruption, hospital system, courts, and the justice system, everything is the same as it was left by the previous governments. There isn't any planning and no concrete steps.

Do something, give a roadmap and take some practical steps, what is the harm in improving the system of police and the hospitals?

All that is needed to accomplish this is compassion and planning along with some administrative abilities but even here your performance is zilch…. extremely disappointing. Even if I agree with the point of view that one year is a very short time period for any planning or practical steps then do you even need five years to answer a simple question that why until now you haven't presented any solid plan for reforming the election commission, reforms that you have been promising since the day one?

Be mindful that the model of Riyasat e Madina will have to be presented practically and not just verbally [Pervez, 2018:1-3]. If you keep dragging your feet then remember that Allah doesn't provide such a chance again and again. Imran Khan Sahib, the awareness that you have given the people might prove to be your undoing ultimately.

There is still time, get rid of inept people around you and include honest and just people like yourself in your team, change this corrupt bureaucracy, and appoint honest officers so that the conspiracy to fail you could be stopped otherwise you won't even be a footnote in the annals of the history.

206

REFERENCES:

Guilia M. [2013], "Plato's Argument for Rule by Philosopher Kings". E-International Relations, University of New York, pp. 1-3.

Isabella et al [2023], "Food Poverty in the U.K: The Causes, Figures and Solutions". The Editorial: The Big Issue Magazine, pp. 1-3.

Khalid B. S [1966], "The Capabilities of Pakistan's Political System". Asian Survey, Vol. 7, No. 2, A Survey of Asia in 1966, Part 2, pp. 102-110.

Noah B. [2023], "What is At Stake in Pakistan's Power Crisis". Council on Foreign Relations, Foreign Affairs, pp. 1-4.

Pervez H. [2018], "Madina State and "Naya" Pakistan". The Editorial: The Dawn Magazine, pp. 1-3.

Global Economic Warfare and Pakistan

Time is changing at a swift pace. The world has altered the tactics of war. New alliances are forming rapidly. There are issues of new strategies among countries, political alliances, distribution of resources, future planning, military cooperation, cognizance of problems, regional integrity, defense of geographical boundaries, water resources, self-sufficiency in oil, gas, science, and technology but more than that the need of the hour is economic development and increase in the trade [Niall, 2021: 469-480]. The country that doesn't acknowledge this fact or even tries to ignore it will become collateral among the nations of the world in the near future.

At present, the economic war is at its zenith in the form of the third world war [Gerald et al, 2006: 1-24]. Powerful countries are facing off against each other. Plans are being made to wreck others economically in order to win the war on the economic front. The coming ten years are crucial in this economic warfare because economic changes are taking place at unimaginably fast speed.

The big world powers are striving hard to improve and buttress their economic and financial position and resources but only that nation will emerge victorious that has the ability to do something practically through effective planning, sound strategy, and tireless hard work. This scenario has clearly divided the world into two parts which I have mentioned on numerous occasions. This division is natural since whenever a suppressor comes in contact with the weak and oppressed his atrocities know no bounds and it might naturally come into play.

It is also the law of nature that when a nation crosses the limits of decency and borders on injustice then that nation is wrecked by Allah verily He doesn't like the transgressors. On the other hand, the justice of nature is that whoever is compassionate towards fellow beings and makes sincere continuous efforts, succeeds. This is an established fact.

In the past century, history has witnessed many nations who considered themselves superpowers, crumble and fall. Today they are subjugated and destitute because nothing is beyond the supreme power of Allah.

He can easily use mosquitoes, birds (ababeel), and pandemics. As the Quran says, "Unto Allah belongs the Sovereignty of the heavens and the earth and whatsoever is therein, and He is able to do all things."

In the new political horizon, China is ready to swoop down like an eagle. By the end of this decade, the world will have to acknowledge the new rising power because China has left America behind in trade and investment [Laura et al, 2022: 1-15]. As per recent statistics issued by the United Nations, China has beaten America in new direct forging investment.

Last year new direct investment by the foreign companies in America has declined to almost half of what it used to be while according to United Nations' data this same investment has increased four times in Chinese firms. This has given China a prominent position globally [Arendse, 2022: 1-5]. United

Nations Conference on Trade and Development has stated in its report that in China the volume of direct foreign investment was 163 billion dollars while American share was just 134 billion dollars.

This is a warning bell for America. In 2019 the American share was 251 billion dollars and China got 140 billion dollars, but now the situation has changed completely. According to the Centre for Economics and Business Research (CEBR) in England, China which is currently locked in a trade war with America will leave the rest of the world behind by 2028[Ryan et al, 2020: 1-6].

After this, it will become impossible to defeat China in the economic sphere. On the other hand, Chinese endeavors in Gwadar are playing a pivotal role in extracting Pakistan from economic destitution and making it a pivotal global economic hub. China is also using its influence in Oil and gas agreements with Iran and Russia and in the Kashmir-Ladakh issue. All these efforts will more or less come to fruition after the current decade.

At this moment China's defense, diplomatic, and trade of help Pakistan will change world history because in addition to Pakistan; Russia, Iran, and Turkey are other important players in this block [Rashida, 2017: 3-22]. Indisputably, currently, Pakistan's worsening economic condition is at its peak. In a recent report the total debt has reached 113 billion dollars out of which only 18 billion is from the last years because when PTI came to power, the debt was 95 billion dollars which are now touching new heights [Jalil et al, 2022: 1-5].

The economic team of the Prime Minister has miserably failed since at times it talks about pledging public parks and then at other times raises prices of petroleum products. It is absolutely pertinent to raise questions about the efficiency of the team that can't ensure just the distribution of resources to the level of the common man.

In fact, the government has no control over the current situation since inflation, corruption, plunder, and black marketing have become the fate of this nation and the government is calmly witnessing this whole drama as a silent spectator.

Perhaps the government has found comfort in quiet. Instead of keeping mum, the government should learn a lesson from the changes that are taking place in the global economic scenario. The cat won't leave a pigeon alone just because it has closed its eyes.

REFERENCE

Policies Aim to Maintain Growth Momentum". China Briefing: Dezan Shira Associates, pp. 1-5.

Gerald S. et al [2006], "War and The World Economy". Journal of Conflict Resolution, Vol. 50, No. 5, pp. 1-24.

Jalil A. et al [2022], "India and Pakistan at 75: Prospects for The Future". United States Institute of Peace, pp. 1-5.

Laura S. et al [2022], "How Global Public Opinion of China Has Shifted in The Xi Era". Pew Research Center, pp. 1-15.

Niall D. et al [2021], "Introduction: The Brics, Global Governance and Challenges for South-South Cooperation in a Post-Westren World". International Political Science Review, vol. 43, No. 4, pp. 469-480.

Rashida H. [2017], "Pakistan and China: Partnership, Prospects and The Course Ahead". Policy Perspectives, Vol. 14, No. 1, Pakistan and Its Neighbours, pp. 3-22.

Ryan H. et al [2020], "More Pain Than Gain: How The US-China Trade War Hurt America". The Brookings, pp. 1-6.

Impoverished Peddlers of Poverty

At the moment, the most daunting challenge facing the people of Pakistan is dealing with hunger, poverty, and inflation that has become a common fixture in their lives. The back-breaking price hike has deprived the poor of basic facilities like food, clothing, and shelter [Fariha et al, 2021: 1-14].

The poor have gone below the poverty line but even the people belonging to the middle classes have been driven to suicide. The households are now maintaining a semblance of dignity by rationing the food so that the children may eat properly while the elders eat one meal a day. Getting one meal a day is now an uphill task let alone one billion jobs.

Most of the hawkers, naan makers, milkmen, and butchers have been driven to sell adulterated goods. Recently the World Bank's 'South Asia Economic Focus Exports Wanted' has predicted that inflation will rise to the tune of 7.1% by the end of the current fiscal year. This report has also revealed that unfortunately, this rate can climb up to 13.5% in the next year. This clearly means that the tsunami of price hikes isn't going to abate in the near future [Prema, 2011: 1-55].

The prices of cooking oil, ghee, and milk have been raised yet again at the Utility Stores while the Prime Minister had ordered the provision of subsidy to the Utility Stores to provide some relief to the people. Similarly, Karachi was ordered to be cleaned but that promise also remained an empty promise. As of now, both the Utility Stores and Karachi are the same as before. The government's claims of being people friendly and good governance stand exposed yet again as the prices of oil and ghee rose by Rs. 4, brand milk packs by Rs. 5, and those of children's cereals by Rs. 20 to Rs. 38 [Laurent, 2014: 1-256]

According to the government notification milk, tea whitener, and coffee prices have also been increased while brand shampoo price has also been raised due to which price of 90ml shampoo bottle reached Rs. 98 from Rs. 89. The price of detergents offered for sale at the Utility Stores has also been raised. On top of that, the prices of 94 medicines have been increased by 262%. Prices of medicines to treat fever, headache, cardiac ailments, malaria, diabetes, sore throat, flu, stomach ache; nose, ear, throat, and blood infection have registered a blood-curdling hike [Fhrizz, 2020: 1-9].

The notification further stated that the prices of medicines have been increased because of supply shortages, which in my view is but a cruel joke on the people. If the government was compelled to raise the prices of medicines was the government invited by the people to raise prices of other items? The current situation makes one feel that persuading the government to do anything is child's play; anyone can blackmail the government to get the desired job done.

This shows not only the weakness of the government machinery but also flawed planning. Dr. Faisal Sultan (Special Advisor to the Prime Minister for Health) has claimed that the government was not influenced by the pharmaceutical industry [Shahina, 2020: 1-2]. This claim seems crazy and seems to be refuting the ground realities. When life-saving drugs vanish from the market and aren't available easily then what does this imply? Isn't this a blatant threat by the pharmaceutical companies? The second claim of the government, that the prices of life-saving drugs have been raised because they weren't available in the market due to low prices; also seems beyond comprehension.

My question is this; Sir! Is the disappearance of medicines from the market not blackmailing by the pharmaceutical companies, and if the medicines are withdrawn from the market and the government is helpless then where is the writ of the government? If in the future, any company fixes arbitrary exorbitant prices or resorts to hoarding in order to raise prices then what will the government do? Will it again burden the public with its incompetence by raising the prices instead of controlling this mafia? It's the government's job to ascertain the availability of medicines and maintain the supremacy of law.

You have the right to raise the prices but first, you need to increase the income of the people. Do you have any idea that which section of society needs these life-saving drugs? For your kind information, they are the underprivileged elderly, the disabled, and the pensioners whose incomes you have not increased even by a rupee this year hence you have no right to raise the prices of the medicines required by them.

On the other hand, the National Electric Power Regulatory Authority (NEPRA) has approved an additional burden of Rs.164 billion and 8.7 million on the consumers.

All this combined amount to denying the people the right to medical treatment. I would say to the public that this government itself is impoverished; one shouldn't expect them to look after the poor. It's a pity that those who should be tending to the wounds of the public are crying about their own wounds to the people. Hanif Rahi has put this beautifully:

> *buhat ghareeb hein mehngaee bantnay walay*

> *(Greatly impoverished are the peddlers of poverty)*

REFERENCE

Farehas S. et al [2021], "Covid-19 in Pakistan: Challenges and Priorities". Cogent Medicine, Vol. 8, No. 1, pp. 1-14.

Fhrizz S. D. J [2020], "Milk Tea Industry: An Exploratory Study". Nueva Ecjia University of Science and Technology, pp. 1-9.

Lauret G. [2014], "Karachi – Ordered Disorder and The Struggle for The City". Centre For International Studies, pp. 1-256.

Prema C. A. [2011], "South-South Trade: An Asian Perspective". Asian Development Bank: ADB Economics Working Paper Series, No. 265, pp. 1-55.

Shahina M. [2020], "Dr. Faisal Sultan Becomes PM's Special Assisant on Health". The Editorial: The News International, pp. 1-2.

Problems after Problems

Pakistan is the only country that has still remained with traces of Dengue and Polio; however, despite commendable efforts resulting in the mitigation of Covid-19 menace in Pakistan, Dengue has emerged to be another epidemic making people fall prey to it, on the other hand [Firdous, 2011: 1-7]. Even in the past, Mian Shahbaz Sharif also took many steps to eradicate Dengue, despite his best efforts this insidious disease could not be eradicated; whereas, during his tenure dedicated paramedic dengue teams used to visit the streets repeatedly and conducted spray drives.

But this time, for a few months after the outbreak of Dengue, no such team, in most of the areas, neither any awareness campaign could be carried out effectively. However, with the increasing number of cases, recently, the government has taken up the matter on critical grounds, showed their dedication to exclusively control the spread in its entirety. In fact, due to Covid-19's severity last year, the dengue campaign could not be carried out as planned; resultantly, social media places the entire responsibility on the government, in contrary to the Covid-19's challenges as justification, by claiming that such mismanagements cannot be anticipated from the governments' end. Since the purpose of governments is to plan in well-advance, keeping all uncertainties and contingencies in consideration, such justifications remained insufficient for the critics [Rahmet, et al, 2020:1-7]. However, in this scenario, I stand by the Prime Ministerthat if the institutions are strong then the government and the people do not face such difficulties.

Therefore, Prime Minister has repeatedly asserted the priority of the government is to let the institutions be independent of the government's influence so that they can formulate independent policies and make recommendations to the government for the welfare of the people; unfortunately, the government has not succeeded in this endeavor yet.

One of the exemplary institutions in this regard is NHS, a British health institution, where the freedom to formulate the policies has been preached within the framework of the constitution and law, to make timely recommendations to the government in order to address future challenges to be handled in a utilitarian way [Jane, et al, 2019: 1-181].

In this regard, the NHS and the British Institute of Health wrote to the government recommending that the flu vaccine shall be administered along with the COVID-19 vaccine, so that Covid accompanied by the flu may not prove to be fatal to the people [Gabriel, et al, 2020: 1-3].

Following these recommendations from the NHS and the British Health Agency, the British government took timely action and launched a flu vaccine campaign from the beginning of winter to keep the public safe from any kind of stress, although currently due to the re-emergence of Covid-19 cases, there is a strong possibility that the UK and Europe might move to another lockdown at any time.

Almost 35,000 Corona cases are being reported in the UK almost every day, which could have repercussions worldwide. In the same way, Pakistan's health department should pursue and support the government by presenting its pharmaceutical recommendations, formulating medicinal strategies likewise, in a timely manner in order to avoid any future adversities [Sania et al, 2013: 2291-2297].

The government should reconsider the fact that the number of patients in the hospitals of Lahore has been steadily increasing over the past several months; thus, aggravating the burden on the medical and paramedical staff. As of now, more than 1300 dengue patients are being treated in different hospitals in Lahore. However, according to the health department, at present more than 7500 dengue cases have been reported across Punjab, most of the cases are from Lahore city, many have gone recovered, whereas, others are confined to their homes [Natasha, et al, 2013: 299-309].

Another issue persisting is the pricing of the tests, during the tenure of the previous government, the prices of the Dengue test were fixed at Rs.50, now the cost of the same test has reached up to Rs. 800 [Nadiya et al, 2018: 3316-3331].

On the other side, privately owned labs are charging the prices as per their own will. Even if anyone wanted to have a detailed report on the disease's test results, the charged amount reaches Rs.3000, these detailed tests usually need to be done almost every other day, hence, clearly shows that thousands of rupees are being wasted on these tests of daily basis. Moreover, if there's a need to have the platelets implanted, then the cost of other tests including cross-match goes up to Rs. 35000.

Furthermore, the entire process is not such convenient due to the long queues in order to make appointments for the lab tests and implantation of platelets too.

On the other hand, the sharp rise in drug prices is enough to be the reason behind the arduously back-breaking of the people. Government employees and pensioners have already seemed ground in the chopper of raising inflations; whereas, the poor are in a state of disarray as they are left with no other hope other than that of their Almighty God [Vincent, 2020:1-5].

Lift up your head and observe, a complete state of chaos and mayhem; inflation and uncertainty, everywhere, taking every daily use and ordinary goods away from the reach of common man day-by-day. On top of that, the fear of Dengue and Covid-19, making people suffer from anxiety and depression; in some instances, the poor are seen selling children on the streets; but, unfortunate is the government's ignorance towards the formulation of any such strategy to save its people from this mayhem, no concrete steps in this regard have been taken so far – people are left with no other option other than to mourn in distress.

The government should reassess and evaluate this deteriorating situation, provide relief to the people on an urgent basis so that the situation can be brought under control and the nation can be saved from any other unfortunate dilemma.

REFERENCE

Firdous J. [2011], "Dengue Fever [DF] in Pakistan ". Asia Pacific Family Medicine, Vol. 10, No. 1, pp. 1-7.

Gabriel S. et al [2020], "The UK's Public Health Response to Covid-19". British Medical Journal, pp. 1-3.

Jane B. et al [2019], "Strenthening Health Systems Through Nursing: Evidence From 14 European Countries [Internet]". Health Policy Series, No. 52, pp. 1-181.

Nadiya T. et al., [2018], "Point-of-care Tests: A Review of Advances in The Emerging Diagnostic Tools for Dengue Virus Infection". Sensors and Actuators B Chemicals, Vol. 255, No. 3, pp. 3316-3331.

Natasha E. et al., [2013], "Epidemiology of Dengue: Past, Present and Future Prospects". National Institutes of Health: National Library of Medicine, Vol. 5, No. 1, pp. 299-309.

Rahmet G. et al., [2020], "Covid-19: Prevention and Control Measures in Communities". Turkish Journal of Medical Sciences: National Library of Medicine, Vol. 50, No. 3.

Sania N. et al., [2013], "Health Reform in Pakistan: A Call to Action". Health Transitions in Pakistan, Vol. 381, No. 9885, pp. 2291-2297.

Vincent S. R. [2020], "The High Cost of Prescription Drugs: Causes and Solutions". Blood Cancer Journal, Vol. 10, No. 71, pp. 1-5.

Fourth Chapter: Issue of International Concern

International Huntsmen

A glance at the past few decades shows that the international balance of power is shifting gradually [Mette, 2009: 347-380]. The world is changing rapidly; new alliances and powers are coming into being. Nations and countries have split up and this will have far-reaching consequences [Dominik, 2020: 193-225]. Even the way the wars have been fought has changed. In this developed era, fifth-generation warfare and the cold war is deciding the fate of nations [Asmaa, 2019: 1-12].

The speech of the Chinese president in front of the nations of the world has clearly enunciated that America is no longer the sole superpower in the world and that power isn't the birthright of any single state. On the other hand, the powerful countries of the world are fervently trying to get hold of the world oil reserves, as soon as possible [Michelle, 2022: 1-6]. The big countries are fighting proxy wars in the battleground of smaller countries in order to achieve their objectives [Andrew, 2013: 40-46].

The recent civil war in Syria is an example of this phenomenon. In this war, America and Israel were backing Syrian rebels while Iran, Turkey, and Russia remained the frontline supporters of the Syrian government [Elizabeth,2018: 1-3]. As a matter of fact, this world is intoxicated by power and wealth. The world and this life aren't everlasting but in complete disregard of this fact, a game of blood and fire is being played. Whole countries are being devastated.

These hot and cold wars have caused anarchy in these countries while destroying their political values. An analysis also opines that all this is taking the world towards a third Great War but I think that this war of the modern era has started way back. Only its dynamics keep changing with time [Sisir, 1969: 54-63].

The lust for resources will cause nothing but destruction and devastation of the whole world. Iraq, Libya, Afghanistan, Egypt, Palestine, Syria, and now Azerbaijan- Armenia conflict all seem to be an outcome of this power-lust [Bishnu, 2004:1-7]. The ups and downs of the past century depict the negative approach of these powerful global predators; the approach that says they should have complete control over everything, none may dare question or oppose them, the riches of the world should be at their feet and no one should even get a whiff of this [Susan, 2011:1-7].

Baku first attracted the attention of these predators when more than half of the oil in the international market was being produced by it [Bulent, 1998:30-50]. Even today Baku is producing a fifth of the world supply. This oil money propelled Azerbaijan to new heights of development and prosperity which didn't sit well with power-drunk countries.

An international conspiracy was hatched which aimed at weakening Azerbaijan by backing Armenia. Azerbaijan is a small country that came into being in 1990 following the breakup of the Soviet Union. Over the past 20 years, this country has made exemplary progress owing to its oil wealth [Laurence, 2022:1-3].

According to the international journal 'Council on Foreign Relations', Azerbaijan produces 800,000 barrels of oil per day and is a big oil exporter to Europe and Central Asia [Fariz,

2020: 1-4]. 1994 is the year that saw the end of a six-year-long conflict between Armenia and Azerbaijan over Nagorno-Karabakh enclave.

This is however still a high conflict area. Nagorno-Karabakh is also important because there are huge oil and gas reserves in the Behr- -e-Gillan or the Caspian Sea but there is another opinion according to which not oil but transportation of oil and gas is the main reason for this importance. Azerbaijan depends on this area for transportation of oil and supply of gas to the West. Nagorno-Karabakh consists of seven areas and is a part of Azerbaijan International Laws.

Since Azerbaijan supplies oil and gas to Turkey, Israel, the western and many other countries; these countries can't afford a long war between Armenia and Azerbaijan. According to an estimate, Azerbaijan sells 100,000 barrels of oil per day to Turkey alone. Russia is taking full advantage of this whole scenario by selling arms to both countries and filling up its coffers.

The longer this conflict continues the more beneficial the suspension of Azerbaijanian oil supply will be for Russia, moreover, since Russia has an army base in Armenia, one reason for Russian interest could be gaining control of western oil supply routes with Armenian help. But now the Russian game is at its end because Pakistan and Turkey have announced their support for Azerbaijan.

Pakistan is the only country in the world that has not acknowledged the state of Armenia and the reason is the same as the one in the case of Israel [Abrar,2018: 1-4]. In this perspective, Azerbaijan has contacted Pakistan for the purchase of the F-17 Thunder-2 which proves Pakistan's dominance in the field of technology. The way things will move and the direction this war of power and oil takes remains to be seen.

The government of Pakistan will have to decide with acumen and foresight because the times ahead can bring new challenges.

REFERENCES:

Abrar M. A. [2018], "Strange Estrangement: Pakistan and Armenia". The Editorial: The Express Tribune, pp. 1-4.

Andrew M. [2013], "Proxy Warfare and The Future of Conflict". The RUSI Journal, Vol. 158, No. 2, pp. 40-46.

Asmaa P. [2019], "The Fifth Generation Warfare and The Definitions of Peace". The Journal of Intelligence Conflict and Warfare, Vol. 2, pp. 1-12.

Bishnu R. U. [2004], "Resource Conflicts and Conflict Resolution in Nepal". Mountain Research and Development, vol. 24, No. 1, pp. 1-7.

Bulent G. [1998], "The Battle for Baku {May-September, 1918}: A Peculiar Episode in The History of The Caucasus". Middle-Eastern Studies, Vol. 34, No. 1, pp. 30-50.

Dominik P. [2020], "Convergence Between Developed and Developing Countries: A Centennial Perspective", Social Indicators Research, Vol. 153, pp. 193-225.

Elizabeth T. [2018], "Inside Israel's Secret Program to Back Syrian Rebels". The Editorial: Foreign Policy Magazine, pp. 1-3.

Fariz I. [2020], "Azerbaijan's Foreign Policy Priorities and The Role of The Middle-East". The Middle-East Institute, pp. 1-4.

Laurence B. [2002], "Is Azerbaijan Planning A Long-term Presence in Armenia?". Russia and Eurasia Programme Chatham House, pp. 1-3.

Mette E. S. [2009], "The End of Balance of Power Theory? A Comment on Wohlforth et al's Testing Balance of Power Theory in World History". European Journal of International Relations, vol. 15, No. 2, pp. 347-380.

Michelle B.   [2022], "Crisis and Fragility of Democracy". United Nartions Human Rights, Opening Workshop for The International Association of Jesuit Universities, Boston College, pp. 1-6.

Sisir G. [1969], "The Third World and The Great Powers". The Annals of the American Academy of Political and Social Sciences, Vol. 386, pp. 54-63: Protagonists, Power and the Third World: Essays on The Changing International System. Sage Publications Inc.

Susan S. F. [2011], "Ups and Downs in the Global City: London and New York in the 21st". DOI: 1002/1978.

Democratic Charlatans

Democracy is in crisis nowadays. The values it embodies—particularly the right to choose leaders in free and fair elections, freedom of the press, and the rule of law—are under assault and in retreat globally [Jin-Young, 2019:1-19]. Most of the countries in the world where the political parties engage in politics in the name of democracy but the fact of the matter is that they are miles away from the spirit of democracy themselves [Richard et al, 2018:1-7]. Democracy is a political system in which all paths to power pass through the citizens [Larry, 2004:1-8].

After God, the people are the source of power as they select their rulers according to their own free will. In a country like Pakistan, the funeral pyre of democracy was lit the day a handful of families changed democracy into dictatorship [Mehlaqa, 2023: 1-3]. The role of the U.S. government was quite critical here, because of unfairly supporting such political parties or dictators around the globe. As an example, In October 1999, Pakistan's Chief of Army Staff Gen. Pervez Musharraf replaced Prime Minister Nawaz Sharif in a bloodless coup [Hasan,1999:208-218].

Following the military overthrow of an elected government. Tim Arango mentioned in his article in the New York Times that, a Turkish newspaper reported that an American academic and former State Department official had helped orchestrate a violent conspiracy to topple the Turkish government from a fancy hotel on an island in the Sea of Marmara, near Istanbul [Elena, 2018:55-74]. The same newspaper, in a front-page headline, flat-out said the United States had tried to assassinate President Recep Tayyip Erdogan on the night of the failed coup.

On the other hand, the U.S. interfered in Egypt, Syria, Japan, North Korea, Vietnam, Afghanistan, Iraq, and Libya is also contradicting his claim. But, the U.S. still repeatedly professing that they are not sporting dictatorship at all. If the U.S. wouldn't support such regimes which are established over the democratic norms, the situation of the world could be different today.

Michael J. Abramowitz wrote in Freedom House, even when he chose to acknowledge America's treaty alliances with fellow democracies, the president spoke of cultural or civilizational ties rather than shared recognition of universal rights; his trips abroad rarely featured any mention of the word "democracy." [Michael, 2017:1-15] Indeed, the American leader expressed feelings of admiration and even personal friendship for some of the world's most loathsome strongmen and dictators.

Democracy doesn't suit these political pundits nor do the democratic norms have any effect on them. The addiction of power and ruling over the people takes away their capacity and strength to take decisions in the national interest [Jim, 2013:1-261]. The love for family rule and monarchy runs in their blood but they raise slogans of democracy and predicaments of the common man even though they haven't been able to come out of the circle of their own gains neither will they ever be able to do so [Latika, 2021: 1-7]. They can neither raise a voice within their own parties nor can they challenge anyone outside of them.

They are so influential that no one can even think of bringing them to book. If anyone can hold them accountable, then that would be the people of the subjective country. But these politically barren parties have tousled the intellect of people in the whirlpool of efforts to make ends meet. They have forgotten everything except a constant struggle to survive.

They will never have enough resources to fulfill their basic requirements and hence will never have the thirst for wisdom neither will they hold these incompetent hereditary kings. When they come to power their only purpose is to collect a fortune, transfer it overseas, and take the influence and wealth of their families to new heights [Brock, 2019: 1-7].

A huge army of slaves is at their beck and call because they are born slaves and still believe in the obsolete theory of slavery across generations. An overwhelming majority of the population has been kept illiterate through proper planning so that they would remain far away from awareness and consciousness, neither will they acquire political wisdom nor will they understand the spirit of democracy and will never become harbingers of real change [Sandra, 2009: 1-5].

Most of our politicians are charlatans who hoodwink people through their political gimmickry [Richard, 2021: 1-10]. This corrupt mafia is using sleight of hand and duping the people for the past seventy years. To this day the people couldn't understand whether there is a snake in the hamper or not, their potions cure any disease or not; all this is a result of greed, lust, self-interest, nepotism.

No party has given party leadership to any member except the hereditary leaders. No one except them and their children have the right to lead the party.

Not a single member of these political parties around the globe has ever developed the ability to challenge the party leadership in the party elections apart few; fight and then win any such election because the leadership of these parties who claim to be champions of democracy, is also selected through a process that is a mere eyewash and not truly democratic at all. Zulfiqar Ali Bhutto was succeeded by his daughter, son in law and now his grandson is heading the party [Stoke, 1999: 243-267].

In PMLN Maryam Nawaz is eager to rule after Mian Nawaz Sharif. ANP is also in the same boat. Bacha Khan, then Wali Khan followed by Asfandyar Wali and now his son Aimal Khan is gearing up to lead the party. On the other hand, recently Jamiat Ulema-e Pakistan has announced that after Maulana Fazal Ur Rehman, his son Asad ul Rehman will lead the party.

PTI won't be any different because how could a party practically implement democracy in a country which has failed to implement democratic norms within its own internal party organization.

The U.S. also some extend followed the same almost 16 years when Bush senior brought Bush junior after him and Hilary swanking Clinton [Tom, 2009:1-5]. Nehru, Indra, Rajeev, Sonia and now her son Rahul is also the biggest example in India. Will someone please make the people understand that why the leadership of the above-mentioned parties is the birthright of these rulers only? What kind of ethics we can see under the umbrella of democracy in the world? The sworn enemies of yore are becoming bosom buddies today. Those who were or are rebels of the nondemocratic approach of the parties end up in different ways.

A world is appreciating their capabilities but they have been pushed into oblivion because the new philosophy is: "if he embezzles he also spends in the right places". In my opinion, only that party can be called democratic that has democracy within its organizational structure. In other words; if the sky falls, then we can catch larks.

REFERENCES:

Brock et al [2019], "Needs in Moral and Political Philosophy". The Stanford Encyclopedia of Philosophy, pp.1-7.

Elena F. [2018], "Disintegrated Selves: Dissociative Disorders and Colonial Anxiety in Orphan Pamuk's The Black Book". A Poetics of Neurosis: Narratives of Normalcy and Disorder in Cultural and Literary Texts, pp. 55-74.

Hasan A. R. [1999], "Pakistan in 1999: Back to Square One". Asian Survey, Vol. 20, No. 1, pp. 208-218. University of California Press.

Jim O. [2013], "Power, Powerlessness, and Addiction". University of Birmingham, Cambridge University Press, pp. 1-261.

Jin Young L. [2019], "Globalization and The Crisis of Liberal Democracy: The Political Dynamics of Neo-liberalism and Populism". ResearchGate, Vol. 21, No. 4, pp. 1-19.

Larry D. [2004], "What is Democracy?". Hilla University for Humanistic Studies, Stanford University, pp. 1-8.

Latika B. [2021], "The Men in Grey: The True Powers Behind the Palace". The Sydney Morning Herald, pp. 1-7.

Mehlaqa S. [2023], "The Death of Democracy in Pakistan". FPIF – Foreign Policy in Focus in Conjunction with Critical Connections, pp. 1-3.

Michael J. A. [2017], "Democracy in Crisis". FreedomHouse, pp. 1-15.

Richard W. et al [2021], "Many in the U.S, Western Europe Say Their Political System Needs Major Reform". Pew Research Center, International Affairs, pp. 1-10.

Richard W. et al [2018], "Many Around the World Are Disengaged from Politics". Pew Research, pp. 1-7.

Sandra J. [2009], "Roman Slavery and The Question of Race". Black Past Magazine, pp. 1-5.

Stokes C. S. [1999], "Political Parties and Democracy". Annual Review of Political Science, Department of Political Science, University of Chicago, Vol. 2, pp. 243-267.

Tom R. [2009], "States of The Union Before and After Bush". Research Editorial: Pew Research Center, pp. 1-5.

American Presidential Election and World Peace

At the moment the American presidential election is the focal point of the whole world's attention [Solomon,2020: 1-4]. This election is important not only for Joe Biden and Donald Trump but also for the world as well. There are many reasons for this but the most crucial is the one that was established by Trump in the past tenure and the way he chartered the future course of action for America [Mihnea, 2019: 1-8].

This is not only a big question mark for the world as a whole but even the American public is also attaching more importance to the Democrat Party instead of the Republican Party.

The graph of Democrat candidate Joe Biden's popularity is still higher than that of Donald Trump. Joe Biden has been taking part in politics for the past 47 years, he has the honor of serving as Vice President under President Obama but it will be premature to say anything at the moment [Katie, 2020: 1-3].

In the previous election, Hillary Clinton seemed to have a definite edge over Trump but with the passage of time, Trump succeeded in convincing the American public [Michael, 2021: 1-3]. The result of the election was quite different from the expectations. According to The Economist, the graph of Joe Biden's success is as clear as that of the win of Obama.

As the time of election is approaching closer, political activities are also gaining momentum. Television debates of the candidates have commenced and public opinion is reaching the whole world via surveys and polls. Since the American presidential election takes place through Electoral College, which will take place in November this year, so electors will choose the President and the Vice President in December, after their selection [Osazee, 2017: 1-22]. That's why the current election is the most significant stage of the American presidential election.

In the Electoral College, every state is given votes proportionate to its population. The number of delegates of the Electoral College is 580. A presidential candidate has to secure 270 votes to win the presidential race [Tim, 2023: 1-4].

According to the BBC Wisconsin, Pennsylvania, and Michigan where Trump won by a margin of only 1% in 2016, now have different circumstances since Joe Biden has emerged more powerfully in these areas. These are entirely industrialized states and they can play a decisive role in the American election [John, 2016: 1-3].

Moreover, there is tough competition in the states such as Ohio and Texas, where Trump had won with a clear majority earlier. Trump's election campaign is facing tough challenges in these states. Some analysts are of the opinion that Trump has made some grave mistakes that can have serious repercussions for his campaign.

Some of them are the burning issues like the reaction of the media and the public to the problem of racism during the Trump era, unreasonable attitude towards media, the biased approach of the police during racial riots, non-serious policies during the pandemic, and like the presentation of the previous election of Trump as representative of the elite; all these things are being severely criticized.

In these circumstances, the people have been forced to think that if the re-election of Trump would damage the interests of American interests. Now Joe Biden has to prove with his strategy that he can put the country on a better path. Although Joe Biden faces problems due to his stutter so at least this much is common between Trump and Biden that they have no control over their tongues.

In this whole scenario, on one hand, Europe, China, Russia, Pakistan, Iran, and Afghanistan are waiting for a government change in America; while on the other Israel and India are awaiting Trump's re-election. The refusal of the Trump government to honor the agreement with Iran and the imposition of severe economic sanctions and pressure on Arab countries to acknowledge Israel can be a warning bell for these countries if Trump comes to power again and this will have far-reaching effects.

Even if Trump wins the election, this won't have any impact on the role of Pakistan in the Afghan peace process because Pakistan's part in this process is very important as leaning of Taliban towards Pakistan and the visit of the former Afghan Prime Minister Gulbadin Hikmatyar to Pakistan has sent a clear signal to America regarding the role of Pakistan in world peace.

The issue of balance of power between China and America is, however, a thought-provoking matter because the bullying attitude of America could push China, Russia, and Iran towards a war which can hinder the process of world peace [Laura, 2019: 1-8]. If Joe Biden wins then this will be a sign of significant change in America. His promise of taking concrete measures against Islamophobia is making him immensely popular among Muslim voters. He has reiterated time and again that after coming to power his first act will be to end immigration restrictions on these seven countries.

REFERENCE

John M. [2016], "Pennsylvania, Wisconsin, and Michigan [Updated]". The Editorial: Washington Examiner, pp. 1-3.

Katie G. [2020], "Joe Biden is Elected The 46th President of The United States". The Editorial: The York News, pp. 1-3.

Laura S. et al [2019], "Views of The Balance of Power beween The U.S. and China". Pew Research Center, pp. 1-8.

Michael L. [2021], "Hillary Clinton Reads Discarded Victory Speech From 2016 Election". The Editorial: The New York Times, pp. 1-3.

Mihnea M. et al [2019], "The Future of Leadership Development". Harvard Business Review, pp. 1-8.

Osazee G. O. [2017], "Elections and Economic Performance in Nigeria". Faculty of Management Sciences, University of Benin, pp. 1-22.

Solomon U. [2020], "Understanding the American Three-stage Presidential Election". The Editorial: The Guardian, pp. 1-4.

Tim L. [2023], "The Electoral College Explained". Brennan Center for Justice, pp. 1-4.

New American Foreign Policy

America has announced a major shift in its foreign policy. It seems to be a positive change but its impact and real features will become clear in the coming days [Richard, 2021: 1-10] . According to a report of the British newspaper, Daily Telegraph, Joe Biden has been highlighting human rights during his election campaign.

Right after assuming power, he issued seventeen executive orders; the most important was to lift travel restrictions for Muslim countries like Iran, Libya, Somalia, Syria, and Yemen [Nile, 2021: 1-2]. A few days ago the American Government while setting direction for its foreign policy, revealed more features that included having zero tolerance for provocative actions of Russia but continuing diplomatic discourse with it. This is completely different from the last government's decision because Trump always talked of moving ahead taking Russia along [Ivo, 2003: 1-8].

The stance of the present government about Russia seems more aggressive. Not only this but America has also invited China to work together but at the same time as per its tradition, termed China's economic development as economic exploitation. This stance is similar to the policies of the Trump era. In this regard, China has already cleared its position that it wants a balance of power in the world [Mu Chunshan, 2021: 1-3].

In fact, this is a reaction to America's defeat in the economic war which compels America to take a harsh position Vis -a-

Vis China. Similarly, refusal to sell modern weapons to Saudi Arabia and Yemen, defense of Saudi Arabia, and proclaiming support for Yemen in the Yemen war are also part of new American foreign policy [Frank, 2019: 1-6]. The issue of the Saudi journalist Jamal Khashoggi is also under discussion.

All this has made Saudi Arabia, and the rest of the Arab countries, realize the importance of Pakistan. It can be rightly said that America's new foreign policy regarding Arabs has burst its bubble.

America has already acknowledged the importance of Pakistan on the Kashmir and Afghanistan issue and wants to work with Pakistan in this regard [Navnita, 2002: 1-9]. Jo Biden has emphasized the need to resolve the Kashmir issue but so far there is no action in this regard.

Pakistan has to take initiative to get this implemented practically. In a complete opposite to Trump's unjust and regrettable policies regarding Iran, the new government recognizing the significance of Iran has emphatically asked Iran to abide by the 2015 agreement promising to lift all sanctions [Carlos, 2020:1-4].

Responding to the American offer the supreme leader of Iran Ayat Ullah Khamenei has categorically stated that Iran won't even think about any agreement until the sanctions are lifted. This is a very realistic approach because the agreements made by President Barak Obama were not honored by the Trump's set up which was a first in American history.

Now Jo Biden wants to restore the agreement also called U 235 agreement, which included limiting Uranium enrichment by Iran. Iran has expressed its misgivings so that American thought and planning could become clearer. The American government has repealed numerous measures of the Trump administration in the wider public interest and has issued new directives.

U.S. Secretary of State has increased the number of immigrants from fifteen thousand to hundred and twenty-five thousand on behalf of Jo Biden, which is a very positive development [Mark, 2021: 1-3].

American foreign policy has always come under criticism because America is notorious for implementing the principle of might is right and is looked down upon in the Muslim world to the extent of hatred. President Jo Biden's humanitarian steps that have come after decades are being acknowledged but the new American foreign policy is being censured in Russia and China.

In this situation, it remains to be seen if Jo Biden will stick to his policies or will he change them with changing times and situations because he is talking about restoring American standing in the world arena and this is a tall task. Only the practical measures in resolving issues of Kashmir, Afghanistan, Palestine, Syria, and Iraq can prove the American claim of humanitarianism. Another way around U.S. government is not taking any step in the current tension between Israel and Gaza as always. The U.S. and the rest of the world must help to find a peaceful solution to this ongoing problem.

As part of the peace process, the U.S. has to forcefully follow the case of giving the power back to the Taliban in Afghanistan and to Brotherhood in Egypt just as emphatically as the way Jo

Biden has stressed upon restoration of democracy in Myanmar. Justice and human rights don't mean that they can be enforced selectively [Wess, 2023: 1-4]. One cannot advocate for them in one place and turn a blind eye towards them in another.

I am very optimistic that things will move towards betterment. China has already jumped in the fray now if America wants to restore its reputation, it will have to change its behavior in the true sense of the word because now people can't be coerced or subjugated.

REFERENCES:

Carlos B.   [2020], "Evaluating the Trump Administration's Iran Policy". Council on Foreign Relations, pp. 1-4.

Ivo H. et al [2003], "The Globalization Politics: American Foreign Policy for a New Era". Foreign Policy: Brookings Education, pp. 1-8.

Frank A. [2019], "The Full Extent of U.S Arms Deals with Saudi Arabia and UAE". Middle East Eye: Opinions, pp. 1-6.

Mark U. et al [2021], "Key Facts About the Changing U.S Unauthorised Immigration Population". Immigration Issues: Pew Resesrch Center, pp. 1-3.

Mu Chunshan [2021], "China- U.S Relations: Views From China". The Debate: The Diplomat, pp. 1-3.

Navnita C. B. [2002], "Kashmir: Redefining The U.S Role". Brookings Resources, No. 110, pp. 1-9.

Nile G. [2021], "Joe Biden Has Been A Monumental Disaster". The Editorial: The Telegraph, pp. 1-2.

Richard W. et al [2021], "America's Image Abroad Rebounds with Transition from Trump to Biden". Pew Research Center, pp. 1-10.

Wess M. [2023], "The Peace Processes: The U.S Peace Processes". United States Institute of Peace, pp. 1-4.

New Regime in Afghanistan

The whole world is stunned, since the Taliban has taken over the reign of Afghanistan within such a short period, after U.S. withdrawal [Scott, 2021: 1-6]. Mike Pence, former vice president of the U.S., strongly criticized the Biden administration for this evacuation, while talking to the Wall Street Journal he declared this act as an embarrassment to foreign policy and framed it in a REFERENCESas with that of Iran hostage crisis [Jill, 2023: 1-4]. Former U.S. president, Donald Trump, also criticized the hasty decision of evacuation by the Biden administration and demanded resignation in return.

Joe Biden has just extended the efforts and executed the already laid road map of evacuation by the Trump administration. Joe Biden declared the U.S. withdrawal from Afghanistan as the finest resolve, blaming Afghan forces for lack of passion to fight despite possessing all resources and trainings [Terri, 2021: 1-5]. With such lousy morale, there remains no doubt whether to keep U.S. troops in Afghanistan or not.

Joe Biden called the withdrawal of U.S. troops from Afghanistan the best decision by the U.S. government, and justified it by blaming the Afghan army, saying that despite all the training and resources, the Afghan army does not have the spirit to fight; thus, U.S. troops cannot be left to die in Afghanistan in this scenario. In other words, the world wants to know what the motive remains and has been gained after 20 years of warfare when the U.S. ultimately had to withdraw with such a mortifying retreat successors, survivors, and families of deceased U.S. and NATO soldiers possess no limits for their agony – in protests.

An outcry of mourning in India, where the media is projecting it as a horrible nightmare, has already propagating sharp criticism over the U.S [Parita, 1999: 25-47]. Moreover, the escape of Ashraf Ghani out of Afghanistan has also drawn much condemnation from various leaders including Abdullah Abdullah.

By defeating two of the world's superpowers in the last forty years, at this moment of time, the Taliban are on their way to design the new history [Neil, 1999: 1-25]. It seems evident too, that the Taliban won't act casual and hurried in their decisions; they seem patient in their approach in the light of two decades worth of lessons and experiences. They have shown flexibility and tolerance by announcing general amnesty, allowing uninterrupted public and private sector businesses to continue as per routine; raising no objections to Afghan TV programs conducted by female anchors; these all are the indications that Taliban are implementing their strategies keeping their past experience of decades in consideration.

Apparently, they are seeking ways to work with new zeal by showing their willingness to revamp political and foreign relations. The most noticeable and important declaration is the assurance that the Afghan land won't be allowed to be a source of threat or offensive to any nation; besides contentment, this declaration has turned up hope to Afghan people, Pakistan, and Muslim nations.

The purpose behind this hope is a concern about the prosperity and development of Afghan people in the fields of education, economy, defense, and foreign policy through every best possible means. Though the Taliban may remain experts of their own bailiwick, Afghanistan, steering the foreign challenges would be the main milestone [Leoni, 2020: 70-86].

Another biggest challenge would be a designation of such a team to control the uncertain situation, both internally and externally; the next couple of days are deemed very important to identify the credibility of the regime.

Since the world, including Afghan people and Pakistan, held higher anticipations, the same way Taliban have set their expectations with the entire world to accept and recognize them, acknowledge their existence with open hearts.

Taliban has reinforced the same during their recent communications about their sovereignty and their resolve to respect the sovereignty of other nations. This could indeed be the ideal beginning for them to form a reliable government, but the only question that arises is whether the Taliban possess such a skill set of officials who may sustain these optimistic expectations.

Pre-requisite before rushing towards the answers to the above-raised questions requires keen examination regarding the organizational structure of Taliban and the skill-set they possess. Out of the anticipated cabinet, some prominent ones are: Hibatullah Akhundzada, current political and religious leader of Taliban, former Chief Justice, having concrete command over religious and military affairs, his excellent war strategy and leadership has led to many achievements for the Taliban.

The second most prominent, Mullah Abdul Hakim, holds a strong command over law and justice; he has also been a top negotiator in Doha, Qatar. Following, Mullah Abdul Ghani Baradar and Siraj Uddin Haqqani are on the list. They are deputy chiefs of the organization having expertise in both political and military affairs.

One of the important members of the council, Mullah Muhammad Yaqoob, son of Mullah Muhammad Omar, has command over education, intelligence, and information matters. In addition to it, there are other experts as Commissioners and members of the Islamic Council from 13 different domains and professions; capable to run the military, educational, religious, political, science and technology, interior, foreign, intelligence, tourism, and cultural affairs.

In spite of all, the role of Pakistan is inevitable in these circumstances; may the Taliban regime overcomes all obstacles, and they look towards Pakistan for diplomacy – being aware of the Afghan situation since inception with such proximity and contiguity – Pakistan might execute their part in getting the regime acknowledged internationally and politically [Nasreen, 2008: 49-73].

Likewise, previously, Pakistan has always assisted Afghanistan in straightening its ties with China and Russia, to maintain the peace and sustainability of the region. Since always and earlier on, Pakistan has always tried Afghanistan to remain abreast with the entire world.

Now it's over to Afghanistan and the Taliban; they should take sane decisions for their nation and people, to retire them out of decades-long war trauma, and induct them to show their skilled potential for prosperous Afghanistan. US and other countries should open the dialogue with Taliban leaders and try to.

REFERENCES:

Jill C. et al [2023], "Former U.S Vice President Mike Pence Opens 2024 Presidential Bid with Denunciation of Trump Over January 6 Insurrection and Abortion". The Editorial: The Globe and Mail, pp. 1-4.

Leoni C. [2020], "U.S Intervention in Afghanistan: Justifying the Unjustifiable?". Sage Journals, Vol. 41, No. 1, pp. 70-86.

Nasreen A. [2008], "Pakistan, Afghanistan and the Taliban". International Journal on World Peace, Vol. 25, No. 4, pp. 49-73. Paragon House.

Neil S. M. [1990], "Superpower Rivalry in the 1990s". Third World Quarterly, vol. 12, No. 1, pp. 1-25. Taylor and Francis Ltd.

Parita M. [1999], "The Civilising Mission: The Regulation and Control of Mourning in Colonial India". Feminist Review, No. 63, pp. 25-47.

Scott N. [2021], "4 Reasons A Taliban Takeover in Afghanistan Matters to The World". Analysis Asia: NPR, pp. 1-6.

Terri M. C. [2021], "Biden Announces Full U.S Troop Withdrawal From Afghanistan By Sept. 11". U.S Department of Defence, No. 2573268, pp. 1-5.

New Regional Play

After the signing of the Basic Exchange and Cooperation Agreement (BECA) between America and India, many changes are expected to take place in the region [Misbah, 2020: 1-4]. Apparently, this agreement is being presented as a bilateral exchange of information but actually, this agreement will facilitate the exchange of sensitive data obtained by satellite imaging. This is the third phase of this process.

Before this, in August 2016, both countries had signed the Logistic Exchange Memorandum of Agreement (LLMOA). As per this agreement, the armed forces of both countries could make use of each other's defense installations for access to airports, seaports, and other services [Ankit, 2016: 1-3]. Similarly, in 2018 Communication and Information Security agreement was signed during the Two Plus Two Dialogue.

After the signing of this agreement, the exchange of information between the Indian and American Commanders regarding safe and secret communication networks has become easier [Theresa et al, 2017: 1-40].

These agreements are being proclaimed as a huge success for India by the media and the defense analysts of India [Yeshi, 2021: 1-12]. The Economic Times has termed these accords as many times deadlier than the Indian missiles. The U.S. shifted its support from Pakistan to India to control China, Russia, Iran, Iraq, Afghanistan, and Pakistan. In terms of taking such decisions will create anarchy in the region. Unfortunately, the U.S. played a very bad game of the era [David, 2013: 1-6].

On the other hand, Pakistan and China are viewing these agreements in a different light since India is completely devoid of goodwill for both China as well as Pakistan. The Modi government especially doesn't let any opportunity slide, which can harm Pakistan and China. India is, however, probably not completely aware of the American strategy or maybe it has gone so far on the path of enmity towards Pakistan that it's not paying any heed to its own future. America is not as simple as India thinks it to be.

In an interview, previous president Trump called India the dirtiest country in the world which should have been a matter of immense embarrassment for India but it's not possible to make the ignorant see the light of reason. India is colossally mistaken if it thinks that it can succeed by becoming an American lapdog [Abhijnan, 2020 :1-4]. In my opinion, India has been completely trapped and it has sold its sovereignty to America. It goes without saying that America knows Pakistan very well. America has seen Pakistan's capabilities in the Afghan war but it has conveniently forgotten Pakistan's assistance on each and every occasion, which has given it a breathing space.

Now, the world is clearly divided into two blocks now. Both Pakistan and China are making preparations to deal with any possible aggression from America and India [Erin, 2022: 1-10]. Pakistan has made a start by experimenting on the anti-ship missile. Pakistan and China have also signed an agreement about intelligence sharing which is a befitting reply to American and Indian moves. In the same perspective, China has gained the capability to monitor America and India's every move by launching Yugan. This can be really helpful for

Pakistan [Jack, 2020: 1-2]. Through these agreements, America wants to pressurize Pakistan and China into rolling back or scrapping CPEC altogether.

The main reason for this is China's economic war with America. Additionally, America wants to limit or end the ever-growing Chinese influence in the region. In this scenario, Pakistan has only two options; it can establish relations with America and move forward by keeping a balance between relations with America and China, following it can try to convince America through diplomatic efforts that it shouldn't share sensitive information with India despite the above-mentioned agreements.

The second option for Pakistan is to consolidate its position in the region by forming an alliance with Russia, Turkey, and Iran alongside China. It can give America the option that any aggression from India can harm the Afghan peace process and Pakistan might even withdraw from the whole process.

America is trying hard to withdraw its forces from Afghanistan because it is financially under severe pressure and the billions of dollars that it is spending in Afghanistan are adding to this pressure.

Pakistan needs to use good judgment in these circumstances. However, it's clear now that U.S. foreign policy is not very impressive for other countries, they are always quite unwelcoming for the U.S.A. Why not superpower should be helpful for others and expel the stress for the other countries.

REFERENCES:

Abhijnan R. [2020], How India Dealt with Donald Trump". The Editorial: The Diplomat, pp. 1-4.

Ankit P. [2016], "India, US SSign Logistics Exchange Agreement: What You Need to Know". The Editorial: The Diplomat, pp. 1-3.

David P. [2013], "The Lessons of the Accord for Modern Times: Think Outside the Box". The Editorial: The Conversation, pp. 1-6.

Erin B. [2022], "Why the Partition of India and Pakistan Still Casts A Shadow Over the Region". The National Geographic, pp. 1-10.

Jack B. [2020], "Pakistan And China Reach New Intelligence Sharing Agreement". The Editorial: The Washington Free Beacon, pp.1-2.

Misbah M. [2020], "India-US Military Agreement: BECA and Its Implications for The Region". India Study Centre [ISC], ISSI.

Theresa H. et al [2017], "International Cybersecurity Information Sharing Agreement". https://www.jstor.org/stable/resrep2046, pp. 1-40.

Yeshi C. [2021], "India's Engagement in Development and Peacebuiding Assistance in The Post-conflict States". Policy and Practice Review: Frontier Political Science, Security, Peace and Democracy, Vol. 3, pp. 1-12.

India Shouldn't Repeat its Failure

During the era of the Soviet and American invasions of Afghanistan, the region witnessed masses of refugees migrating in a state of bafflement and confusion [Leoni, 2021 : 1-17].

According to the statistics given by United Nations High Commission for Refugees (UNHCR), there are approximately 1.4 million registered refugees in Pakistan, resultantly, this study has ranked Pakistan on top of the list of host countries that have been a second home to these temporary displaced Afghan families [Mateen, 2014: 1-4].

Moreover, the same report reflects statistics for other regions that include approximately one million refugees migrating to Iran, although the total number of refugees is estimated to be approximately five million, it is reported that the majority of these refugees have not been registered officially.

On the other hand, India also sanctioned asylum to Afghan refugees but on a limited scale, projecting its image as the white knight of human rights, however, under the garb of this seemingly histrionic human rights activists during the times of Russian invasion, the Indian intelligence compassed the heinous act of spotting persons of influence from these asylum seekers and wheedling the same to become their agents [Qadri et al, 2022: 1-3]. These Afghan-Turned-Indian agents were later infiltrated back into Afghanistan during the American regime after 9/11, and by virtue of the Indian-American nexus, these agents were later honored with key positions in the puppet government of Afghanistan.

This strategy bolstered India to gain strong footings in Afghanistan, thus resulting in the establishment of numerous terror-breeding camps alongside the western border of Pakistan, that were not just functioning as propaganda houses but also as training academies and launching pads of their guerrilla warfare trained terrorists from Afghanistan into the Pakistan territory [Sheikh, 2021: 1-4].

A thread of Indian hostility was witnessed in the recent past, at the Gwadar East Bay Expressway project in Baluchistan, Pakistan, whereby a Chinese worker lost his life in an attack by a suicide bomber.

Such instances of targeting Chinese officials, involved in the construction of Dam, occurred prior to this attack as well; the same has been confessed by an Indian apprehended spy, Kulbhushan Yadav, regarding the existence of these terror breeding networks identified alongside borders.

Addressing a recent press conference in Islamabad following a meeting of the federal cabinet Information Minister Fawad Chaudhry said that the banned Tehreek-i-Taliban Pakistan (TTP) was in a state of "disarray" after Indian funding for the militant outfit had stopped [Bashir, 2022: 1-4].

Nevertheless, 16 December will always be remembered as black day, one of many monstrosities carried out by TTP in Pakistan, Peshawar school massacre, terrorist attack in which seven heavily armed Taliban fighters stormed an army-run primary and secondary school in Peshawar, Pakistan, on

December 16, 2014, killing 150 people, of whom at least 134 were students.

Moreover, Pakistan's Foreign Minister Shah Mehmood Qureshi, accompanied by military spokesman Maj Gen Babar Iftikhar, while sharing salient features of the dossier with the media at a presser at the Foreign Office, emphasized that the world could not afford to ignore India's rogue behavior and stated that Pakistan reserved the right to defend itself in every possible way [Edith, 2021: 1-5].

They further added that there is exclusive evidence that provides concrete proof of Indian financial and material sponsorship of multiple terrorist organizations, including UN-designated terrorist organizations Jamaat-ul-Ahrar, Balochistan Liberation Army, and Tehreek-i-Taliban Pakistan. May India not refrain from propagating its noxious foreign policy, its dissolution is inevitable; since its ties with China, Pakistan, Iran, Russia, Nepal, and Bangladesh are already in shambles – now the U.S. has left them alone in Afghanistan [Naveed, 2020:1-10].

As the Taliban took control of Kabul, the Modi government foreign office representative, Arindam Bagchi, said India will prioritize Sikhs and Hindus of Afghanistan in providing e-visas for their emergency evacuation with all required assistance. Hence, India has again proved by repeating the history of providing shelter to Afghan refugees, specifically of its own interests, to promote their Hindutva doctrine [Ahmad et al, 2021: 1-4]. However, if it would have been on humanitarian grounds, then the assistance of the same scale must have been extended to Muslims of Afghanistan as well; which is not the case here.

The options for India increasingly look limited. It had long pursued a policy of siding with the groups of erstwhile Northern Alliance. India was never able to make any substantial linkages with the Taliban regime and take-over in Kabul by the Taliban has left India out of its diplomatic influence in the region.

According to an ex-Indian Ambassador to Afghanistan Mr. Gautam Makhupadhyay, the old debate in India on whether to talk or not to the Taliban is now academic.

Three questions loom uppermost in the minds of observers in India. First, what accounts for the near-total capitulation of the 300,000-350,000 U.S. and NATO trained and equipped Afghan Army and Police forces, the ANDSF, without much of a fight barring a few honorable exceptions in Lashkargah, Herat, and Taloqan, against lightly armed insurgents estimated to be around 60,000.

Second, what can explain the U.S. decision to pull out its troops unconditionally without waiting for a negotiated political settlement regardless of consequences that were almost entirely predictable other than the speed with which it occurred?

And third, what can explain India's reluctance to engage the Taliban and what can it do? [Gautum, 2021: 1-4]

Indian foreign policy is based on the philosophy of ancient scholar Chanakya Kautilya, according to him your neighbor is your natural enemy and the neighbor's neighbor is your friend. India has issues and conflicts with all neighboring counties including China, Pakistan, Sri Lanka, Bangladesh, and Myanmar [Muhammed et al, 2019: 1-10].

India has a long history of supporting Tamil tigers against Sri Lanka. Also, in 1962, there was a limited war between China and India. With all these differences and hegemonic behavior, Indian foreign policy is considered a threat to the neighboring countries and also for sustainable peace in the region. Furthermore, the U.S. deteriorating relations with Iran are a threat to India's overall stability as well.

As the U.S. withdrawal from Afghanistan nears completion, India needs to prepare for tumultuous times. It was in India's interest to see the U.S. remain longer in the region. Furthermore, the U.S.'s deteriorating relations with Iran are a threat to India's overall stability as well.

Human rights groups and some Indian politicians have criticized the country's asylum policy toward Afghanistan saying that it was in line with BJPs controversial Citizenship and Amendment Bill, championed by Indian Prime Minister Narendra Modi. The bill excludes Muslims, signaling that the Hindu nationalist government harbored a discriminatory sentiment toward the country's Muslim minority [Adnan, 2021: 1-12].

Indian Foreign Minister Dr. Subramanian Jaishankar has also recently reached New York for an emergency meeting of the UN Security Council on the situation in Afghanistan. India - a non-permanent member of the Security Council - holds its Presidency for this month. This was the second time in 10 days that the UN body met to discuss the situation in the war-torn country.

In the thick of the current situation, for India, in Afghanistan under the Taliban regime, the only option left is to work with its neighboring countries to ensure that a political settlement is reached.

India has to open the path for mutual discussion with China and Pakistan, and the need of the time suggests tolerating the views over Kashmir as well. Non-compliance, defiance, and rigidness may cost India terms of losing its identity in the future of global politics.

REFERENCES:

Adnan A. [2021], "India: Government Policies, Actions Target Minorities". The Editorial: Reuters News Agency, pp. 1-12.

Ahmad S. et al [2021], "Taliban Sweep into Afghan Capital After Government Collapses". The Editorial: The Associated Press, pp. 1-4.

Bashir A. A. [2022], "India-Pakistan Dialogue: Past Trends and Future Prospects". South Asia: The Diplomat, pp. 1-4.

Edith M. L. [2021], "The AP Interview: Don't Isolate The Taliban, Pakistan Urges". The Editorial: Associated Press News, pp. 1-5.

Gautam M. [2021], "An Expert Explains: What Kabul Means in Delhi". Indian Strategic Studies, pp. 1-4.

Leoni C. [2021], "US Intervention in Afghanistan: Justifying the Unjustifiable". South Asia Research, Vol. 41, No. 1, pp. 70-86.

Mateen H. [2014], "Pakistan – World's Largest Host of Refugees: UNHCR". The Editorial: The Dawn News, pp. 1-4.

Muhammed R. et al [2019], "Chanakya Kautila's Philosophy and its Influence on Currrent Indian Foreign Policy". Riphah International University, vol. 13, pp. 1-10.

Naveed S. [2020], "Irrefutable Evidence: Dossier on India's Sponsorship of State Terrorism in Pakistan Presented". The Editorial: The Dawn News, pp. 1-10.

Qadri I. et al [2022], "The School in A Basement That is Changing Lives". The Editorial: Foreign Policy News, pp. 1-3.

Sheikh J. H. [2021], "India's Failures". The Editorial: The Nation, pp. 1-4.

Thank You Pakistan

Without any doubt, diplomacy is considered to be the most vital element of politics, as propagation of stances. However, its success is entirely based upon the decisions and timings of its enactment [Dan et al, 2020:1-26].

In the view of the recent decision by the Pakistani government, endorsed by Information Minister Fawad Chaudhary, regarding the presence of U.S. troops in Pakistan; while the numbers remain unsure as the government has claimed the presence of only 42 troops; whereas, BBC reveals that 150 rooms are being reserved in a private hotel of the capital city of Pakistan, Islamabad.

It seems most probable that this could be just a momentary stay for those troops before they depart back for the U.S. and finally, the even last soldier exits from Afghanistan before the deadline. Furthermore, Information Minister also claimed that 10302 people have arrived in Pakistan on transit-visa, out of which, 9032 from NATO have already been left for their respective countries [Katherine, 2022: 4].

He also emphasized that, since Pakistan is committed to the peace and betterment of Afghanistan, these evacuation assistances will be continued through borders and air routes – by whatever means possible.

However, the social media of Pakistan is agonizing over this situation and posing challenging questions. There's not even a bit of room in doubting that the decision of facilitating U.S.

troops on the land of Pakistan, despite evacuation, is a staggering move by the government [Niha et al,2020:1-5]. Commenting on this stance would be premature as of yet, as the repercussions of this act would emerge to be perceptible after a while. The concerns are being raised against the sanity of such a decision, as what strategy the government worked upon by resorting this retreat of the U.S., who has unscrupulously and tyrannically slew millions of Afghans, Iraqis, and Pakistanis during its stay. But, as per my opinion Pakistan did well to provide safe exit to NATO and American forces. Joe Biden vision is truly appreciable here.

Pakistani social media is raising questions like, what good strategy could be behind to escort them with such honor and protection? Despite experiencing their exposed agendas in the face of Blackwater and Raymond Davis, which led to cause severe law and order disturbances, the government chose to facilitate them.

It too remains obscure, whether the Cabinet was informed of this decision, or if this is a democratic decision approved by the parliament?

Social media further reporting that, if this decision has opted on the humanitarian grounds, the killing of millions of civilians in Vietnam, Iraq, Afghanistan, and Pakistan (specifically Waziristan), stimulates deep thinking on American human rights ideology- Anyhow, it remains incomprehensible why instead of going to Qatar, Pakistan is chosen for the transit stay; moreover, despite having 83 billion dollars' worth military equipment left behind – sufficient to escort their exit to Qatar [Paul et al, 2019: 1-9].

Is it because the U.S. planes and flying machinery are so rusted and corroded that they couldn't even make their flights directly to their Headquarters in Qatar? Thus, the decision of escorting their retreat with an escorted transit stay raises concerns over the government's claim of silencing "do more" voices, and refusal to grant Pakistani land for any escalation in Afghanistan. This seems suspicious!

This strategy of dubiety is leading towards harsh criticism by the opposition party in Pakistan; the U.S. must have routed its troops towards their strategic partner, India, instead of Pakistan [Ram et al, 1973:1-6]. If India is profoundly sincere with the U.S., they must have allowed their own land for the troops strategically, U.S. Even assuming this with the anticipation of getting rewarded by the U.S. against these efforts, might eventually appear to be in vain. Certainly, what the U.S. might have observed, and realized, is the importance of Pakistan, and the reality of India in this scenario.

Despite knowing the fact that Pakistan has faced the loss of almost seventy thousand lives in the U.S.-led war, what appeared to be more regretful is the ever-ignorant behavior of the U.S. against Pakistan, and remain submissive towards India [Rabia, 2021: 1-3]. It had never recognized even a flake of our nation's sacrifices, the martyrdom of our soldiers, our dedication, and honesty towards the fulfillment of their own agenda. The U.S. still considers Pakistan responsible, censuring, for their humiliating retreat and defeat in Afghanistan.

When the U.S. never wastes a single chance in holding Pakistan accountable for their own mess every time, then why should we have to pacify and console them up with continuous assistance. May the government had reserved any covert or sensitive strategy behind this decision, the people and opposition must have been taken into confidence prior to its implementation.

On the other hand, with the dire situation of COVID-19 prevailing all over the country, the vaccine certificates of every individual landing on the soil of Pakistan must be verified religiously; so that these returnees might not end up bringing any new variant of the virus to our society, and become a source of its spread [Nistha et al, 2020: 1-9].

This inspection is required in the wake of Pakistan's incumbent position in the red-list; whereas, despite being the originator of new variant and perpetrator of the loopholes, our neighbor has been removed from the red-list. Merely this is nothing, but a sheer depiction of injustice and biases [Madiha, 2019:1-13].

Hence, the situation now is entailing to some inevitable and stern measures, that the Pakistan government has to lay hold of, by taking people of the nation, along with the opposition, in confidence. Moreover, on parallel, the government must dispatch these troops back to their homes to avoid any anarchy, to stay safe-and-shielded by any unforeseen deplorable incidence/s in the future.

As it is rightly said: "All Good is forgotten, when Evil return."

REFERENCES:

Dan H. et al [2020], "The Meaning of Diplomacy". Journal of International Negotiation, Vol. 26, No. 2, pp. 1-26.

Katherine S. [2022], "A Year Later, A Look at Public Opinion About the US Military Exit from Afghanistan". Politics and Policy: Pew Research Center, pp. 1-4.

Madiha A. [2019], "An Inflection Point for Pakistan's Democracy". The Brookings Centre: Foreign Policy Analysis, pp.1-13.

Niha D. et al [2020], "Toothless and Terrified: The State of Pakistan's Media". The Editorial: The Diplomat, pp. 1-5.

Nistha S. et al [2020], "The Impact of Covid-19 on Globalisation". National Library of Science: National Centre for Biotechnology Information, Vol. 11, No. 10, pp. 1-9.

Paul S. et al [2019], "The Qatar's Foreign Policy: Relevance and Shortcomings". Covenant University, Ota, Ogun, State, Nigeria, Vol. 10, No. 2, pp. 1-9.

Rabia A. [2021], "Pakistan and The Taliban 2.0: The Good, The Bad and The Ugly". The Atlantic Council, South Asian Center, pp.1-3.

Ram J. et al [1973], "The Opposition: Problems and Prospects". Economic and Political Weekly, Vol. 8, No. 42, pp. 1-6.

If American can't see inside

If we take a closer look at the racial riots in America, history teaches us that racial riots aren't a new problem for the U.S [Zara, 2021: 1-48]. The American government, American police, and African Americans have faced this situation several times in the past as well. In fact, this is a basic social principle that if viciousness isn't stopped the first time around then after one or two incidents this brutality becomes a tradition in the society which encourages the oppressor and makes it a matter of routine for the oppressed.

A few days back I went through a book by Philip Kotler in which he said that humans have a very weak memory, maybe this is the reason that African Americans put up with this injustice time and again and then repeatedly forget about it. If this viciousness was countered with full might the first time around then maybe the African Americans didn't have to live this day again and they wouldn't have been brutalized in this way, now it may take many more centuries to uproot this brutal system.

Anyway, I don't see an immediate end to this in American society. Rather I feel that this may never end and there are many reasons for it but the major reason is the inherent racism in human nature since if it is in his power every person wants to prioritize his own race and nation in every matter.

There is only one way out of this predicament that Islam has taught the world i.e. no black has any superiority over white and no white has any superiority over any black except by piety and fear of God. The Holy Prophet Muhammad (Peace Be Upon Him) gave the world a practical illustration of these teachings by being affectionate towards Hazrat Bilal (Black background friend and companion), May God be pleased with him) and by treating him exceptionally well.

In any case, racism started centuries ago in America when we see the struggle of African leader Kunta Kinte against racism and the practical form of his sacrifices but its second stage started a little bit earlier than the modern era in 1824 and later in 1831 when the homes of the blacks were brutally razed in the areas of Hardscrabble and snow town, the ensuing movement resulted in the destruction of many buildings and countless people were injured and incarcerated [William, 2021: 1-10]. Following that, these incidents kept happening regularly after every year or two and this is still going on. Until now almost 159 black movements against racism have been documented on the national level.

During these protests, thousands were jailed and thousands of others died. In these 159 black movements, many leaders raised the issues of human rights and the end of racism but some black leaders deserve to be named and we will talk about them later on, lamentably these leaders were either murdered or made to commit suicide over the past century, which has kept the black community deprived of real leadership.

Whenever the blacks raised the voice for equal rights it took the form of a mob or riots because there is no comprehensive purpose to guide them and no proper course is determined, there is just anger and grief that results in making looting, arson, and plunder, the destiny of America.

Another episode in this connection was witnessed a few days back in Minneapolis when racial riots broke out across America following the murder of George Floyd by the police after brutal torture. As a result, things haven't come back to normal as of yet. Special Forces have been called up to assist the police in 24 states. Arson and violence are going on everywhere, more than 200 buildings have been set on fire, more than 300 police vehicles have been torched and this is still going on. To top it all President Trump is adding fuel to the fire [Erik, 2020: 1-4].

It would have been better had he handled things sensibly but he recently gave another proof of his irresponsible behavior by saying that where there are riots there will be bullets by the government.

After this, the American government, which claims the Americans to be a civilized nation, stands fully exposed. After this pat on the back by the government, the American police started treating its own people like the enemy. The sky even witnessed such scenes where the policemen were dragging the African American women on the roads. This was the frightful face of the American police.

Anyways, a discussion was about the prominent personalities who raised their voices against racism, one of these was Malcolm X who later on embraced Islam [Allison, 2007: 261-272]. He said that Islam was the only religion of the world that teaches equality among humans. He even said that only Islam gives the solution to racism and racial riots. He further wrote that he has never seen love, brotherhood, and equal human rights anywhere but among Muslims.

Another outstanding figure was that of Martin Luther King who raised his voice against American prejudice and talked about equal rights, converting black African Americans from a race into a nation [Clayborne, 1987: 448-454]. Despite being black, he won the love and admiration of the American public more than anyone else and even reached the American National Assembly. In 1955 with Montgomery Bus Boycott, he started the civil rights movement and in 1962 this morphed into a movement to end racism. In a few years, Martin Luther King made this into a national movement so much so that he started working on naming the national department of Washington DC after the movement of the poor people.

In 1964, he won the Nobel Peace Prize, he was also given the Presidential Award but a conspiracy led to his death in 1964. He didn't even live to see his 40th birthday but he contributed so much towards ending racial prejudice from the world that he will always be remembered in American history.

The need of the hour is that all the communities in America should work together and take practical steps for ending this racial prejudice. In this regard, the most appreciable efforts were made by the Pakistani Muslims in America. Sajid Tarrar the advisor to the American President has not only taken particle steps but has also given superb suggestions for solving the issues between the police and the black community [David, 2006: 1-3]. They have stressed upon giving all Americans equal rights free of racial discrimination, perhaps the American President will understand their stance.

DFW has started its work from a few cities and has shown positive results by increasing police-public interaction on a public level. At the moment, American city ALVES is among one of those cities where not even a single incident of confrontation between the police and the public has been reported yet, not even stone-throwing or arson, or any other kind of racial unrest has surfaced which is due to the efforts of the Pakistani community which is really admirable [Mario, 1998: 128-144].

Now it's time for America to correct its course which is desperately needed so that the American economy doesn't get devoured by the Corona as well as the racial riots. The words of Hazrat Ali (AS) keep reverberating in the mind that enunciate that a system based on refuting the presence of Allah can survive but a system based on oppression cannot.

If America can't see the writing on the wall even after the defeat in Afghanistan, the crisis of Corona, and now these racial riots then I think that this system of oppression is not going to last long as well. I think Joe Biden should work hard to tackle the internal problems of the U.S. instead of inferring in other countries matters. It will help the U.S. to build a better society and prospers America, which could set a precedent for new superpowers in the future.

REFERENCES:

Allison J. [2007], "Giving Voice to Children's Voices: Practices and Problems, Pitfalls and Potentials". American Anthropologists New Series, vol. 109, No. 2, pp. 261-272.

Clayborne C. [1987], "Martin Luther King Jr: Charismatic Leadership in a Mass Struggle". The Journal of American History, vol. 74, No. 2, pp. 448-454. Oxford University Press.

David R.S [2006], "Religious Contributions to Peacemaking: When Religion Brings Peace Not War". Peace, Religion and Peacemaking Initiative, vol. 1, pp. 1-3.

Erik O. [2020], "Racial Violence and a Pandemic: How the Red Summer of 1919 Relates to 2020". The Editorial: NBC News Digital, pp. 1-4.

Mario G. [1998], "The City as the Object of Architecture". Assemblage, No. 37, pp. 128-144. The MIT Press.

William S. [2021], "The Game is Changing for Historians of Black America". The Inheritance Project: The Atlantic Project About American History and Black Life, vol. 618747, pp. 1-10.

Zara A. [2021], "The Fight against Racism Must Continue". American Psychological Association, vol. 52, No. 1, pp. 1-48.

The Next Mistake of American

At present when the whole world is in the clutches of COVID 19 and is prepared to work hand in hand to fight this menace, every day spurs the world on to learn something both individually and collectively from each other's experience to serve humanity. There is only one topic under discussion for the whole world and that is to make every possible effort for keeping humans and humanity safe from this pandemic.

On the one hand, the developed countries are working round the clock to produce a better vaccine or medication against the new variants of COVID-19, but, even in these highly troubling times, history is still waiting to witness the expression of solidarity, brotherhood, and humanity from the powerful countries towards rest of the countries of the world.

Now the things have reached a point where many countries, nations, and their citizens, as well as neighbors, friends, and family members, have opted to stay away from seeing each other and socializing for the greater common good to defeat this noxious infection. The aim is to stop the spread of the virus at the moment. Unfortunately, new mutations of COVID-19 are still creating dangerous situations for the world [Angela et al, 2021: 1-90].

In Britain and America, whole towns and cities appear deserted and desolate from time to time according to the circumstances. Europe is in the firm grip of the clutches of this pandemic. Undoubtedly the situation is very complex, dangerous, and distressing so far. The vaccination certificate is a new travel document now [John et al, 2022: 169-190].

Despite these hard days, there is hope that God will show a path and with the blessings of the Creator of the world will overcome this deadly sickness. It is our firm belief that none can give life or death except God. His help and support are the only means of getting out of this predicament and we have no other escape. God is enough for us, and despondency is akin to denying the existence of God.

Now the baffling thing is that during these chaotic times some countries are pursuing self-interest but on the other hand many countries are cooperating with each other. Even in a materialistic society like Europe, generally, the neighbors, friends, and family are helping each other, history bears testimony to the fact that one nation is still fighting for survival single-handedly.

This nation is facing these trying times with courage and steadfast belief in God and waiting for Divine relief and assistance. The current situation is that, in Iran, the death rate is quite high due to the new wave of COVID 19 and the nation is picking up a dead body every ten minutes but still, they haven't asked for anyone's assistance except for God. These noble and dignified people are laudable for their fortitude as they look towards the heavens for help and mercy with teary eyes but there is no complaint on their lips. Being grateful under every adversity and burying their loved ones with courage. The graveyards are getting full of graves but the storm of CORONA is showing no signs of letting up.

At this moment Iran is the most affected country from COVID after America, France, Spain, and Italy [Amin, 2020: 1-3]. The vaccinations are playing a vital role to bring life back slowly and gradually.

In these harsh times, the silence of the world in general and that of the U.S., in particular, is playing a very condemnable role as a whole. Regrettably, the economic sanctions that were imposed by America in the regime of Trump were getting stricter by the day and there are no signs of any imminent relaxation in these sanctions [Jennifer et al, 2015: 1-7]. But, Joe Biden is a man of principles, he showed his wisdom after taking over the American presidency.

Iran is the second-highest oil-producing country of the region preceded by Saudi Arabia and due to these sanctions, it can't sell its oil in the open market [Sukru, 2019: 1-5]. The rest of the world is also paying the price of these sanctions as it has to pay exorbitant prices for oil imports.

If Iran gets to sell its oil in the open market, it will not only be beneficial for Iran but will also benefit the underdeveloped and poor countries in the current financial crisis.

Since their industrial production will increase and their overall living standards will get better. But what can one say even in these critical days there are a few countries that have no regard for moral values and are so drunk on power that they can't see anything except their own interests. The life or death of others is not their concern.

I am surprised at their insensitivity can't they see the dying multitudes in Iran? Can't they feel their suffering and misery? Can't they perceive the hardships and agony that Iran is going through because it can't even import medicines and medical equipment due to economic sanctions in a pandemic?

The United Nations should take strict notice of this callousness and America should reconsider its sanctions. Even if America doesn't lift the sanctions, it should at least allow Iran to import medicines, medical equipment, and life-saving drugs that have been given on humanitarian grounds [Denis, 2002: 346-354]. The fact of the matter is that the biggest concern at present is saving human lives.

America and the rest of the world have to forgo the conventional obduracy and set new examples of humanitarianism and philanthropy. The international law for war also says that even during combat situations provision of medical facilities can't be restricted or prohibited for the opposing country but as Aristotle had opined.

'written laws are like spiders' webs, and will like them, only entangle and hold the poor and weak, while the rich and powerful will easily break through them in these circumstances, the new president of Iran has recently written to prime minister Imran Khan asking him to play a role in waking up the world's consciousness and helping in the lifting of sanctions at least till the end of Covid 19. It is time for the world to choose between obstinacy and humanity.

Justice and injustice can't go hand in hand, only impudicity and lack of conscience can. Prime Minister of Pakistan Imran Khan has raised this matter but not forcefully enough. As I have mentioned earlier the issue is not that of Iran but humanity, humanitarianism, and justice.

The guiding principle for humankind is humanity and in the present scenario, we can save the world only by acting in the light of this principle. I salute the Edhi Foundation that has recently given the Iranian Government a hefty amount for dealing with the effects of Corona Virus [Sami, 2019: 1-3]. Take a moment and consider the point that if a small philanthropist organization can think about the people forsaken by the world then why can't world powers like the U.S. see the wretchedness of these destitute people? The need of the hour is that all countries of the world should join hands regardless of any distinctions or prejudices and help each other.

No one can deny the fact that these difficult days will pass but if the people of Iran aren't treated at par with the rest of the world then indisputably the history will consider this conduct of the world as brutal and criminally negligent.

There is still time and the world should play its role effectively for saving these eighty-two million people and changing history. Britain, China, and Russia should play their role for humanity. And, the U.S needs to justify its role here and work to develop harmony and cooperation between nations for peace.

It's creating more tension in the region instead of resolving issues. Pakistan should also give a loud and clear message by coming forward and playing its due role in saving the world equally.

May God help us all and be the Benefactor of all the helpless and persecuted people of the world.

REFERENCE

Amin M. C [2020], "Iran and The Economic Fallout of Covid-19". The Middle-East Institute, pp. 1-3.

Angela M. et al [2021]," How Covid-19 is Changing The World: A Statistical Perspective". UNCTAD: CCSA, pp. 1-90.

Denis J. H. [2002], "The United Nations: The Embarrassment of International Law". Medicine, Conflict and Survival, pp.346-354. Taylor and Francis Ltd.

Jennifer D. et al [2015], "Harsh Laws and Violence Drive Global Decline". The Editorial: Freedom House Press, pp. 1-7.

John B. et al [2022], "Placed-based Politics and Nested Deprivation in The UK; Beyond Cities, Towns," "Two Englands" and "The Left Behind". Routhledge: Francis and Taylor Group, Vol. 58, No. 2, pp. 169-190.

Sami S. [2019]," Remembering Edhi: The Exception to Pakistan's Faults". The Editorial: The Dawn Press, pp. 1-3.

Sukru C. [2019], "How Saudi-Iranian Oil Rivalry Has Been Shaped by American Power". The Editorial: The Conversation Press, pp. 1-5.

Economic Sanctions Against Iran Need to End

At present when the whole world is in the clutches of COVID 19 and is prepared to work hand in hand to fight this menace, every day spurs the world on to learn something both individually and collectively from each other's experience serve humanity [Ben R. et al,2020:1-10].

There is only one topic under discussion for the whole world and that is to make every possible effort for keeping humans and humanity safe from this pandemic [Borge ,2020:1-6]. On the one hand, the developed countries are working round the clock to produce a vaccine and on the other hand, even in these highly troubling times, history is still waiting to witness the expression of solidarity, brotherhood, and humanity from the powerful countries towards rest of the countries of the world.

Now the things have reached a point where many countries, nations, and their citizens, as well as neighbors, friends, and family members, have opted to stay away from seeing each other and socializing for the greater common good to defeat this noxious infection. The aim is to stop the spread of the virus.

In Britain and America, whole towns and cities appear deserted and desolate. Europe is in the firm grip of the clutches of this pandemic. Undoubtedly the situation is very complex, dangerous, and distressing.

Despite these hard days, there is hope that Allah will show a path and with the blessings of the Creator, the world will overcome this deadly sickness.

It is our firm belief that none can give life or death except Allah. His help and support are the only means of getting out of this predicament and we have no other escape. Allah is enough for us, and despondency is akin to denying the existence of Allah.

Now the baffling thing is that during these chaotic times while some countries are pursuing self-interest but on the other hand many countries are cooperating with each other. Even in a materialistic society like Europe, generally, the neighbors, friends, and family are helping each other, history bears testimony to the fact that one nation is still fighting for survival single-handedly.

This nation is facing these trying times with courage and steadfast belief in Allah and waiting for Divine relief and assistance. The current situation is that, in Iran, the death rate is very high due to COVID 19 and the nation is picking up a dead body every ten minutes but still, they haven't asked for anyone's assistance except for Allah.

These noble and dignified people are laudable for their fortitude as they look towards the heavens for help and mercy with teary eyes but there is no complaint on their lips. Being grateful under every adversity and burying their loved ones with courage. The graveyards are getting full of graves but the storm of CORONA is showing no signs of letting up. At this moment Iran is the most affected country from COVID after America, China, and Italy [Edouard et al, 2021:1-20].

In these harsh times, the silence of the world in general and that of America, in particular, is criminal. Regrettably, the economic sanctions that were imposed by America after Trump is getting stricter by the day and there are no signs of any imminent relaxation in these sanctions [Nicholas, 2022:1-10].

Iran is the second-highest oil-producing country in the region preceded by Saudi Arabia and due to these sanctions, it can't sell its oil in the open market [Sukru, 2019:1-5]. The rest of the world is also paying the price of these sanctions as it has to pay exorbitant prices for oil imports. If Iran gets to sell its oil in the open market, it will not only be beneficial for Iran but will also benefit the underdeveloped and poor countries since their industrial production will increase and their overall living standards will get better [Eric, 2020:1-4].

But what can one say even in these critical days there are a few countries that have no regard for moral values and are so drunk on power that they can't see anything except their own interests. The life or death of others is not their concern.

I am surprised at their insensitivity can't they see the dying multitudes in Iran? Can't they feel their suffering and misery? Can't they perceive the hardships and agony that Iran is going through because it can't even import medicines and medical equipment due to economic sanctions?

The United Nations should take strict notice of this callousness and America should reconsider its sanctions. Even if America doesn't lift the sanctions, it should at least allow Iran to import medicines, medical equipment, and life-saving drugs in view of the raging Covid 19[Denis, 2002: 346-354]. The fact of the matter is that the biggest concern at present is saving human lives.

America and the rest of the world have to forgo conventional obduracy and set new examples of humanitarianism and philanthropy. The international law for war also says that even during combat situation provision of medical facilities can't be restricted or prohibited for the opposing country [Larry, 2020:1-15] but as Aristotle had opined,

'Written laws are like spiders' webs, and will like them, only entangle and hold the poor and weak, while the rich and powerful will easily break through them'

In these circumstances, Hassan Rouhani the president of Iran has recently written to prime minister Imran Khan asking him to play a role in waking up the world's consciousness and helping in the lifting of sanctions at least till the end of Covid 19 [Ali, 2021: 1-8]. It is time for the world to choose between obstinacy and humanity.

Justice and injustice can't go hand in hand, only impudicity and lack of conscience can. Prime Minister Imran Khan has raised this matter but not forcefully enough. As I have mentioned earlier the issue is not that of Iran but of humanity, humanitarianism, and justice. The guiding principle for humankind is humanity and in the present scenario, we can save the world only by acting in the light of this principle.

I salute the Eidhi Foundation that has recently given the Iranian Government a hefty amount for dealing with the effects of the Corona Virus [Mohammed, 2018:1-4]. Take a moment and consider the point that if a small philanthropist organization can think about the people forsaken by the world then why can't the world powers see the wretchedness of these destitute people? The need of the hour is that all countries of the world should join hands regardless of any distinctions or prejudices and help each other.

No one can deny the fact that these difficult days will pass but if the people of Iran aren't treated at par with the rest of the world then indisputably the history will consider this conduct of the world as brutal and criminally negligent [Ebad,2022:1-7]. There is still time and the world should play its role effectively in saving these eighty-two million people and change history. Pakistan should also give a loud and clear message by coming forward and playing its due role in saving the Iranian people. May Allah help us all and be the Benefactor of all the helpless and persecuted people of the world.

REFERENCES:

Ali A.D [2021], "Iran's Foreign Policy Under Raisi". Centre For Strategic Studies, Tehran, Vol. 7, pp.1-8.

Ben R.M et al, [2020], "Innovation, Development and Covid-19: Challenges, Opportunities and Ways Forward". OECD Policy Responses, United Kingdom, pp. 1-10.

Borge B. [2020], "Global Cooperation Is More Vital Than Ever: This is Why". World Economic Forum, The Japan Times, pp.1-6.

Denis J.H [2002],"The United Nations : The Embarrassment of International Law". Medicine, Conflict and Survival, vol. 8, No. 4, pp.346-354.

Ebad E. [2022], "The Iranian Economy's Challenges amid the Pandemic and Sanctions". Ebadi Institute of Policy-making, Tehran, Iran, pp. 1-7.

Eduoard et al. [2021], "Iran: Coronavirus Pandemic Country. Profile". Our World in Data.

Eric R. [2020], "How Iran Impacts the Price and Supply of Oil". The Editorial, Investopedia, pp. 1-4.

Larry L. [2020], "Protecting Medical Care in Conflict: A Solvable Problem". Office of The Directorate, Action on Armed Violence, pp. 1-15.

Mohammed A. [2018], "Edhi Foundation: Serving Humanity". Edhi Foundation for Humanitarian Services, Pakistan, pp. 1-4.

Nicholas M. [2022], "The History of Economic Sanctions as a Tool of War". Department of Modern European History,

Cornell University: "The Economic Weapon: The Rise of Sanctions as a Tool of Modern War". Yale University Press, pp.1-10.

Sukru C. [2019], "How Saudi-Iranian Oil Rivalry Has Been Shaped by American Power". Lancaster University: National Research Foundation, pp. 1-5.

Europe: The Destruction Wrought By Corona and Its Reasons

The coronavirus has firmly gripped more than 2 million people worldwide nearly and 300,000 have perished [Amelia et al., 2020: 1-25]. Uncertainty reigns supreme all over, God knows what devastations will the future unfold. There is a pervading sense of anxiety in the whole world, every new day is bringing new problems and hardships but there is still hope the Allah Almighty will deliver us from these troubling times. The biggest challenge facing the world right now is economic degradation.

All over the world small businesses and companies are going bankrupt. Recently a famous airline 'Virgin Atlantic' also gave up in Australia which may end up in unemployment of millions. In England, 'Primark' and 'British Airways' are accumulating heavy losses. In Europe, the number of unemployed has reached 1 million, in spite of the fact that Europe has set aside a budget of 100 billion Euros to counter this exact situation. In England, 2 million people have lost their jobs.

There could be two main reasons for this, firstly the exit of England from the European Union and secondly the situation created as a result of Corona [Harold et al., 2016:1-4]. Britain had announced a budget of 32 billion Pounds to respond to this situation. On the other hand, if we look at America, we see that more than 5 million people lost their jobs due to the economic fallout of Corona and more than 74000 people have lost their lives, which is the highest number of deaths in the world.

In this backdrop, if we look at Italy, we see those 30,000 deaths until a few days back. France and Spain have lost around 27000 lives each. In Belgium and Germany 9000 while in Britain more than 33000 perished. In the light of these devastations, different expert opinions and analysis are surfacing [Chirag et al., 2021:1-9]. Recently a Cambridge University professor Sir David Speckle Halter has said that the reported figures of deaths resulting from Corona Virus are far less than the actual number [Pippa, 2022: 1-2].

Evan Doil, the medical director of British Public Healthcare says that different countries estimate the deaths from virus differently and that is why it is difficult to estimate these numbers globally, surprisingly this was also affirmed by the British Health Chief Adviser Chris Wity and this is raising many questions [Dan, 2021: 1-7].

If we closely look at the high magnitude of the spread of the virus in Britain then according to an analysis the main cause of this wide and rapid spread of the virus in Britain is that the British Government took too long to respond and to control the virus [Ayo et al., 2021: 1-10]. For example, the decision to lockdown came quite late. The reason for the delay was the thought of herd immunity i.e. the people should be allowed to mingle, their bodies will gradually develop immunity against the virus, and the government won't have to take any measures in this regard this could have been a huge risk. Another thing worth mentioning here is that Sweden is still following the principle of herd immunity, they also have around 30000

Corona patients but astonishingly the rate of death is very low [Sigurd, 2020:1-7].

Anyways if we consider the second big decision of the British government which is also thought to be a prime reason for the spread of the Coronavirus that is the decision to keep the flight operation open for an extended period of time. Due to this decision, more than 500 people traveled to the UK from China only and the first Chinese Corona patient surfaced in 'Brighton', and then within no time it spread all over the country. According to another research, those countries that adopted extensive testing right from the start have been able to check the spread of Corona but England was in two minds about adopting this formula as well, as compared to Italy the number of patients, as well as deaths, increased tenfold.

In spite of having the ability to carry out 100000 tests per day, even now the number of people tested per day is very low than its capability. The government was severely criticized by the member of the opposition, Roseanna Elian, for all these laxities. Apart from that the government also failed to provide protective kits to the health workers. In contrast, those countries that took timely decisions including Germany and Korea largely adopted all these preventive measures and as a result, their death rate has remained relatively low [Ryanti et al, 2020: 1-15].

Italy also opted for lockdown a little later but they carried out test drives for testing more and more people but they made the same mistake as the british government and increased testing only when the pandemic had spread up to a dangerous level [Martin, 2021: 149-165]. In the present scenario, the big powers seem apprehensive about the future and they have no idea which way the chips will fall.

After taking into account, the expert opinion, the question now arises, whether the coronavirus cases are being accurately recorded in Europe and other countries or not? Are testing kits giving results? It can't be denied that the deaths are registered properly in the hospitals but in contrast, the deaths occurring in care homes can't be accurately assessed that whether they are a result of coronavirus or not. Let's consider the opinions of some other experts as well.

A few days ago, according to Belgium's virologist and government's spokesman Prof. Steven Van Coach, the people are making flawed comparisons about the coronavirus, which is distorting the facts [Jean, 2021:1-4]. Similarly, according to BBC, Oxford University's Prof. Jason Oak has also stressed upon the importance of the fact that all countries should present accurate facts in front of the world in order to assess the situation correctly and to make correct decisions.

This thought raises another question when the World Health Organization has published all the exact procedures then which countries aren't following these instructions properly? It is imperative to make the names of these countries public and I ask why these countries aren't being guided to collect the statistics by the book? In any case, it is now undisputed that we need to learn from the mistakes of these countries. We should comprehend the opinion of Prof. Jason Oak, the analysis will have to be tested on the touchstone of experiments so that the situation is accurately judged and the right decisions are taken for the future.

The counties where lockdown has ended or has been relaxed, need to be extra careful because the scientists are in agreement that if there is a second wave of coronavirus it is going to be deadlier than the first wave and as a result, the deaths could exceed millions in every country. In Pakistan especially, the public should be made aware of the impact of abusing smart lockdown and its possible effects so that they don't make any mistakes and Pakistan can emerge as a safe country.

REFERENCES:

Amelia C.et al., [2020], "Rising Hunger: Facing a Food-Insecure World". Council of Foreign Relations: Foreign Affairs, CFR Education, pp.1-25.

Ayo S.et al., [2021], "The Spread of Covid-19 Outbreak in the First 120 Days: A Comparison Between Nigeria and Seven Other Countries". National Library of Science: National Centre for Biotechnology Information, PMC7802991, pp.1-10.

Chirag M. et al., [2021], "Estimating Covid-19 Mortality in Italy Early in the Covid-19 Pandemics". Nature Communications, Vol. 12, No.2729, pp.1-9.

Dan T. et al., [2021], "Coronavirus and the Social Impacts on Great Britain: 24 September 2021". Office For National Statistics, Policy Evidence Analysis: Team UK, pp.1-7.

Harold D. et al [2016], "Why Britain Really Voted to Leave the EU". University of Essex Research Team, U.K, pp.1-4.

Jean M. [2021], "Belgium's Van Ranst: Covid Scientist Targeted by a Far-right Sniper". BBC Editorials, Vol.5, pp.1-4.

Martin B. [2021], "The Italian Government Response to Covid-19 and the Making of a Prime Minister". Contemporary Italian Politics, Vol. 13, No.2, pp.149-165.

Pippa C. [2020], "Coronavirus: Top Scientist Accuses Government of Number Theatre". Daily Mirror: Political Editorials, U.K, Vol.2.

Riyanti D. et al., [2020], "Covid-19 and ASEAN Responses: Comparative Policy Analysis". National Library of Medicine: National Centre for Biotechnology Information, PMCID: PMC 7577870, pp.1-15.

Sigurd B. [2020], "Sweden's Experiment with Herd Immunity is Unethical and Undemocratic". Swedish Science Forum for Covid-19, pp. 1-7.

Your Sacrifices Will Bear Fruit

Many months have passed but neither India has lifted the curfew in Kashmir nor had it to face any condemnation on the international level. The role of Pakistan also didn't exceed from passing resolutions and holding protests throughout the country on the 5th of February. The government of Pakistan didn't take any practical steps. The moot point here is why aren't these resolutions and protests producing desired results? [Saadat, 2021]

The international community has shown supreme indifference to the plight of the Kashmiris [Arsene, 2011:1-12]. Talking about my feelings, whenever I think of this I spend a tough sleepless night. I try to relax and divert my attention through a million means but sleep stays far away from me. The whole night is spent in anguish thinking that if I could have bought freedom and peace for the Kashmiris and even any oppressed nation. I would have, no matter what the price but regrettably that's not possible.

Freedom can neither be bought nor can it be gained without paying the homage of blood and sacrificing lives. The sacred blood that is being given by the Kashmiris will one day bear fruit [William,1973:421-438]. How can I silence my restless and anguished heart that is beating still, this body still has breath left, the pulse is beating still, but the eyes have turned to stone. The wait is endless. Cries and painful groans follow me the entire night.

The screams of mothers lamenting their sons who only wished for freedom keep ringing in my ears, those who lost their husbands who have no ray of hope left in their lives, whose young sons sacrificed their lives for truth like Hazrat Ali Akbar (AS), who have taken vows from their sons that they will emulate the way of Imam Hussain (AS), the torn headscarves of the sisters who have sacrificed their honor and dignity for upholding the faith don't let me sleep, the cries of small children who are weeping for a drop of milk and dying of thirst and hunger, who are awaiting the arrival of a Mohammad Bin Qasim or a Salah ud Din Ayubi who could rid them of this oppression of barbaric Indian forces, the tears of that old father keep me awake who has buried his grown son, whose eyes have grown weary of waiting for the golden dawn of freedom, the wailing of the daughters who are awaiting the return of their fathers don't let me sleep.

When will the oppressed Kashmiris get their rights? [Angana, 2020:1-7]

When will their voice rouse the sleeping conscience of the world?

When will these so-called Muslim rulers and democrates practically side with the Kashmiris?

How long will this night of brutality and tyranny last?

When will Pakistan gather enough courage to send its army for helping these sufferers?

Did the Kashmiris side with us to see this day when their blood is flowing like water, their daughters are being raped and we are silent spectators? I believe that, one day the whole world will be answerable on this oppressive situation.

I am sure Kashmiri's thinking that the death is better than the life that can't take its right back from the cunning usurping enemy who is killing the Kashmiris in their millions with complete impunity [Maria, 2021:1-14].

Ever since the curfew was imposed no Kashmiri has slept a peaceful night's sleep. How could these rulers of the world sleep peacefully in this injustice?

How can they not hear the cries of the suffering victims who are wailing and crying their hearts out just a few steps away?

Leaving aside the rulers if we have a look at the actions of some political sections, we see that no one can beat them in brazenness, shamelessness, and remorselessness. These sellers of conscience have buried the Kashmiri freedom struggle at such a critical juncture when the rulers were gaining some success in waking up the slumbering world conscience. Their Freedom March took place and they effectively stabbed the Kashmir movement in the back.

It was nothing more than an untimely call for prayer. Jamat e Islami is far better than them as it is regularly taking out rallies, protests, and public gatherings in a bid to get the voice of Kashmiri's heard. On the other hand Peoples Party, Pakhtunkhwa Milli Awami Party, and JUI (F) are proving to be completely deaf in this regard [Asma, 2022:1-7]. Their Freedom March was nothing more than a stunt.

Not even once have they mentioned Kashmir after that march, they merely had to become tools of foreign powers so they became exactly that. India and other foreign powers wanted to push the Kashmir issue on the back burner and that happened [Erin, 2019:1-4]. These powers easily attained their objective. What more can I say? Apparently, Most of the heads of Kashmir committee had nothing to do with the Kashmiris during his ten-year tenure as the Chairman of Kashmir Committee and neither is he concerned with their plight now.

All he needs is his perks and facilities, and something to grease the wheels only then he comes into action. All the political parties should have taken a joint stand, had strengthened the stance of the government, and played their role in the freedom struggle of the Kashmiris but exactly the opposite happened. Those who have damaged the cause of Kashmir when it was on the brink of success will be haunted by the voices of the brutalized Kashmiris mothers, sisters, daughters, children, and elders until the day they die. The attention of the world media was diverted towards the march in the same way that the lists of Sikhs were given to India to destroy the Khalistan movement right when it was about to divide India into pieces [Carolina, 2012:1-15]. This act effectively buried the Khalistan movement forever.

This act is unforgivable. Now the government also got a chance to get rid of this bone and it did. No one to know and none to question, but all of them will have to answer for their deeds one day. I have done my part through my pen, now it is between you and these rulers. I am ordained to call attention to what is right.

REFERENCE

Angana P. C [2020], "Kashmir: A Place Without Rights". The Editorial: Just Security Network, vol. 71840, pp. 1-7.

Arsene B. D. [2011], "Understanding the International Community". Hekima Review, No. 44, pp. 1-12.

Asma F. [2022], "The Peculiar Case of The Pakistan People's Party as An Oppositon". Carnegie Endowment for International Peace, pp. 1-7.

Carolina M. [2012], "Mass Media and Globalization". In the Book: Wiley- Blackwell's Encyclopedia of Civilizations, pp. 1-15.

Erin B. [2019], "The Kashmir Conflict: How Did it Start?". National Geographic, pp. 1-4.

Maria E. [2021], "Right of Self Determination and Kashmiris: A Conceptual Understanding and Perspective". National Defence University, Islamabad, pp. 1-14.

Wiliam T. [1973], "The Concept of Political Freedom". Social Theory and Practice, vol. 2, No. 4, pp. 421-438. Florida State University, Department of Philosophy.

Saadat K. B. [2021], "Role of Establishment in Pakistan Politics". Thesis For B.sc Political Science, Forman Christian College.

Fall of Dhaka

16th December is the day that can't be lamented enough. This is the heartrending day when East Pakistan parted ways from us and our kids were brutally massacred in the APS catastrophe [Choudhury, 1958: 298-306]. To this day I feel as if someone has ripped me apart or as if my heart was cut into two; its beating suspended forever.

These two incidents have left a lasting effect and heartache. Those beautiful flowers were trampled upon even before they could bloom but we will never forget that black day. We will never let the light of the lamps die which were lighted by the blood of those martyrs.

On the other hand, was the Bengali Muslims who were geographically far away from the four provinces of Pakistan, whose language, culture, way of life, appearance, caste and color, and even diet was different but these Bengali Muslims answered the call of Quaid e Azam (May Allah shower him with His blessings) as one and joined hands to write a new history [Amrita, 2015: 588-592]. Bengali Muslims stood shoulder to shoulder with us for a separate homeland and paid the debt of brotherhood and being Muslims with their blood. They sacrificed hundreds of thousands of lives and enriched Pakistan. They stood tall and never once did they back down.

These Muslims had taken Dhaka to new heights of progress with their untiring efforts even before Pakistan came into being. Even Quaid e Azam (May Allah shower him with His blessings) spent many precious years of his professional life as a lawyer, in Dhaka. At that time Dhaka held its own in the trade and industrial sector [Touhidur, 2021:1-101]. The question is what happened that the whole Bengali nation became the puppet of outsiders.

In my opinion, on one hand, it was an outcome of conspiracies of the foes but on the other hand; narcissism of friends and individual personalities also played a significant role in this debacle. Those who raised the slogan of idhar hum udhar tum (this part is ours and that part is yours) left this transitory abode but Pakistan lost Bengal; its pride [Bengi, 2022:1-10].

Al- Badar that stood fast against the onslaught of Mukti Bahni was the crucially significant asset of Pakistan. Each and every member of this organization went all out for protecting Pakistan. Major Retd. Riaz Hussain Malik has thrown light on the role of the members of Al-Badar and Al-Shams in many of his interviews. These brave, graceful, loyal, patriotic beacons of greatness were in no way less than any soldier fighting in the path of Allah.

Captain AbulKarim also gave similar remarks about these youngsters. In the history of Pakistan, Shiber. which was a Bengali student organization trained their youth in the form of Al-Badar and Al-Shams who didn't hesitate to sacrifice their livelihoods and lives for Pakistan.

Many members trained by this organization like Mateeul Rehman Nizami, Abdul Qadir Mulla, Ali Hassan Mujahid, Qamar Ul Zaman, Ghulam Azam, Dilawar Hussain Saeedi, Salah Ud Din Choudhary, and many other unknown soldiers, gave practical proof of their love for Pakistan. The present Bengali government picked up 1971 era leaders of JI one by one and sentenced them to death for siding with Pakistan. These leaders, who embraced the hangman's noose for the sake of Pakistan, neither regretted their actions nor did they flee the country to avoid facing cases and jails. So much so that they laid down their lives but their love for Pakistan didn't see an iota of decline nor did their loyalty lessen with time.

The enemy divided Pakistan into linguistic lines at that time and is trying its level best to hit on the foundations of Pakistan in order to harm our beloved homeland but it has forgotten that the blood of the martyrs has reinforced these foundations and it will ensure impregnability of Pakistan. The nation is now aware of the conspiracies of the enemy. The brotherhood, love, and unison of the people are the real souls of Pakistan and God is Willing it will keep Pakistan prosperous and in high spirits for all eternity.

REFERENCES:

Amrita H. [2015], "Football and Communalism in Colonial Bengal: Mohemmedan Sporting Club and Bengali Muslim Society, 1891-1947". Proceedings of The Indian History Congress, Vol. 76, pp. 588- 592.

Bengi Uk. Et al [2022], "The Relation of Individual and Collective Narcissism and Belief in Covid-19 Conspiracy Theories: The Moderating Effects of Need for Uniqueness and Belonging". Department of Psychology, Istanbul Medipol University, Goztepe, pp. 1-10.

Choudhury G. W. [1958], "Democracy on Trial in East Pakistan ". International Journal, Vol. 13, No. 4, pp. 298-306.

Mohammed A. et al [2022], "The Liberation War of Bangladesh: Emergence of Nationalism in The Political Context". ResearchGate Publishers, pp. 1-14.

Touhidur R. [2021], "Significance of Conserving the Dhaka New Market". Thesis for: Bachelor of Urban and Regional Planning: Advisor; Professor Golam Muinuddin, PhD, pp. 1-101.

A Man from Haven

Hazrat Allama Muhammad Iqbal gave the Muslims impetus to take back their rightful place [Muhammed, 2021:1-23]. He did all this when the Muslims f the subcontinent desperately needed this guidance and assistance and their future was clouded in despondency. In those trying times, Iqbal revived the dying soul of the Muslim nation through his wisdom and sagacious poetry in such a way that Muslims of the whole of India rose as one for their right, then after millions of sacrifices, Pakistan emerged on the world map as an Islamic welfare state.

The independence of Pakistan; Iranian, Turkish and Egyptian revolutions all are results of the deliberations of Iqbal [Ilhan, 2019:1-16]. Iqbal specifically addressed the Muslim youth and equated them to the eagle which in fact was more than a mere epithet; it was a philosophy of awakening. Iqbal's endeavor was to make each and every youngster realize the true spirit of this philosophy so that they could become aware of the Philosophy of Khudi (self-actualization).

Undoubtedly his poetry carries the message of awakening for Muslims of all times and eras. In the bleakest hour of despair, it was the distinction of only Iqbal that he lit a candle of hope for the Muslims and put salve on their wounded hearts. His poetry carries a unique elucidation of the Quran that we can never hope to find in the poetry of any other poet the route that he chartered out for the reform of the ummah; every path to this destination leads to the Quran.

Many critics have presented an analysis that the actions of many poets don't match their words, but a unique feature of Iqbal's personality is that his religious training was drenched in the grooming of his father; Sheikh Noor Muhammad. This grooming is markedly visible in his poetry. That is why his similarity of thought and action, loyalty with the religion, wisdom, and sagaciousness put the nation on the path that resonates with love for the Prophet Muhammad (May Allah bless him and his progeny and bring him peace).

It was the acumen of Iqbal that he spotted the deception of the Hindus, laid this fact bare in front of Quaid e Azam Muhammad Ali Jinnah, and requested him to lead the Muslims of the Indo-Pak subcontinent [Saleem, 1975: 71-82]. We can never thank him enough for this benevolence that he illuminated the darkness with the light of truth.

Praise be to Allah that He sent Iqbal and Quaid; otherwise, the dream of Pakistan could never have been realized.

It's a pity that our ancestors succeeded in realizing the dream of Iqbal and Quaid by establishing Pakistan but we still have to build a Pakistan that truly reflects their vision because we haven't worked on the real base of Pakistan in the way that was envisioned by Iqbal [Jacob, 2004: 319-341]. He wanted the establishment of an Islamic Welfare State where the Muslims of India could lead their lives in the light of the Islamic decrees.

He dreamed of a state which would be recognized as a democratic state among the comity of Muslim nations, where justice, civilization, and social values prevail and where a practical example of the Islamic way of life could be given [Sureyya, 2021: 282-297]. The state where the youth were the center of Iqbal's hopes could serve as beacons of light in the darkness of ignorance and slavery.

Sadly, the youth of today has wandered far away from his real purpose. They can't even spare a thought for their parents and family let alone the whole Muslim ummah. Lost in the frivolities this youth is making fun of the philosophy of Iqbal. Those who were supposed to aspire to the high mountain peaks and conquer the stars are busy devouring the meat of their own like vultures.

The responsibility for this lies with those who have the power because whatever has been sown has to be reaped. It is high time to groom the eagles of Iqbal and to expose them to the true spirit of religion, sincerity, and moral values that were taught by Iqbal. Keeping in view the importance of this month we will have to reiterate the fact that we need to understand the thought of Iqbal, we should explain the philosophy of Iqbal to the youth, make the philosophy of Iqbal a part of the curriculum and mold every facet of life in this God gifted land according to the luminous system of Islam.

Now that more than 80 years have passed since Iqbal has left us, we will have to reform our ways collectively as a nation. We should be ashamed of our actions of the past 70 years that we have kept our beloved homeland away from the vision of Iqbal and Quaid. The interest-based system, profusion and scarcity, westernized education system, way of life, and culture; all negate Islamic principles [Fethi, 2020: 1-23].

Now the critics say that Iqbal has criticized the western way of life but this is in fact a result of the partial study of Iqbal because he only criticized those facets of western civilization that are in conflict with Islam. Today we need to ponder over Iqbal's love for Islam, his philosophy, and his Sufi thought.

> *Lift through love, all humble to lofty heights.*
> *Illuminate the world with the love of Muhammad.*

REFERENCES:

Fethi K. [2020], "Curiosity and Interest Based Learning". Educational Sciences, Erzincan University, pp. 1-23.

Ilhan N. [2019], "History of Pakistan 1947-2019". Europa World Regional Series, pp. 1-16.

Jacob B. et al [2004], "On Catharasis: From Fundamentals of Aristotle's Lost Essay on The Effect of Tragedy 1857". American Image, Vol. 61, No. 3, pp. 319-341.

Muhammed U. R. [2021], "Allama Dr. Muhammed Iqbal's Philosophy of Islamic Culture and Moral Values and Contemporary Muslim World: An Analytical and Critical Study ". Pakistan Journal of International Affairs, Vol. 4, No. 4, pp. 1-23.

Saleem K. [1975], "Iqbal- Philosophic Poet". Indian Literature, Vol. 18, No. 3, pp. 71-82.

Sureyya   Y. [2021], "The Concept of Citizenship and The Democratic State". Electronic Journal of Social and Strategic Studies, vol. 2, No. 3, pp. 282-297.

POWERLESS HUMANITY

BIBLIOGRAPHY

BOOK:

Louise M.B. [2013], "The All-India Muslim League, 1906-1947: A Study of Leadership in The Evolution of a Nation". Karachi: Oxford University Press.

Lucy N. [2020], "Dying for the Nation: Death, grief and Bereavement in Second World War Britain". Cultural History of Modern War: Manchester University Press.

Shamim I [2019], "The British vs American Education Systems". REFERENCESto IGCSE vs SAT Exams.

Alasdair et al [2017], "Secrets of Successful Change Implementation." Mckinsey's Sydney Office, Mckinsey & Company.

Maleelah et al., [2022], "The Role of the Private Sector in, Pakistan, pp.1-6. Pakistan's School Education". Education Sector Development, Pakistan, pp.1-6.

Milton F. [1955], "Role of Government in Education: Capitalism and Freedom". University of Chicago Press, pp.123-144.

Abdul M.O [2021], "The Whole-of-Nation Approach: The Case of Brunei Darussalam, Wawasan 2035, and the 4th Industrial Revolution". Handbook of Global Challenges for Improving Public Services and Government Operations, pp. 291-309.

Imran N. [2010], "Pakistan's Standing in the Global Village". Research Gate Publication, pp.1-17.

Maxwell C. [2019]. "Aristotle and the Good Ruler". Centre for the Study of Democratic Institutions, University of British Columbia. Oxford University Press, No. 13, pp. 1-8.

Nate R. [2019], "Alone in a Foreign Land: The Emotional Challenges of Living Abroad Alone". Ascent Publication, pp. 1-5.

Seumas M. [2017], Bribery, Nepotism, Fraud and Abuse of Authority". Cambridge University Press, pp. 106-124:

A Book Chapter: Institutional Corruption: A Study Applied in Philosophy.

Nicholas M. [2022], "The History of Economic Sanctions as a Tool of War". Department of Modern European History, Cornell University: "The Economic Weapon: The Rise of Sanctions as a Tool of Modern War". Yale University Press, pp.1-10.

JOURNAL:

Jeffrey E. G. [1989], "Japan and Germany: American Concerns". Jstor: Foreign Affairs, Vol. 68. No. 5 (Winter,1989), pp. 84-101.Council of Foreign Relations.

Kuznets P. W. [1988], "An East Asian Model of Economic Development: Japan, Taiwan, and South Korea". Jstor: Economic Development and Cultural Change, Vol. 36, No.3 [April 1988] pp. s11-s43.

Adeline I. A. et al, [2015], "Roles of The Youths in Nation building". Journal of Policy and Development Studies, vol 9, No 5, November 2015.

Erum H. [2018], "Growing Population of Pakistani Youth: A Ticking Time Bomb or a Demographic

Dividend". Journal of Educational Development, Institute of Business Management, Pakistan.

Alan P. [1962], "Education, Muslim Elite and the Creation of Pakistan". Jstor: Comparative Education Review, Vol. 6, No 2, pp.152-159. University of Chicago Press.

Prakash O.M. [2003], "Roots of Islamic Separatism in Indian Subcontinent". Jstor: Proceedings of The Indian History Congress, Vol. 64, pp.1049 - 1065. Indian History Congress.

Kutty B.M. [1996], "Quaid-e-Azam's Presidential Address to Pakistan's First Constituent Assembly". Jstor: Pakistan Horizon, Vol. 49, No 4, pp. 9-15. Pakistan Institute of International Affairs.

Khalid B.S. [1959], "Martial Law Administration in Pakistan". Jstor: Far Eastern Studies, Vol. 28, No 5, May 1959, pp. 72-79. Institute of Pacific Relations.

Siphesihle E.M et al. [2019], "Political Parties and Students Union Government Elections in South Africa's Tertiary Institutions: The Case of University of Zululand". Journal of African Renaissance, vol. 16, No 3, pp. 91-104.

Rathman I. [2004], "Musharraf's Regime in Pakistan: The Praetorianism Faces an Uncertain Future". The Indian Journal of Political Science, Vol. 65, No 2, pp. 259-282. Indian Political Science Association.

Samuel E.N.O[1980], "Education as a Source of Economic Growth and Development". Jstor: The Journal of Negro Education, vol. 49, No, pp. 203-206.

Sharon K. et al [2019], "Improving 21st Century Teaching Skills: The Key to Effective 21st Century Learners". Research in Comparative and International Education, vol. 14, Issue 1.

Taiwo M. [2005], "Problems of Policy Implementation in Developing Nations: The Nigerian Experience". Journal of Social Sciences, Vol. 11, No 1, pp. 63-69.

Adeniyi et al [2015], "Corollary of Government Policies On University Admission: A Review of Nigerian Universities". International Journal of Management and Social Sciences, vol. 3, No. 8, pp. 205-217.

Maria et al. [2010], "Teacher-Student Relationship: The Meaning of Teacher's Experience Working with Underachieving Students". Journal of Pedagogy, pp.1-16.

Faruqi K.A [1979], "Iqbal- The Humanist". Indian Literature, 22, No 3; Aspects of Modern Poetry, vol pp. 97-107.

Hans K. [1940], "The Genesis and Character of English Nationalism". Journal of History of Ideas, Vol. 1, No. 1, pp. 69-94. University of Pennsylvania Press.

Richard P.et al., [2018], "The Seminar-Workshop Experience in Journalism Class: A Best Practice?". Rizal Technological University, Mandaluyong, Philippines. International Journal Humanities and Social Sciences, Vol. 10, No. 3, pp. 45-55.

Sawaf M. [2020], "The US-Iran Conflict and the Consequences of International Law-breaking". The Conversation International Journal, pp1-7.

Samad A. [2019], "Academic and Religious Services of Mohammed Maqsood llahi [Mahboobllahi] and Its Effects on the Society". The International Research Journal, Department of Usooluddin, Vol. 3, No. 2, pp. 1-14.

Devendra [2014], "Role of Opposition in a Parliamentary Democracy". The Indian Journal of Political Science, Vol. 75, No. 1, pp. 165-170: Indian Political Science Association.

Muhammed N. [2021], "National Integration: Challenges and Options for Pakistan". Islamabad Policy Research Institute [IPRI], Vol. 7, No. 1, pp. 1-36.

Ali A.D [2021], "Iran's Foreign Policy Under Raisi". Centre for Strategic Studies, Tehran, Vol. 7, pp.1-8.

Ahmed B. et al., [2014], "Islamic Finance in The United Kingdom: Factors Behind its Development and Growth". Islamic Economic Studies, vol. 22, No. 1, pp.37-78.

Allison J. [2007], "Giving Voice to Children's Voices: Practices and Problems, Pitfalls and Potentials". American Anthropologist, Vol.109, No. 2, pp. 261-272.

Samuel H. [1945], "Principles of Social Interaction". American Sociological Review, vol. 10, No. 1, pp. 6-12.

Khaled D. [2018], "Trump Adding Fuel to Fire". Al-Ahram Weekly Journal, 2018 Edition, pp. 1-2.

William E. [2019], "The President and Intelligence Communities". Vol. 36, No. 2, pp. 95-98. National Military Intelligence Foundation.

Zara A. [2021], "The Fight Against Racism Must Continue". American Psychological Association, vol. 52,

No. 1, pp. 1-48. Continue". American Psychological Association, vol. 52, No. 1, pp. 1-48.

Beat S. [2007], "The Spirit of Geneva; Humanitarian Diplomacy and Advocacy". Refugee Survey Quarterly: vol. 26, No. 4, "The Spirit of Geneva in a Globalized World: The Twelfth Annual Conference of Webster University, Geneva (2007), pp.163-165. Oxford University Press.

Michael S. [1994], "A Guide to Truth Predicates in the Modern Era". The Journal of Symbolic Logic, vol. 59, No. 3, pp.1032-1054. Association of Symbolic Logic.

Seth B. [2021], "How to Prevent the Next Pandemic". Public Health Opinion: Scientific American Journal, pp. 1-5.

Christopher H. [2022], "Mapping the Notting Hill Riots: Racism and the Streets of Post-War Britain". History Workshop Journal, Vol. 93, No. 1, pp. 47-68.

Cross R.S. [1950], "The Modern Predicament". The Philosophical Quarterly, Vol.6, No.25, pp.359-365, University Press.

Maryam T.et al [2016], "Reforming a Broken System: A New Performance Evaluation System for Pakistan Civil

Servants". The Pakistan Development Review, Vol. 55, No. 1, pp. 49-72.

Vest C.M. [1945], "A Critique of Criticism or The Critic Criticised". Peabody Journal of Education, Vol. 23, No. 3, pp. 162-168. Taylor and Francis Ltd.

Anthony A. [1983], "The British Government and the Media,1937-1938". Journal of Contemporary History, Vol. 18, No. 2, pp.281-297. Sage Publications Ltd.

Ruma C. [2009], "Printer Hugh Gaine Crosses and Re-Crosses the Hudson". Jstor: New York History, Vol. 90, No. 4, pp.271-285. Cornell University Press.

Yamamoto T. [1989], "The Press Clubs of Japan". The Journal of Japanese Studies, Vol. 15, No. 2, pp. 371-388.

Donald et al. [1957], "Estimates of the Infection Rates for Poliomyelitis Virus in the Years Preceding the Poliomyelitis Epidemics of 1916 in New York and 1945 on Mauritius". The Journal of Hygiene, Vol. 55, No. 2, pp. 254-265. Cambridge University Press.

Ednak et al. [2014], "Progress Toward Polio Eradication". National Library of Medicine: National Centre for Biotechnology Information, Microbiology and Mortality Weekly Report, Vol. 63, No. 21, pp. 468-472.

Siang et al. [2019], "Jonas Salk [1914-1995]: A Vaccine Against Polio". Singapore Medical Journal, Vol. 60, No. 1, pp.1-10.

Denis J.H [2002], "The United Nations: The Embarrassment of International Law". Medicine, Conflict and Survival, Vol. 8, No. 4, pp.346-354.

Martin J. et al., [2021], "Areas of Global Importance for Conserving Terrestrial Biodiversity, Carbon and Water", Nature, Ecology and Evolution, vol. 5, pp. 1499-1509.

Fritz L. [1970], "Urdu Literature and Mughal Decline". Mahfil, Vol. 6, No. 2/3, 1970, pp. 125-131: Asian Studies Centre, Michigan State University.

Kohade V. [2021], "Impact of Second Wave Covid-19 in the World", College of Pharmacy: Department of Pharmaceutics, Latur College of Pharmacy, Hasegaon, Vol. 8, No. 3, pp. 1-10.

Rokus D. [2011], "Rumi and The Abyss of Longing". Mawlana Rumi Review, Vol. 2, pp. 61-93.

Sayed B. [2019], "The Future of Pakistan and Its Overseas Diaspora", Journal of International Affairs, Pakistan, pp. 1-7.

Schurman J. G. [1894], "The Consciousness of Moral Obligation". The Philosophical Review, Vol. 3, No. 6, pp. 641-654. Duke University Press, pp. [1-15].

Veronica S. [1971], "The Myth of The Middle-class Family in American Family Sociology". The American Sociologist: Vol. 6, No. 1, pp. 14-18.

Sidrah R. [2010], "Human Rights and Decolonization: New Perspectives and Open Questions". International Journal of Human Rights: Anthropology, Applied Ethics and Historical Studies; pp. 1-26.

Stratos P. [2009], "Corruption in Our Courts: What it Looks Like and Where it is Hidden". The Yale Law Journal, Vol.118, No.8, pp.1900-1943. The Yale Journal Company, Inc.

James S. [1911], "The Problem of Destitution: A Plea for the Minority Report". International Journal of Ethics, vol. 22, No.1, pp.39-50.

Mncube D. et al., [2021], "Novice Teachers' Experiences of Teaching Visually Impaired Learners in the Foundation Phase", Universal Journal of Educational Research, Vol.9, No. 6, pp.1179-1189.

Sharif S. [2007], "Pakistan: Islam, Radicalism and the Army". International Journal on World Peace, Vol. 24, No. 2, pp. 25-35.

Syed M. [2007], "Pakistan and the War Against Terrorism". Pakistan Horizon, vol. 60, No. 2, pp.85-107. Pakistan Institute of International Affairs.

Thathiah R. [2006], "Pakistan Army and Regional Peace in South-Asia". Journal of Third World Studies, Vol.23, No.1, pp.119-146. University of Florida Press.

Malcolm R. [1979], "The British Government and Mormon Question, 1910-1922". Journal of Church and State, Vol.21, No. 2, pp.305-323. Oxford University Press.

Shahid A.et al [2006], "Economics of Regaining Office: The Case of Pakistan [1947-2005]". The Pakistan Development Review, Vol. 45, No. 4, pp. 913-923: Pakistan Institute of Development Economics, Islamabad.

Glenn V. [1968], "Pakistan: Discontinuity and the Majority Problem". Geographical Review, Vol.58, No.2, pp.195-213.

Sharif S. [2007], "Pakistan: Islam, Radicalism and the Army". International Journal on World Peace, Vol. 24, No. 2, pp. 25-35.

Syed M. [2007], "Pakistan and the War Against Terrorism". Pakistan Horizon, vol. 60, No. 2, pp.85-107. Pakistan Institute of International Affairs.

Thathiah R. [2006], "Pakistan Army and Regional Peace in South-Asia". Journal of Third World Studies, Vol.23, No.1, pp.119-146. University of Florida Press.

Foluke O.   [2004], "Environmental Sustainability in Nigeria The Awareness Initiative". African Issues, vol. 31/32, No. ½, pp. 41-52. Cambridge University Press.

Haibo R. et al., [2022], "Government Trust, Environmental Pollution Perception and Environmental Governance Satisfaction". National Library of Medicine: National Centre for Biotechnology Information, Vol. 19, No. 16, pp. 1-10, PM/D: 36011557.

Jianghan Z. [2018], "Elite Power Competition and Corruption Investigation in China: A Case Study". The University of Hong Kong: Modern China; Vol. 46, No.3, pp.1-46.

Chirag M. et al., [2021], "Estimating Covid-19 Mortality in Italy Early in the Covid-19 Pandemics". Nature Communications, Vol. 12, No.2729, pp.1-9.

Ted B. [2021], "The Massacres of the Jews Under Richard [A.D 1189-1190]". Department of History and Religion, Lincoln Memorial University, Harrogate, Vol.12, No.10, pp.1-821.

Vivekanandam B. [1982], "Riots in Britain: An Analysis". India Quarterly, Vol.38, No.1, pp.51-63.

Saroosh A. [2022], "A Philosophical Significance of Karbala". Research Gate: Aligarh Muslim University, pp. 1-3.

Jean M. [2021], "Belgium's Van Ranst: Covid Scientist Targeted by a Far-right Sniper". BBC Editorials, Vol.5, pp.1-4.

Martin B. [2021], "The Italian Government Response to Covid-19 and the Making of a Prime Minister". Contemporary Italian Politics, Vol. 13, No.2, pp.149-165.

Om P. [2003], "The Roots of Islamic Separation in Indian Sub-continent". Proceedings of the Indian History Congress, vol. 64, pp.1049-1065. Indian History Congress.

Gayle M. et al [2023], "Recession in 2023?". The Editorial: World Economic Forum, pp. 1-3.

Malarvizhi P. [2021], "Humanity on Calamity". V.V. Vanniaperumal College for Women, International Journal of Scientific and Engineering Research, Vol. 12, No. 11, pp.1-8.

Andrew M. [2013], "Proxy Warfare and The Future of Conflict". The RUSI Journal, Vol. 158, No. 2, pp. 40-46.

Andreas M. [2021], "Violence, Communication, and Civil Disobedience". An International Journal of Legal and Political Thought, Vol. 12, No. 4, pp. 491-511.

Battilana et al., [2021], "Don't Let Power Corrupt You". The Magazine, Harvard Business Review Analytical Services, Vol. 9, pp. 1-10.

Devendra K.   [2014], "Role of Opposition in a Parliamentary Democracy". The Indian Journal Political Science, Vol. 75, No. 1, pp. 165-170.

Endalcachew B. [2017], "The Legacy of Colonialism in The Contemporary Africa: A Cause for Intra-state and Inter-state Conflicts". Bahir Dar University, pp. 1-8. International Journal of Innovative and Applied Research, Vol. 3, No. 2.

Olaoluwa et al [2014], "Living Conditions and Public Health Status in Three Urban Slums of Lagos, Nigeria".

South East Asia Journal of Public Health, vol. No. 4, pp.1-7.

Tony P. [2013], "Street Crime: A View from The Left". Social Justice and Global Options, Vol. 40, No. 1-2, pp. 216-230.

Aatif A. M. [2008], "Iqbal's Vision of a Muslim State". International Iqbal Society, Vol. 944, No. 1656, pp. 1-3.

Charles H. K. [1984], "Policies of Ethnic PREFERENCESin Pakistan ". Asian Survey: University of California Press, Vol. 24, No. 6, pp. 688-703.

Manzoor H. et al [2016], "Ethics and Education in Pakistan: Principles, Policies and Practice". Children and Sustainable Development Journal: Chapter 10, pp. 385-396.

Peter C. [2018], "How to Nurture A Democracy". Institute for The Study of Complex Systems, Vol. 459, No. 2, pp. 1-2.

Tariq R. [1997], "Language and Ethnicity in Pakistan". Asian Survey: University of California Press, Vol. 37, No. 9, pp. 833-839.

Asmaa P. [2019], "The Fifth Generation Warfare and The Definitions of Peace". The Journal of Intelligence Conflict and Warfare, Vol. 2, pp. 1-12.

Bishnu R. U. [2004], "Resource Conflicts and Conflict Resolution in Nepal". Mountain Research and Development, vol. 24, No. 1, pp. 1-7.

Bulent G. [1998], "The Battle for Baku {May-September, 1918}: A Peculiar Episode in The History of The Caucasus". Middle-Eastern Studies, Vol. 34, No. 1, pp. 30-50.

Dominik P. [2020], "Convergence Between Developed and Developing Countries: A Centennial Perspective", Social Indicators Research, Vol. 153, pp. 193-225.

Sisir G. [1969], "The Third World and The Great Powers". The Annals of the American Academy of Political and Social Sciences, Vol. 386, pp. 54-63: Protagonists, Power and the Third World: Essays on The Changing International System. Sage Publications Inc.

Jin Young L. [2019], "Globalization and The Crisis of Liberal Democracy: The Political Dynamics of Neo-liberalism and Populism". Research Gate, Vol. 21, No. 4, pp. 1-19.

Amrita H. [2015], "Football and Communalism in Colonial Bengal: Mohemmedan Sporting Club and Bengali Muslim Society, 1891-1947". Proceedings of The Indian History Congress, Vol. 76, pp. 588- 592.

Muhammed N. et al., [2023], "Maulana Fazal-ur-Rehman as an Alliance Maker: A Case-study of Pakistan Democratic Movement". Pakistan Journal of Humanities and Social Sciences, Vol. 11, No. 2, pp. 1009-1013.

Stokes S. C. [1999], "Political Parties and Democracy". Annual Review of Political Science, Vol. 2, pp. 243-267.

Badamasi Z. et al., [2019], "Restructuring and the Dilemma of State Police in Nigeria: To Be or Not to Be?". Journal of Business and Social Review in Emerging Economies, Vol. 5, No. 1, pp. 41-50.

Hongying W. et al., [2001]," Transparency International and Corruption as an Issue of Global Governance". Global Governance, Vol. 7, No. 1, pp. 25-49.

Devine T. M. [2006], "The Breakup of Britain? Scotland and The End of Empire: The Prothero Lecture". Transactions of The Royal Historical Society, Vol. 16, No. 6, pp. 163-180.

Gerald S. et al [2006], "War and The World Economy". Journal of Conflict Resolution, Vol. 50, No. 5, pp. 1-24.

Mint U. [2000], "Corruption: Causes, Consequences and Cures". Asia-Pacific Development Journal, Vol. 7, No. 2, pp. 1-26.

Adela S. et al., [2013], "Remittances and Their Impact on Economic Growth". Periodica Polytechnica Social and Management Sciences, Vol. 21, No. 1, pp. 3-19.

Farzana S. [2015], "Fighting to The End: The Pakistan Army's Way of War". A Reviewed Work, International Affairs [Royal Institute of International Affairs 1944], Vol. 91, No. 3, pp. 665-667.

Choudhury G. W. [1958], "Democracy on Trial in East Pakistan ". International Journal, Vol. 13, No. 4, pp. 298-306.

Farrukh F. [2021], "Identity and Interests: History of Pakistan's Foreign Policy and The Middle-Eastern Muslim States, 1947 to 1956". Cogent Social Sciences, Vol. 7, No. 1, pp. 1-12.

Glenn V. S. [1968], "Pakistan Discontiguity and the Majority Problem". National Geographical Review, Vol. 58, No. 2, pp. 195-219.

Jacob B. et al [2004], "On Catharasis: From Fundamentals of Aristotle's Lost Essay on The Effect of Tragedy 1857". American Image, Vol. 61, No. 3, pp. 319-341.

Muhammed U. R. [2021], "Allama Dr. Muhammed Iqbal's Philosophy of Islamic Culture and Moral Values and Contemporary Muslim World: An Analytical and Critical Study ". Pakistan Journal of International Affairs, Vol. 4, No. 4, pp. 1-23.

Saleem K. [1975], "Iqbal- Philosophic Poet". Indian Literature, Vol. 18, No. 3, pp. 71-82.

Sureyya Y. [2021], "The Concept of Citizenship and The Democratic State". Electronic Journal of Social and Strategic Studies, vol. 2, No. 3, pp. 282-297.

Justice M. [2019], "Sustainable Development: Meaning, History, Principles, Pillars and Implications for Human Action: Literature Review". Cogent Social Sciences, Vol. 5, No. 1, pp. 1-21.

Nelson M. [2017], "On the Coloniality of Human Rights". Revista Critica de Sciences Socials, vol. 114, No. 114, pp. 117-136.

Firdous J. [2011], "Dengue Fever [DF] in Pakistan ". Asia Pacific Family Medicine, Vol. 10, No. 1, pp. 1-7.

Gabriel S. et al., [2020], "The UK's Public Health Response to Covid-19". British Medical Journal, pp. 1-3.

Nadiya T. et al., [2018], "Point-of-care Tests: A Review of Advances in The Emerging Diagnostic Tools for Dengue Virus Infection". Sensors and Actuators B Chemicals, Vol. 255, No. 3, pp. 3316-3331.

Natasha E. et al., [2013], "Epidemiology of Dengue: Past, Present and Future Prospects". National Institutes of Health: National Library of Medicine, Vol. 5, No. 1, pp. 299-309.

Rahmet G. et al., [2020], "Covid-19: Prevention and Control Measures in Communities". Turkish Journal of

Medical Sciences: National Library of Medicine, Vol. 50, No. 3.

Sania N. et al., [2013], "Health Reform in Pakistan: A Call to Action". Health Transitions in Pakistan, Vol. 381, No. 9885, pp. 2291-2297.

Vincent S. R. [2020], "The High Cost of Prescription Drugs: Causes and Solutions". Blood Cancer Journal, Vol. 10, No. 71, pp. 1-5.

Alex S. [2002], "Civil Service Reform in Post-Independence Nigeria: Issues and Challenges". Public Administration Quarterly, Vol. 25, No. 4, pp. 498-517.

Raja Q. et al., [2020], "The Rise of Peripheral Nationalism in Pakistan and The Pashtun Tahafuz Movement". Asian Ethnicity, Vol. 23, No. 2, pp. 215-229.

Ali A. [2022], "The Burden of Cancer, Government Strategic Policies and Challenges in Pakistan: A Comprehensive Review". Frontiers in Nutrition, Vol. 9, No. 7, pp. 1-18.

Hyuna S. et al [2021], "Global Cancer Statistics 2020: GLOBOCAN Estimates of Incidence and Mortality Worldwide For 36 Countries". American Cancer Society: A Cancer Journal for, Clinicians, Vol. 71, No. 3, pp. 209-249.

Muhammed R. S. [2017], "Cancer Prevalence, Incidence, and Mortality Rates in Pakistan in 2012". Cogent Medicine, Vol. 4, No. 1, pp. 1-13.

Rebecca L. et al., [2020], "Cancer Statistics 2020". American Cancer Society: A Cancer Journal for Clinicians, Vol. 7, No. 1, pp. 7-30.

Farehas S. et al [2021], "Covid-19 in Pakistan: Challenges and Priorities". Cogent Medicine, Vol. 8, No. 1, pp. 1-14.

Angana P. C [2020], "Kashmir: A Place Without Rights". The Editorial: Just Security Network, Vol. 71840, pp. 1-7.

Khalid B. S [1966], "The Capabilities of Pakistan's Political System". Asian Survey, Vol. 7, No. 2, A Survey of Asia in 1966, Part 2, pp. 102-110.

Stokes C. S. [1999], "Political Parties and Democracy". Annual Review of Political Science, Department of Political Science, University of Chicago, Vol. 2, pp. 243-267.

Leoni C. [2020], "U.S Intervention in Afghanistan: Justifying the Unjustifiable?". Sage Journals, Vol. 41, No. 1, pp. 70-86.

Nasreen A. [2008], "Pakistan, Afghanistan, and the Taliban". International Journal on World Peace, Vol. 25, No. 4, pp. 49-73. Paragon House.

Yeshi C. [2021], "India's Engagement in Development and Peace Building Assistance in The Post-conflict States". Policy and Practice Review: Frontier Political Science, Security, Peace and Democracy, Vol. 3, pp. 1-12.

Leoni C. [2021], "US Intervention in Afghanistan: Justifying the Unjustifiable". South Asia Research, Vol. 41, No. 1, pp. 70-86.

Muhammed R. et al., [2019], "Chanakya Kautila's Philosophy and its Influence on Current Indian Foreign Policy". Riphah International University, vol. 13, pp. 1-10.

Dan H. et al., [2020], "The Meaning of Diplomacy". Journal of International Negotiation, Vol. 26, No. 2, pp. 1-26.

Nistha S. et al., [2020], "The Impact of Covid-19 on Globalisation". National Library of Science: National Centre for Biotechnology Information, Vol. 11, No. 10, pp. 1-9.

Paul S. et al., [2019], "The Qatar's Foreign Policy: Relevance and Shortcomings". Covenant University, Ota, Ogun, State, Nigeria, Vol. 10, No. 2, pp. 1-9.

Ram J. et al., [1973], "The Opposition: Problems and Prospects". Economic and Political Weekly, Vol. 8, No. 42, pp. 1-6.

Allison J. [2007], "Giving Voice to Children's Voices: Practices and Problems, Pitfalls and Potentials". American Anthropologists New Series, Vol. 109, No. 2, pp. 261-272.

Clayborne C. [1987], "Martin Luther King Jr: Charismatic Leadership in a Mass Struggle". The Journal of American History, Vol. 74, No. 2, pp. 448-454. Oxford University Press.

David R.S [2006], "Religious Contributions to Peace Making: When Religion Brings Peace Not War". Peace, Religion and Peace Making Initiative, Vol. 1, pp. 1-3.

William S. [2021], "The Game is Changing for Historians of Black America". The Inheritance Project: The Atlantic Project About American History and Black Life, vol. 618747, pp. 1-10.

Zara A. [2021], "The Fight against Racism Must Continue". American Psychological Association, vol. 52, No. 1, pp. 1-48.

John B. et al., [2022], "Placed-based Politics and Nested Deprivation in the UK; Beyond Cities, Towns," "Two Englands" and "The Left Behind". Routledge: Francis and Taylor Group, Vol. 58, No. 2, pp. 169-190.

Madiha H. et al., [2020], "A National Survey of Critical Care Services in Hospitals Accredited for Training in a Lower-middle Income Country: Pakistan". National Library of Medicine: National Center for Biotechnology Information, Vol. 60, pp. 273-278.

Farrukh F. et al., [2021], "Identity and Interests: History of Pakistan's Foreign Policy and Middle-Eastern Muslim States: 1947-1956". Politics and International Relations: Taylor and Francis Online, Cogent Social Sciences, Vol. 7, No. 1, pp. 1-12.

Gil F. [2008], "Identifying the Place of Democratic Norms in Democratic Peace". International Studies Review, Vol. 10, No. 3, pp. 548-570. Oxford University Press.

Gerasimos S. [2007], "Plato's Criticisms of Democracy in The Republic". Social Philosophy and Policy, Vol. 24, No. 2, pp. 70-89.

Chris N. [2005], "Recognizing States and Governments". Canadian Journal of Philosophy, vol. 35, No. 1, pp. 27-82. Cambridge University Press.

Glenn V. [1968], "Pakistan: Discontiguity and the Majority Problem". Geographical Review, Vol.58, No.2, pp.195-213.

Stephen H. et al., [2020], "Locational Analysis of Slums---". GeoJournal, Vol. 86, pp. 2467-2481.

Deborah P. [1995], "Shall We Go Home? Increasing Urban Poverty in African Cities and Migration Processes". The Geographical Journal, vol. 161, No. 3, pp. 245-264. The Royal Geographical Society.

John H. [2021], "Good Leadership is About Asking Good Questions". Harvard Business Review: Global Peter Drucker Forum, pp. 1-3.

ONLINE:

Jawad S. H. [2020], "Politics and Moral Values". [https://academia.edu/477755671/politics-and-moral-values/].

Adnan N. [2014], "Police Capacity and Insurgency in Pakistan". Policing Insurgencies, Oxford Academic Journal Online, pp. 177-202. Comparative Politics, International Relations.

Andreas R. [2016], "The Zia ul-Haqq Era, 1977-1988". Sociology and Anthropology of Religion. Oxford Scholarship Online.

Gurmeet K. [2013], "Pakistan's Internal Security Challenges: Will the Military Cope?". Jstor: https://www.jstor.org/stable/resrep 09151//., pp. 1-8.

POLICY PAPER:

Forbig J. [2005], "Revisiting Youth Political Participation". Europe: Council of Europe.

Institute of Strategic Studies [1998], "Text of Prime Minister Nawaz Sharif's Speech At the UN: September 23, 1998".

Liugi S. [2021], "From Partners to Rivals? The Future of EU-Turkey Relations" Policy Brief [pdf].

UNESCO [2021], "Global Education Monitoring: What is Neck?". Global Education Monitoring Report, UNESCO Office.

Hassan A. [2016], "Role of Pakistan Police in Counterinsurgency". Belfer Centre, Harvard University. Counterinsurgency and Pakistan Paper Series, No. 5, pp. 1-8.

Catherine B. [2018]," A Beginner's Guide to the Office for Students". Whonke Policy Watch, pp.1-10.

Evans R.S. [2016], "Electronic Health Records: Then, Now and in the Future". National Library of Science: National Centre for Biotechnology Information, pp. 48-61.

Simon W. [2019], "The Inside Story of How Three Unlikely Allies Won World War 11". National Geographic Project.

Carlo M. [2022], "The Tragic Murder of Daniel Pearl Explained". The Grunge Archives.

Geo E. [2015], "71 Journalists Killed in Pakistan Since 2001". PPF Media Violence Index Report.

Think Tank [2020], "Next Generation or Lost Generation? Children, Young People, and the Pandemic" European Parliament.

Ben R.M et al., [2020], "Innovation, Development, and Covid-19: Challenges, Opportunities and Ways Forward". OECD Policy Responses, United Kingdom, pp. 1-10.

Ebad E. [2022], "The Iranian Economy's Challenges amid the Pandemic and Sanctions". Ebadi Institute of Policy-making, Tehran, Iran, pp. 1-7.

Eduoard et al. [2021], "Iran: Coronavirus Pandemic Country. Profile". Our World in Data.

OTHER SOURCES

R. Geraid H. Ryan S. [2021], "The Bhutto Family and Pakistan: Power, Politics and the Deep State". Independent Scholar: Department of International Politics.

Ahmad A.S. [2019], "Understanding the Quaid's Vision of Pakistan". School of International Service, American University, Washington D.C.

Al-Mujahid S. [2001], "Ideology of Pakistan". Islamic Research Institute, International Islamic University.

Chari P.R. [2014], "Can India Be Cunning?". Institute of Peace and Conflict Studies [IPCS].

Cohen S.P. [1995], "Kashmir: The Roads Ahead" Seminar Organized by MCISS, Asia 1992.

Kumar S. [1999], "India-US Relations: From Estranged Democracies to Strategic Partnership". Southern Asia Studies Programme, School of Social Sciences and International Studies, Pondicherry Central University.

Laura S. et al. [2022], "How Global Public Opinion of China Has. Shifted in The Xi Era". Pew Research Centre.

Mazhari M. [2021], "Iran, Turkey, Pakistan Have Great Task to Solve Afghanistan Problem: Turkish Politician". International Multimedia Tourism.

Ningthoujam A. [2021], "India-Israel Ties: New Opportunities in the Middle-East". Symbiosis School of International Studies, Pune, India.

Roy T.T. [2020], "The Indian Empire of Burma, 1909". The Churchill Project, Hillsdale College, Cambridge Review of International Affairs, 2018.

Singh S. [2012], "India's China Policy Is Confused". Centre for Policy Research in India.

Marianna P. [2021], "Philosophy of Education in Times of Crises and Pandemics". Philosophy of Education

Today: Diagnostics, Prognostics, Therapeutics and Pandemics.

Ishrat A. A. [2013], "Pakistan's Participation in the War on Terror and US Concerns: An Analysis". Department of International Relations, University of Sindh.

Chris H. [2014], "Understanding Student Loans: How Exactly Do They Work?". Students' Award Agency for Scotland.

Madeline B. [2022], "Polio Vaccines: New Developments on the Road to Eradication". American Society for Microbiology, pp. 1-5.

Keisha N. [2020], "The Fight Against Racism Has Always Been Global". Civil Rights International: Department of History, University of Pittsburgh, pp. 1-8.

Melissa D. [2022], "Examining Systemic Racism: Advancing Racial Justice in America". Stanford University Communications, pp. 1-15.

Sintayehu T.T [2022], "The Disease That Re-emerged----
-". Infectious Disease Epidemiology, Infection Biology,
Phytochemical Analysis, Ethiopia, pp. 1-6.

WHO-a- [1994], "Summary of 1994 Activities of the
WHO Collaborating Centres in the Western Pacific
Region". Language: English, pp.414.

WHO-b- [2019], "Pakistan and Afghanistan: The Final
Wild Poliovirus Bastion". Language: English.

Jamee H. [2015], "Mehbub-e-ilahi's Spiritual Legacy
Continues to Foster the Sufi Way of Life in India: Syed
Mohammed Ashraf Kichauchwi". All India Ulma &
Mashaikh Board.

Jess S. et al. [2022], "The Legislative Process in
Parliament". Institute for Government, United Kingdom.

Sajjad H.M. [2018], "Mujhey Kyun Nikala [Why Was I
Ousted?]". Office of the Directorate: Delta Technology
Consulting Ltd, pp. 1-3.

Yifeng et al. [2021] "Self Sacrifice at Work: A
Synthesized Definition and An Identity-Based

Framework". Academy of Management Annual Meeting Proceedings, pp.1-6.

Larry L. [2020], "Protecting Medical Care in Conflict: A Solvable Problem". Office of The Directorate, Action on Armed Violence, pp. 1-15.

Becca B. et al., [2021], "Understanding the Impact of Covid-19 on UK Population". Directorate of the Centre for International Migration, UK, pp. 1-4.

Jenny B. [2007], "Lewisham'77: Success or Failure". The Institute of Race Relations, UK, pp. 1-4.

Amelia C.et al., [2020], "Rising Hunger: Facing a Food-Insecure World". Council of Foreign Relations: Foreign Affairs, CFR Education, pp.1-25.

Ayo S.et al., [2021], "The Spread of Covid-19 Outbreak in the First 120 Days: A Comparison Between Nigeria and Seven Other Countries". National Library of Science: National Centre for Biotechnology Information, PMC7802991, pp.1-10.

Dan T. et al., [2021], "Coronavirus and the Social Impacts on Great Britain: 24 September 2021". Office for National Statistics, Policy Evidence Analysis: Team UK, pp.1-7.

Harold D. et al [2016], "Why Britain Really Voted to Leave the EU". University of Essex Research Team, U.K, pp.1-4.

Riyanti D. et al., [2020], "Covid-19 and ASEAN Responses: Comparative Policy Analysis". National Library of Medicine: National Centre for Biotechnology Information, PMCID: PMC 7577870, pp.1-15.

Sigurd B. [2020], "Sweden's Experiment with Herd Immunity is Unethical and Undemocratic". Swedish Science Forum for Covid-19, pp. 1-7.

Rabia A. [2021], "Pakistan and the Taliban 2.0: The Good, the Bad and the Ugly". Office of the Directorate, the Atlantic Council's South-Asia Centre for Security, Strategy and Policy Research, University of Lahore, pp.1-4.

Christophe J. [2002], "A History of Pakistan and its Roots". London Anthem Press, 2002, ISBN:1843310309, pp.1-352.

Deondre S. [2021], "Erasing Indigenous History: Then and Now", Stanton Foundation, Ohio State University, pp.1-15.

Salim B. [2022], "Put an End to U-turns and Play with a Straight Bat, Khan Sahib!", from the Desk of Salim Bokhari, pp.1-2.

Abel I. [2017], "Education of People with Special Needs". Department of Economics, National Open University, Jabi-Abuja, Nigeria. The 3rd International Conference on Social Science, pp.1-12.

Emma C. et al., [2019], "The Challenges of Inclusion for Children with Disabilities: Experiences of Implementation in Eastern and Southern Africa". UNICEF Think Piece Series, pp. 1-12.

Hilary S. [2019], "Social Exclusion". Brown University Publications, pp. 1-7.

Sarah C. [2018], "Stephen Hawking's Final Theory About the Big Bang", SciTech Daily: The University of Cambridge, pp.1-5.

Zaeem M. [2017], "Legal Rights of Children Under Laws of Pakistan". Pakistan's 1st Legal News and Analysis Portal: Courting the Law, pp.1-2.

Gabriel G.et al., [2019], "Every Year Nearly 6 Million People Die". Global Health: World Economic Forum, pp.1-4.

ENCYCLOPAEDIA

Brock et al., [2019], "Needs in Moral and Political Philosophy". The Stanford Encyclopaedia of Philosophy, pp.1-7.

Clayborne C. [2023], "American Civil Rights Movements". The Editors of Encyclopedia Britannica.

Cohen R. [2018], "Hume's Moral Philosophy". Stanford Encyclopaedia of Philosophy, pp. 1-20.

Eric R. [2020], "How Iran Impacts the Price and Supply of Oil". The Editorial, Investopedia, pp. 1-4.

Jeff W. [2023], "Boston Massacres: United States History". The Editors of Encyclopaedia Britannica, pp.1-20.

Kwame G. [2010], "African Ethics". Stanford Encyclopaedia of Philosophy, The Metaphysics Research Lab, Centre for the Study of Language and Information.

NEWSPAPER:

Samir T. [2013], "Remembering Ashfaq Ahmad: Through His Stories, He Will Live Forever in Our Hearts". The Express Tribune, 2013.

Melissa D.W[2020], "When Thomas Jefferson Penned---
-". Stanford News Service.

Timothy J.S. [2003], "The Truth About the War Memorial to Fallen Journalists". Boston Globe.

Sarah B. [2002], "Polio is Eradicated from Europe". Health Editorial, The Guardian International Edition, pp.1-3.

Collen W.   [2021], "Solving Racial Disparities in Policing". The Harvard Gazette, pp. 1-10.

Farrah T.   [2020], "After the Fires: Re-building Minneapolis in the Wake of Black Lives Matter". The Sidney Morning Herald, pp.1-9.

Shahzeb A. [2023], "Can Pakistan's Military Dispense Justice?" Asia News Network.

Mohammed A. [2018], "Edhi Foundation: Serving Humanity". Edhi Foundation for Humanitarian Services, Pakistan, pp. 1-4.

Sukru C. [2019], "How Saudi-Iranian Oil Rivalry Has Been Shaped by American Power". Lancaster University: National Research Foundation, pp. 1-5.

Al Muntazar [2020], "Hazrat Imam Husain (A.S) and Hazrat Imam Mahdi (a.s)". Al Muntazar Online Islamic Course, Pakistan, pp. 1-10.

Vikas D. [2021], "Review of Select Contributions of Philip Kotler to Marketing Theory and Practice". Neville Wadia Institute of Management Studies and Research, pp. 1-6.

Sadaf F. [2022], "Al Hassan: The Beloved Grandson of The Prophet Mohammed". Online Islamic Library, Karachi, Pakistan, pp. 1-6.

Sheikh J.H [2020], "A Battle for Justice ". The Nation Editorial, pp. 1-3.

Antoine J.et al., [2020], "How Do Black People Channel Their Anger----". Washington Post, June 2019 Edition, pp. 1-5.

Rafiullah M. [2022], "Olive Farming is Key to Saving the Forests in Balochistan". Olive Oil Times, Pakistan, pp. 1-5.

Patrick B.   [2021], "Row Over UK Tree Planting Drive". The Editorial: The Guardian, pp. 1-3.

Chris A. [2011], "Pakistan Military Denies BBC Report on Taliban Links". Reuters: South-Asia News, pp.1-3.

Ivana K. et al., [2022], "What is NATO and When Does it Act?". CNN Editorials, pp.1-6.

Muhammed S. [2023], "Is Terrorism Returning to Pakistan?". The Conversation Editorials, pp.1-6.

Myra M. [2016], "On India-Pakistan: Hope for the Best, and Prepare for the Worst". Reuters Editorials and Commentaries, pp.1-6.

Ivana K. et al., [2022], "What is NATO and When Does it Act?". CNN Editorials, pp.1-6.

Muhammed S. [2023], "Is Terrorism Returning to Pakistan?". The Conversation Editorials, pp.1-6.

Myra M. [2016], "On India-Pakistan: Hope for the Best, and Prepare for the Worst". Reuters Editorials and Commentaries, pp.1-6.

Chris A. [2011], "Pakistan Military Denies BBC Report on Taliban Links". Reuters: South-Asia News, pp.1-3.

Pippa C. [2020], "Coronavirus: Top Scientist Accuses Government of Number Theatre". Daily Mirror: Political Editorials, U.K, Vol.2.

Melissa D. [2021], "Anger and Sadness Soared Following George Floyd's Death". Directorate of Stanford Report, pp.1-3.

Jason S. [2021], "The Global Impact of George Flyod----". The CBS News International, UK, pp.1-4.

Borge B. [2020], "Global Cooperation Is More Vital Than Ever: This is Why". World Economic Forum, The Japan Times, pp.1-6.

Aminah H. [2021], "Iqbal: A Visionary for All Times". The Express Tribune Editorial, No: 2315451.

Danyal A.K [2018], "Quiet Burns the Fire: The Baldia Tragedy". The Editorial: Herald Magazine, pp. 1-10.

Ebrahim B. [2022], "Adverse Effects Following Covid-19 Vaccination in Iran". BMC Infectious Diseases, pp. 1-8.

Radhakrishnan R.K [2002], "Passage to India: Arrival of Economic Refugees from Sri Lanka Looms Large". The Editorial: The Hindu News, pp. 1-3.

Mercy A. [2022], "The China-Russia Triangle: Alternative World Order?". The Editorial: The Diplomat, pp. 1-3.

Neve G. [2012], "No Justice for Rachel Corrie". The Editorial: The Nation Newspaper, pp. 1-2.

Laura D. [2022], "What Is Fear of Time Chronophobia". The Editorial: Very Well Health Magazine, pp. 1-5.

Michael E. P. [1990], "The Competitive Advantage of Nations". The Editorials: Harvard Business Review, pp. 1-15.

Nick O. [2018], "How Germany Was Divided: A History of Partition Plans". The Editorial: Never Was Magazine, pp. 1-7.

Sarah E. [2023], "The Rights of Children Over Parents". Aljumuah Magazine, pp. 1-10.

Arsene B. D. [2011], "Understanding the International Community". Hekima Review, No. 44, pp. 1-12.

Hannah R. [2020], "Climate Change and Flying: What Share of Global CO2 Emissions Come from Aviation". The Editorials: Our World in Data, pp. 1-4.

Bravo A. [1987], "The Driving Forces of Environmental Change". United Nations University Website: http;//unu.edu/, pp.1-5.

Bruce L. [2020], "The Pros and Cons of Planting Trees to Address Global Warming". Yale Climate Connections: Bruce Liberman Freelance Archives, pp. 1-4.

Malcolm S. [2019], "The Fiscal Responsibilities of Government". A Modern Guide to State Intervention: University of Leeds, pp. 85-96.

Alan B. [2019], "Examining the Viability of Planting Trees to Help Mitigate Climate Change". Global Climate Change: NASA's Jet Propulsion Laboratory, pp. 1-10.

Jackie S. [2019], "How Artificial Intelligence Can Tackle Climate Change", National Geographic, pp. 1-4.

Muhammed H. [2020], "Climate Change and Health in Pakistan: Impacts and Adaptation Policy". PMAS and Agriculture University, pp. 1-16.

Samiullah S. et al., [2017], "Causes of Delay in The Construction of Dams in Pakistan". First International Conference on Industrial Engineering and Management Applications, Mehran University of Engineering and Technology, Jamshoro, Sindh, Pakistan, pp. 1-6.

Asma F. [2022], "The Peculiar Case of The Pakistan People's Party as An Opposition". Carnegie Endowment for International Peace, pp. 1-7.

Carolina M. [2012], "Mass Media and Globalization". In the Book: Wiley- Blackwell's Encyclopedia of Civilizations, pp. 1-15.

Erin B. [2019], "The Kashmir Conflict: How Did it Start?". National Geographic, pp. 1-4.

Maria E. [2021], "Right of Self Determination and Kashmiris: A Conceptual Understanding and Perspective". National Defence University, Islamabad, pp. 1-14.

Salman G. [2017], "An Environmental Analysis of the Billion Tree Tsunami Project in Khyber-Pakhtunkhwa Pakistan". South-Asia Forestry and Environmental Sustainability, Himalayas, pp. 1-7.

William T. [1973], "The Concept of Political Freedom". Social Theory and Practice, vol. 2, No. 4, pp. 421-438. Florida State University, Department of Philosophy.

Saadat K. B. [2021], "Role of Establishment in Pakistan Politics". Thesis For B.sc Political Science, Forman Christian College.

Guilia M. [2013], "Plato's Argument for Rule by Philosopher Kings". E-International Relations, University of New York, pp. 1-3.

Isabella et al [2023], "Food Poverty in the U.K: The Causes, Figures and Solutions". The Editorial: The Big Issue Magazine, pp. 1-3.

Noah B. [2023], "What is At Stake in Pakistan's Power Crisis". Council on Foreign Relations, Foreign Affairs, pp. 1-4.

Pervez H. [2018], "Madina State and "Naya" Pakistan". The Editorial: The Dawn Magazine, pp. 1-3.

Secunder K. [2022], "Imran Khan: What Led to Charismatic Pakistan P.M's Downfall". The Editorial: BBC News, Islamabad, pp. 1-5.

Shah M. B. [2021], "Imran Khan Is Crushing the Poor: Anger Rises as Inflation Grips Pakistan". The Editorial: The Guardian News, Islamabad, pp. 1-4.

Abrar M. A. [2018], "Strange Estrangement: Pakistan and Armenia". The Editorial: The Express Tribune, pp. 1-4.

Elizabeth T. [2018], "Inside Israel's Secret Program to Back Syrian Rebels". The Editorial: Foreign Policy Magazine, pp. 1-3.

Fariz I. [2020], "Azerbaijan's Foreign Policy Priorities and The Role of The Middle-East". The Middle-East Institute, pp. 1-4.

Laurence B. [2002], "Is Azerbaijan Planning A Long-term Presence in Armenia?". Russia and Eurasia Programme Chatham House, pp. 1-3.

Mette E. S. [2009], "The End of Balance of Power Theory? A Comment on Wohlforth et al's Testing Balance of Power Theory in World History". European Journal of International Relations, vol. 15, No. 2, pp. 347-380.

Michelle B. [2022], "Crisis and Fragility of Democracy". United Nations Human Rights, Opening Workshop for The International Association of Jesuit Universities, Boston College, pp. 1-6.

Susan S. F. [2011], "Ups and Downs in the Global City: London and New York in the 21st". DOI: 1002/1978.

Elena F. [2018], "Disintegrated Selves: Dissociative Disorders and Colonial Anxiety in Orphan Pamuk's The Black Book". A Poetics of Neurosis: Narratives of Normalcy and Disorder in Cultural and Literary Texts, pp. 55-74.

Hasan A. R. [1999], "Pakistan in 1999: Back to Square One". Asian Survey, Vol. 20, No. 1, pp. 208-218. University of California Press.

Jim O. [2013], "Power, Powerlessness, and Addiction". University of Birmingham, Cambridge University Press, pp. 1-261.

Larry D. [2004], "What is Democracy?". Hilla University for Humanistic Studies, Stanford University, pp. 1-8.

Latika B. [2021], "The Men in Grey: The True Powers Behind the Palace". The Sydney Morning Herald, pp. 1-7.

Mehlaqa S. [2023], "The Death of Democracy in Pakistan". FPIF – Foreign Policy in Focus in Conjunction with Critical Connections, pp. 1-3.

Michael J. A. [2017], "Democracy in Crisis". Freedom House, pp. 1-15.

Richard W. et al., [2021], "Many in the U.S., Western Europe Say Their Political System Needs Major Reform". Pew Research Center, International Affairs, pp. 1-10.

Richard W. et al., [2018], "Many Around the World Are Disengaged from Politics". Pew Research, pp. 1-7.

Sandra J. [2009], "Roman Slavery and The Question of Race". Black Past Magazine, pp. 1-5.

Tom R. [2009], "States of The Union Before and After Bush". Research Editorial: Pew Research Center, pp. 1-5.

John M. [2016], "Pennsylvania, Wisconsin, and Michigan [Updated]". The Editorial: Washington Examiner, pp. 1-3.

Katie G. [2020], "Joe Biden is Elected The 46th President of The United States". The Editorial: The York News, pp. 1-3.

Laura S. et al [2019], "Views of The Balance of Power between The U.S. and China". Pew Research Center, pp. 1-8.

Michael L. [2021], "Hillary Clinton Reads Discarded Victory Speech From 2016 Election". The Editorial: The New York Times, pp. 1-3.

Mihnea M. et al [2019], "The Future of Leadership Development". Harvard Business Review, pp. 1-8.

Osazee G. O. [2017], "Elections and Economic Performance in Nigeria". Faculty of Management Sciences, University of Benin, pp. 1-22.

Solomon U. [2020], "Understanding the American Three-stage Presidential Election". The Editorial: The Guardian, pp. 1-4.

Tim L. [2023], "The Electoral College Explained". Brennan Center for Justice, pp. 1-4.

Carlos B. [2020], "Evaluating the Trump Administration's Iran Policy". Council on Foreign Relations, pp. 1-4.

Ivo H. et al [2003], "The Globalization Politics: American Foreign Policy for a New Era". Foreign Policy: Brookings Education, pp. 1-8.

Frank A. [2019], "The Full Extent of U.S Arms Deals with Saudi Arabia and UAE". Middle East Eye: Opinions, pp. 1-6.

Mark U. et al., [2021], "Key Facts About the Changing U.S Unauthorised Immigration Population". Immigration Issues: Pew Research Center, pp. 1-3.

Mu Chunshan [2021], "China- U.S Relations: Views from China". The Debate: The Diplomat, pp. 1-3.

Navnita C. B. [2002], "Kashmir: Redefining The U.S Role". Brookings Resources, No. 110, pp. 1-9.

Nile G. [2021], "Joe Biden Has Been A Monumental Disaster". The Editorial: The Telegraph, pp. 1-2.

Richard W. et al [2021], "America's Image Abroad Rebounds with Transition from Trump to Biden". Pew Research Center, pp. 1-10.
Wess M. [2023], "The Peace Processes: The U.S Peace Processes". United States Institute of Peace, pp. 1-4.

Jill C. et al [2023], "Former U.S Vice President Mike Pence Opens 2024 Presidential Bid with Denunciation of Trump Over January 6 Insurrection and Abortion". The Editorial: The Globe and Mail, pp. 1-4.

Neil S. M. [1990], "Superpower Rivalry in the 1990s". Third World Quarterly, vol. 12, No. 1, pp. 1-25. Taylor and Francis Ltd.

Parita M. [1999], "The Civilising Mission: The Regulation and Control of Mourning in Colonial India". Feminist Review, No. 63, pp. 25-47.

Scott N. [2021], "4 Reasons A Taliban Takeover in Afghanistan Matters to The World". Analysis Asia: NPR, pp. 1-6.

Terri M. C. [2021], "Biden Announces Full U.S Troop Withdrawal from Afghanistan By Sept. 11". U.S Department of Defence, No. 2573268, pp. 1-5.

Abhijnan R. [2020], How India Dealt with Donald Trump". The Editorial: The Diplomat, pp. 1-4.

Ankit P. [2016], "India, US SSign Logistics Exchange Agreement: What You Need to Know". The Editorial: The Diplomat, pp. 1-3.

David P. [2013], "The Lessons of the Accord for Modern Times: Think Outside the Box". The Editorial: The Conversation, pp. 1-6.

Erin B. [2022], "Why the Partition of India and Pakistan Still Casts A Shadow Over the Region". The National Geographic, pp. 1-10.

Jack B. [2020], "Pakistan And China Reach New Intelligence Sharing Agreement". The Editorial: The Washington Free Beacon, pp.1-2.

Misbah M. [2020], "India-US Military Agreement: BECA and Its Implications for The Region". India Study Centre [ISC], ISSI.

Theresa H. et al [2017], "International Cybersecurity Information Sharing Agreement". https://www.jstor.org/stable/resrep2046, pp. 1-40.

Adnan A. [2021], "India: Government Policies, Actions Target Minorities". The Editorial: Reuters News Agency, pp. 1-12.

Ahmad S. et al., [2021], "Taliban Sweep into Afghan Capital After Government Collapses". The Editorial: The Associated Press, pp. 1-4.

Bashir A. A. [2022], "India-Pakistan Dialogue: Past Trends and Future Prospects". South Asia: The Diplomat, pp. 1-4.

Edith M. L. [2021], "The AP Interview: Don't Isolate the Taliban, Pakistan Urges". The Editorial: Associated Press News, pp. 1-5.

Gautam M. [2021], "An Expert Explains: What Kabul Means in Delhi". Indian Strategic Studies, pp. 1-4.

Mateen H. [2014], "Pakistan – World's Largest Host of Refugees: UNHCR". The Editorial: The Dawn News, pp. 1-4.

Naveed S. [2020], "Irrefutable Evidence: Dossier on India's Sponsorship of State Terrorism in Pakistan Presented". The Editorial: The Dawn News, pp. 1-10.

Qadri I. et al., [2022], "The School in A Basement That is Changing Lives". The Editorial: Foreign Policy News, pp. 1-3.

Sheikh J. H. [2021], "India's Failures". The Editorial: The Nation, pp. 1-4.

Katherine S. [2022], "A Year Later, A Look at Public Opinion About the US Military Exit from Afghanistan". Politics and Policy: Pew Research Center, pp. 1-4.

Madiha A.   [2019], "An Inflection Point for Pakistan's Democracy". The Brookings Centre: Foreign Policy Analysis, pp.1-13.

Niha D. et al [2020], "Toothless and Terrified: The State of Pakistan's Media". The Editorial: The Diplomat, pp. 1-5.

Rabia A. [2021], "Pakistan and The Taliban 2.0: The Good, The Bad and The Ugly". The Atlantic Council, South Asian Center, pp.1-3.

Erik O. [2020], "Racial Violence and a Pandemic: How the Red Summer of 1919 Relates to 2020". The Editorial: NBC News Digital, pp. 1-4.

Mario G. [1998], "The City as the Object of Architecture". Assemblage, No. 37, pp. 128-144. The MIT Press.

Amin M. C [2020], "Iran and The Economic Fallout of Covid-19". The Middle-East Institute, pp. 1-3.

Angela M. et al [2021]," How Covid-19 is Changing the World: A Statistical Perspective". UNCTAD: CCSA, pp. 1-90.

Denis J. H. [2002], "The United Nations: The Embarrassment of International Law". Medicine, Conflict and Survival, pp. 346-354. Taylor and Francis Ltd.

Jennifer D. et al [2015], "Harsh Laws and Violence Drive Global Decline". The Editorial: Freedom House Press, pp. 1-7.

Sami S. [2019]," Remembering Edhi: The Exception to Pakistan's Faults". The Editorial: The Dawn Press, pp. 1-3.

Sukru C. [2019], "How Saudi-Iranian Oil Rivalry Has Been Shaped by American Power". The Editorial: The Conversation Press, pp. 1-5.

Ali A. et al., [2019], "Ideology and Iran's Revolution: How 1979 Changed the World". The Global Institute, pp. 1-8.

Caspar P. et al., [2020], "Monitoring Physical Distancing for Crowd Management: Real Time Trajectory and Group Analysis". Research Gate, pp. 1-13.

Christopher B. [2021], "Political Sociology in a Time of Protest". Sage Journals, Vol. 69, No. 6, pp. 919-942.

Cyril A. et al., [2022], "Pakistan's New Government Struggles to Consolidate Control". United States Institute of Peace, pp.1-4.

Daniel F. R. [2020], "US Foreign Assistance in the Age of Strategic Competition". Center for Strategic and International Studies, pp. 1-5.

Muhammed K. [2021], "Impact of The Coronavirus [Covid-19] Pandemic on Retail Sales in 2020". Office for National Statistics, pp. 1-14.

Abdul R. [2020], "Pakistan: How Accountability Became a Tool for Political Oppression". The Diplomat: South East Asian Politics, pp. 1-3.

Alec T. et al [2020], "Two-thirds of Americans Think Government Should Do More on Climate". Pew Research Center, pp.1-12.

John G. [2017], "How Countries Around the World View Democracy, Military Rule and Other Political Systems". Pew Research Center, International Political Values, pp. 1-3.

David F. L [2019], "What Does Fair and Impartial Judiciary Mean and Why is it Important". Bolch Judiciary

Institute, An Institute of Duke Law School, Duke University, pp. 1-8.

Katy W. [2016], "A Brief Inglorious History of "Not Politicizing Tragedy". The Editorial: The Slate Press, pp. 1-4.

Morgan K. [2021], "Political Polarization and Its Echo Chambers: Surprising New Cross-disciplinary Perspectives from Princeton". High Meadows Environmental Institute, pp. 1-5.

Neha N. [2009], "Kashmir: The Clash of Identities". The Editorial: Beyond Intractability, pp. 1-20.

Ctherine H. [2020]," Ministerial Accountability". Institute for Government, pp. 1-4.

Mosharraf Z. [2017]," The Downfall of Nawaz Sharif and the Triumph of Stupidity". The Editorial: Foreign Policy Press, South Asia, pp. 1-5.

Arif R. [2022], "Pakistan's Political Crisis and The Imperatives of Economic Reform". Middle East Institute, pp. 1-4.

Bruce S. [2016], "Brexit Vote Highlighted UK's Discontent with the EU, But Other European Countries Are Grumbling Too". Pew Research Center, pp. 1-3.

James M. [2019], "What Brexit Means". Council on Foreign Relations, pp. 1-10.

Madiha H. [2023], "Pakistan: Five Major Issues to Watch in 2023". Brookings Educational Press, pp. 1-5.

Rashid S. [2004]," Pakistan-European Union Relations". Pakistan Horizon, Vol. 57, No. 4, pp. 29-36. Pakistan Institute of International Affairs.

Arendse H. [2022], "China 2022 FDI Round Up: Stronger Policies Aim to Maintain Growth Momentum". China Briefing: Dezan Shira Associates, pp. 1-5.

Jalil A. et al., [2022], "India and Pakistan at 75: Prospects for The Future". United States Institute of Peace, pp. 1-5.

Laura S. et al [2022], "How Global Public Opinion of China Has Shifted in The Xi Era". Pew Research Center, pp. 1-15.

Niall D. et al [2021], "Introduction: The Brics, Global Governance and Challenges for South-South Cooperation in a Post-Westren World". International Political Science Review, vol. 43, No. 4, pp. 469-480.

Rashida H. [2017], "Pakistan and China: Partnership, Prospects and The Course Ahead". Policy Perspectives, Vol. 14, No. 1, Pakistan and Its Neighbours, pp. 3-22.

Ryan H. et al [2020], "More Pain Than Gain: How The US-China Trade War Hurt America". The Brookings, pp. 1-6.

Dev Vrat S. [2022], "The Indian Media @2047". Central University of Jharkhand, pp.299-307.

Dhrubajyoti B. [2015]," Gilgit Baltistan, China and Pakistan". SSRN Electronic Journal: Indian Council of World Affairs, pp. 1-10.

Hermann K. [2013], "Preservation of Gilgit-Baltistan's Cultural Heritage as a Key to Development". Freie Universitat Berlin, pp. 1-43.

Martin S. [1997], "Migration and Society in Gilgit Northern Areas of Pakistan". Anthropos, pp. 83-90.

Stephanie J. [2022], "The Partition of India: Division and Violence in 20th Century". The Editorial: The Collector, pp. 1-15.

Bengi Uk. Et al [2022], "The Relation of Individual and Collective Narcissism and Belief in Covid-19 Conspiracy Theories: The Moderating Effects of Need for Uniqueness and Belonging". Department of Psychology, Istanbul Medipol University, Goztepe, pp. 1-10.

UNPUBLISHED MATERIALS

Touhidur R. [2021], "Significance of Conserving the Dhaka New Market". Thesis for: Bachelor of Urban and Regional Planning: Advisor; Professor Golam Muinuddin, PhD, pp. 1-101.

Celcia B. [2021], "Travelling is Resuming but Not for Everyone". Foreign Policy: Centre on The United States and Europe, pp. 1-6.

Mohammed A. et al., [2022], "The Liberation War of Bangladesh: Emergence of Nationalism in The Political Context". Research Gate Publishers, pp. 1-14.

Jayshree B. et al [2011], "The ISI and Terrorism: Behind the Accusations". Council of Foreign Relations, Foreign Affairs, pp. 1-3.

Fethi K. [2020], "Curiosity and Interest-Based Learning". Educational Sciences, Erzincan University, pp. 1-23.

Ilhan N. [2019], "History of Pakistan 1947-2019". Europa World Regional Series, pp. 1-16.

Iftikhar M. [2008], "The History of Pakistan". The Greenwood Histories of The Modern Nations, Greenwood Press, pp. 1-262.

Madiha H. [2023], "Pakistan: Five Major Issues to Watch in 2023". The Brookings Press, pp. 1-3.

Neha S. et al., [2021], "Religion in India: Tolerance and Segregation". Pew Research Center, pp. 1-20.

Ziad H. [2011], "Islam and The Early History of Pakistan". Middle East and The Islamic World Working Group: Hoover Institution, pp. 1-4.

Jane B. et al., [2019], "Strengthening Health Systems Through Nursing: Evidence From 14 European Countries [Internet]". Health Policy Series, No. 52, pp. 1-181.

David B. [2023], "Consumer Price Inflation, UK: July 2023". Office for National Statistics, pp. 1-44.

Hugo S. [2020], "You Don't Have to Be Neutral to Be a Good Humanitarian". The New Humanitarianism, pp. 1-3.

ja T. R. [1972], "Some Foreign Policy Problems of Pakistan". Pakistan Horizon, Vol. 25, No. 3, pp. 17-22. Pakistan Institute of International Affairs.

Rakesh K. [2015], "A Global Middle Class is More Promise Than Reality". Economy and Work: Pew Research Center, pp. 1-10.

Tahir K. [2019], "Ashfaq Ahmad's Warning and The Apathy of The Educated". The Editorial: The News on Sunday, pp. 1-4.

Nausherwan K. B. [2019], "Establishing A Tertiary Care Cancer Hospital in a Developing Country: The Story of The Shaukat Khanum Memorial Cancer Hospital and Research Centre", Cancer Control, Shaukat Khanum Memorial Cancer Hospital and Research Centre, Pakistan, pp. 1-10.

Fhrizz S. D. J [2020], "Milk Tea Industry: An Exploratory Study". Nueva Ecjia University of Science and Technology, pp. 1-9.

Lauret G. [2014], "Karachi – Ordered Disorder and The Struggle for The City". Centre for International Studies, pp. 1-256.

Prema C. A. [2011], "South-South Trade: An Asian Perspective". Asian Development Bank: ADB Economics Working Paper Series, No. 265, pp. 1-55.

Shahina M. [2020], "Dr. Faisal Sultan Becomes PM's Special Assistant on Health". The Editorial: The News International, pp. 1-2.

www.ingramcontent.com/pod-product-compliance
Lightning Source LLC
Chambersburg PA
CBHW061028250726

48653CB00001B/3